International Political Economy Series

General Editor: **Timothy M. Shaw**, Professor of Commonwealth Governance and Development, and Director of the Institute of Commonwealth Studies, School of Advanced Study, University of London

Titles include:

Hans Abrahamsson
UNDERSTANDING WORLD ORDER AND STRUCTURAL CHANGE
Poverty, Conflict and the Global Arena

Morten Bøås, Marianne H. Marchand and Timothy M. Shaw (*editors*)
THE POLITICAL ECONOMY OF REGIONS AND REGIONALISMS

Sandra Braman (*editor*)
THE EMERGENT GLOBAL INFORMATION POLICY REGIME

James Busumtwi-Sam and Laurent Dobuzinskis (*editors*)
TURBULENCE AND NEW DIRECTIONS IN GLOBAL POLITICAL ECONOMY

Martin Doornbos
GLOBAL FORCES AND STATE RESTRUCTURING
Dynamics of State Formation and Collapse

Bill Dunn
GLOBAL RESTRUCTURING AND THE POWER OF LABOUR

Myron J. Frankman
WORLD DEMOCRATIC FEDERALISM
Peace and Justice Indivisible

Barry K. Gills (*editor*)
GLOBALIZATION AND THE POLITICS OF RESISTANCE

Marieke de Goede (*editor*)
INTERNATIONAL POLITICAL ECONOMY AND POSTSTRUCTURAL POLITICS

Richard Grant and John Rennie Short (*editors*)
GLOBALIZATION AND THE MARGINS

Graham Harrison (*editor*)
GLOBAL ENCOUNTERS
International Political Economy, Development and Globalization

Patrick Hayden and Chamsy el-Ojeili (*editors*)
CONFRONTING GLOBALIZATION
Humanity, Justice and the Renewal of Politics

Axel Hülsemeyer (*editor*)
GLOBALIZATION IN THE TWENTY-FIRST CENTURY
Convergence or Divergence?

Helge Hveem and Kristen Nordhaug (*editors*)
PUBLIC POLICY IN THE AGE OF GLOBALIZATION
Responses to Environmental and Economic Crises

Takashi Inoguchi
GLOBAL CHANGE
A Japanese Perspective

Kanishka Jayasuriya
STATECRAFT, WELFARE AND THE POLITICS OF INCLUSION

Dominic Kelly and Wyn Grant (*editors*)
THE POLITICS OF INTERNATIONAL TRADE IN THE 21st CENTURY
Actors, Issues and Regional Dynamics

Mathias Koenig-Archibugi and Michael Zürn (*editors*)
NEW MODES OF GOVERNANCE IN THE GLOBAL SYSTEM
Exploring Publicness, Delegation and Inclusiveness

Craig N. Murphy (*editor*)
EGALITARIAN POLITICS IN THE AGE OF GLOBALIZATION

George Myconos
THE GLOBALIZATION OF ORGANIZED LABOUR
1945–2004

John Nauright and Kimberley S. Schimmel (*editors*)
THE POLITICAL ECONOMY OF SPORT

Morten Ougaard
THE GLOBALIZATION OF POLITICS
Power, Social Forces and Governance

Richard Robison (*editor*)
THE NEO-LIBERAL REVOLUTION
Forging the Market State

Timothy J. Sinclair and Kenneth P. Thomas (*editors*)
STRUCTURE AND AGENCY IN INTERNATIONAL CAPITAL MOBILITY

Fredrik Söderbaum and Timothy M. Shaw (*editors*)
THEORIES OF NEW REGIONALISM

International Political Economy Series
Series Standing Order ISBN 0–333–71708–2 hardcover
Series Standing Order ISBN 0–333–71110–6 paperback
(*outside North America only*)

You can receive future titles in this series as they are published by placing a standing order. Please contact your bookseller or, in case of difficulty, write to us at the address below with your name and address, the title of the series and the ISBN quoted above.

Customer Services Department, Macmillan Distribution Ltd, Houndmills, Basingstoke, Hampshire RG21 6XS, England

International Political Economy and Poststructural Politics

Edited by Marieke de Goede
University of Amsterdam, The Netherlands

palgrave
macmillan

First published 2006 by
PALGRAVE MACMILLAN
Houndmills, Basingstoke, Hampshire RG21 6XS and
175 Fifth Avenue, New York, N. Y. 10010
Companies and representatives throughout the world

PALGRAVE MACMILLAN is the global academic imprint of the Palgrave Macmillan division of St. Martin's Press, LLC and of Palgrave Macmillan Ltd. Macmillan® is a registered trademark in the United States, United Kingdom and other countries. Palgrave is a registered trademark in the European Union and other countries.

ISBN-13: 978–1–4039–4932–5 hardback
ISBN-10: 1–4039–4932–8 hardback

This book is printed on paper suitable for recycling and made from fully managed and sustained forest sources.

A catalogue record for this book is available from the British Library.

Library of Congress Cataloging-in-Publication Data
International political economy and poststructural politics / edited by Marieke de Goede.
p. cm. – (International political economy series)
Includes bibliographical references and index.
ISBN 1–4039–4932–8 (c1)
1. International economic relations. 2. International finance. 3. Globalization. I. Goede, Marieke de, 1971- II. International political economy series (Palgrave Macmillan (Firm))

HF1411.I51758 2006
337–dc22 2005056371

10 9 8 7 6 5 4 3 2 1
15 14 13 12 11 10 09 08 07 06

Printed and bound in Great Britain by
Antony Rowe Ltd, Chippenham and Eastbourne

Contents

List of Figures

Acknowledgments

Many thanks to all contributors, who made this volume possible. Many thanks to Tim Shaw and Jen Nelson at Palgrave, who were enthusiastic about this project from the very beginning. I am indebted to an anonymous referee for Palgrave, who helped shape this volume in important ways. For comments on my introduction, as well as general help and advice, I am grateful to Louise Amoore, David Campbell, Martin Coward, Matt Davies, Christiane Hiley, Paul Langley and Erna Rijsdijk. Special thanks to Gunther Irmer, who contributed to the volume in innumerable ways.

Chapter 2 previously appeared as part of Michael J. Shapiro (1993) *Reading 'Adam Smith': Desire, History, and Value*. London: Sage. Many thanks to Rowman Littlefield for permission to reprint.

Chapter 10 previously appeared in *Studies in Political Economy* 63 (2000). Many thanks to *Studies in Political Economy* for permission to reprint.

Marieke de Goede,
Amsterdam
July 2005

Notes on Contributors

Rob Aitken currently teaches in the Division of Social Science at York University in Toronto, Canada. His research focuses on cultural economy and performativity in the context of private financial spaces. His research has appeared in the *Review of International Political Economy* and *Consumption, Markets and Culture*.

Louise Amoore is Lecturer in Political Geography at the University of Durham. She is author of *Globalisation Contested* (2002) and editor of the *Global Resistance Reader* (2005).

Martin Coward is a lecturer in International Relations at the University of Sussex. His recent work includes 'The Imperial Character Of Our Times' (*Theory and Event* 8 (1), 2005) and 'Urbicide in Bosnia,' in S. Graham (ed.) *Cities, War and Terrorism: Towards an Urban Geopolitics* (2004).

Glyn Daly is Senior Lecturer in Politics and Sociology at the University of Northampton. He is author (with Slavoj Žižek) of *Conversations with Žižek* (2004). His research engages widely with the theory of ideology, the notion of the political and the question of impossibility.

Matt Davies is a lecturer in International Relations at the University of Newcastle-upon-Tyre. He has published on culture and political economy in Latin America and on labor in the global political economy, and is currently working on a book with Michael Niemann on everyday life and International Political Economy (IPE).

Marieke de Goede is Lecturer in Political History and International Relations, Department of European Studies at the University of Amsterdam. Her book *Virtue, Fortune and Faith: a Genealogy of Finance* (2005), reads the cultural history of modern financial markets from a poststructural perspective. She is currently working on a book about the war on terrorist finance.

Earl Gammon is a PhD candidate at the University of Sussex, International Relations and Politics Department. His dissertation explores the psychogenesis of modern political economy in the context of nineteenth-century Britain.

Bob Jessop is Director of the Institute for Advanced Studies at Lancaster University. He works on state theory, political economy, and social theory. His most recent books are *The Future of the Capitalist State* (2002) and, with Ngai-Ling Sum, *Beyond the Regulation Approach: Putting Capitalist Economies in their Place* (2006).

Wendy Larner is Professor of Human Geography and Sociology, School of Geographical Sciences, University of Bristol. She has published widely in the fields of political economy, governmentality, economic geography and social policy. She is also coeditor (with William Walters) of *Global Governmentality: New Perspectives on International Rule* (2004).

Bice Maiguashca is a lecturer in Politics at the University of Exeter. Her coedited book *Critical Theories, International Relations and the Anti-Globalisation Movement* explores the interface between diverse social movement resistances to neoliberalism and a range of IR critical theories. She is currently working on a coauthored book with Catherine Eschle on feminist activism within 'the anti-globalization movement'.

Ronen Palan is a professor of International Political Economy at the University of Sussex. His recent publications include: *The Offshore World* (2003) and, with Angus Cameron, *The Imagined Economies of Globalization* (2004).

V. Spike Peterson is a professor in the Department of Political Science, University of Arizona, with courtesy appointments in Women's Studies, Comparative Cultural and Literary Studies, Center for Latin American Studies, and International Studies. Her most recent book, *A Critical Rewriting of Global Political Economy: Reproductive, Productive and Virtual Economies* (2003), introduces an alternative analytics for examining connections among ethnicity/race, class, gender and national hierarchies in the context of today's globalizing dynamics.

J. Magnus Ryner is Senior Lecturer of Political Science and International Studies at the University of Birmingham. His publications include *Capitalist Restructuring, Globalisation and the Third Way* (2002); *A Ruined Fortress? Neoliberal Hegemony and Transformation in Europe* (with Alan Cafruny, 2003); and *Poverty and the Production of World Politics* (with Matt Davies, 2005).

Michael J. Shapiro is a professor of Political Science at the University of Hawaii. Among his recent publications are *For Moral Ambiguity: National Culture and the Politics of the Family* (2001) and *Methods and Nations: Cultural Governance and the Indigenous Subject* (2004).

Ngai-Ling Sum is a lecturer in the Department of Politics and International Relations in Lancaster University. She works on international political economy, globalization and informational capitalism. Her most recent publications are an edited book (with Marcus Perkmann) on *Globalization, Regionalization and Cross-Border Regions* (2002) and, with Bob Jessop, *Beyond the Regulation Approach: Putting Capitalist Economies in their Place* (2006).

Marysia Zalewski is Director of the Centre for Gender Studies at the University of Aberdeen. She has written widely on feminist theory and gender and international relations. More recent research reflects on the conflict in Northern Ireland using feminist poststructuralism. *Intervening in Northern Ireland: Critically Representing the Conflict* (coedited with Dr John Barry) will be published in 2006.

Introduction: International Political Economy and the Promises of Poststructuralism

Marieke de Goede

Engagements between International Political Economy (IPE) as a field of thought that thinks critically about 'the unique problematic of the operation of the modern economy within a fragmented political system' (Palan 2000: 17), and poststructural politics, have been sporadic and antagonistic. It is possible to say that IPE has been particularly resistant to poststructural intervention. Simply put, if poststructuralism has come to be understood as foregrounding analyses of discourse, identity and culture in the study of global politics, a number of IPE authors have expressed concern that these theoretical moves will (a) distract from the study of real material inequality that critical IPE endeavors to study and to transform; and (b) amount to a political relativism that suspends the ontological ground on which judgments concerning the desired agenda of transformation can be made (see for example, the engagement between Krasner 1996 and Ashley 1996; the engagement between Laffey 2000, 2004 and de Goede 2003; see also Gills 2001; Patomäki and Wight 2000). Barry Gills (2001: 238), for example, while sympathetic to poststructural work on agency and identity, nevertheless expresses concern that such analysis would *displace* political economy's 'true subject matter – which is the political economy of the world (historical system) which some call "global capitalism."' Moreover, a focus on identity and a poststructural conceptualization of power are sometimes read as disabling IPE's critique of capital and capitalism, while presenting a worldview of flux and diffused power that is in league with capitalist discourse itself (Laffey 2000; 2004).

This volume offers a sustained engagement between IPE and poststructuralism, that takes seriously the criticisms voiced above, but that moves beyond a polarization of the debate. The resistance of IPE to poststructural intervention can partly be seen as a disciplinary politics that seeks to regulate IPE's agenda of study and to define its core subject matter. All too often, boundaries set in these debates expel from enquiry those themes so important to this volume: identity, cultural representation, discourse, everyday life, the ambiguity of political dissent. In this manner, the primary subject-matter of political economy is settled in particular ways that work to relegate to secondary importance, in the words of Amin and Palan (2001: 560), the 'powers of behaviour rooted in emotions, cultural and social norms, historical lock-in, serendipity and accident.'

However, IPE and poststructural politics *both* endeavor to challenge 'the idea that the character and the location of the political must be determined by the sovereign state,' and to broaden 'the political imagination and the range of political possibilities for transforming international relations' (Devetak 2001: 204; see also Coward this volume). It is to be expected, then, that they may fruitfully engage. Thinking through IPE's traditional concerns of financial and economic practices, states and firms, power and (class) inequality with the help of poststructural insights on representation, performativity and dissent, may yield rich new conceptualizations of political economy that have the potential to resonate far beyond IPE. For example, a sophisticated theorization of the commercialization of security and of economic practices such as subcontracting, that does not simply invoke a mythical and coherent capitalism, is becoming increasingly important for political analyses of the current war on terror. (e.g. Amoore and de Goede 2005).

Challenging boundaries

In this volume, leading poststructural, IPE and feminist scholars debate the promises of poststructural politics for the study of the global political economy. The authors collected here regard the supposed dangers of poststructuralism as a challenge, which may articulate the political in IPE in rich, new ways. They are guided by a set of questions, including: Does a focus on identity and representation distract from the study of material structures and distributive justice?; Are there facts of economics which remain prior to discourse and representation?; What is the role of culture and representation in political economy?; How does the question of identity become important to the study of global restructuring?; How is resistance rethought through poststructural politics? Through engaging with these questions, the volume challenges the boundaries that some established IPE tries to protect, and explores, amongst other issues, gender performativity (Zalewski), psychoanalytic theory (Gammon and

Palan), financial identity (Aitken), governmentality (Larner), everyday life (Davies) and art as a site of resistance (Amoore).

This is not to say that all authors collected here are self-identified post-structuralists, nor that they singularly dismiss the reservations that Gills, Laffey and others have voiced towards aspects of poststructural theory. Magnus Ryner, for example, in his contribution, considers it 'dangerous' to emphasize, as post-Marxists Laclau and Mouffe do, the contingency between class and political consciousness, precisely for the reasons of relativism and the problem of political action that may result from such a theoretical position. The collection presented here then, includes a diversity of opinions on, and practices of, poststructural politics and IPE, in order to constitute a real dialogue. It is not the objective of this volume to develop *a* poststructural IPE, but to engage with those authors and those issues generally thought to be poststructuralist, as well as to engage with some of the criticisms discussed above.

The debate in this volume partly draws upon the ways in which post-structuralism has been appropriated within the study of global politics more generally – not because IPE is to be seen as a 'sub-field' of International Relations (IR), but because the problematizations of agency, sovereignty and boundaries developed in poststructural IR are highly relevant to rethinking these issues in IPE. Challenging boundaries is at the heart of the ways in which poststructuralism has been appropriated in IR. As Michael Shapiro (1996: xvi) writes, challenging 'bordered state sovereignties' through literary intervention and a remembrance of the excluded and the violently suppressed in the formation of the modern state system was at the heart of the task of taking seriously poststructural perspectives from the humanities in IR. Concern for the marginalized sites in global politics leads to the politicization of limits and the way they are articulated. For Ashley and Walker (1990: 263), the dissident work of global political theory needs 'to interrogate limits, to explore how they are imposed, to demonstrate their arbitrariness, and to think *other*-wise, that is, in a way that makes possible the testing of limitations and the exploration of excluded possibilities' (emphasis in original).

But it is not just a concern for the *margins* that inspires a politics of the limits. As Etienne Balibar (1999) argues in his reflections 'At the Borders of Europe,' the border is not necessarily the 'outer limit' of a political sphere but is 'dispersed a little everywhere, wherever the movement of information, people and things is happening and is controlled.' Thus, according to Balibar, the border constitutes *the center* of the political sphere: 'In this sense, border areas – zones, countries, and cities – are not marginal to the constitution of a public sphere but rather are at the center.' Similarly, it is through the border of a discipline that its identity is constituted and its agenda is regulated. A concern for the margins, then, goes to the center of the discipline.

Before moving on to discuss three poststructural themes that are promising to the study of the global political economy, it should be clarified what, in this volume, is meant by the term poststructuralism. Clearly, it is neither possible nor particularly useful to define poststructuralism as if it were a coherent theory or school of thought. Poststructuralism as a philosophical term developed to signify a break with structuralism as a linguistic theory that challenges the direct correspondence between language and the real world, and instead sees meaning as arising within the human system of language and signification. The work of Michel Foucault, for example, can be seen to be indebted to, but to go beyond, structural linguistics in the sense that it accepts a structural understanding 'of both discourse and the speaker as constructed objects,' while rejecting the formal model of rule-governed human behaviour developed by structural linguists, in favour of studying the social and historical contingency of human practice (Dreyfus and Rabinow 1982: xxiii). Foucault rejects the notion that a deep, hidden truth is to be discovered in human practice through critical theory, and focuses, instead, on a critical analysis of the discursive strategies 'which yield justified truth claims' (Dreyfus and Rabinow 1982: xx).

Neither Foucault, nor other philosophers such as Jacques Derrida, are easily and irrevocably captured under the label 'poststructuralist,' and there are important differences between them. However, and especially in the context of the study of global politics, it is possible to identify poststructuralism as having made a particular set of contributions to the debate, most notably the problematization of sovereignty, boundaries and seemingly secure (state) identities (Devetak 2001). What unites thinkers as diverse as Foucault, Derrida and Lyotard under the label poststructuralism, for George and Campbell (1990: 280), is 'a search for thinking space within the modern categories of unity, identity and homogeneity; the search for a broader and more complex understanding of modern society, which accounts for that which is left out – the "other," the marginalized, the excluded.'

In the context of thinking about the global political economy, poststructuralism as a term is chosen to distinguish this volume's concerns from work on 'postmodernism,' which is often understood to signify a new historical era, supposed to be emerging since the 1970s, and marked by 'new experience[s] of space and time' and 'new forms of capital accumulation' (Harvey 2001: 124).[1] Rather than a new (capitalist) era, then, poststructuralism here is to be understood as an interpretative analytic that problematizes sovereignty in world politics as well as in research practice itself (Campbell 1998: 213; see also Edkins 1999: xi). This interpretative analytic invites us to reconsider and destabilize not just the conceptual categories that IPE deploys (the state, the firm, the financial system, the economic actor, capitalism), but also the way knowledge is produced and legitimized in this disciplinary practice. This volume foregrounds the work of post-Marxist and poststructuralist philosophers including Michel Foucault, Judith Butler, Jacques Derrida, Gilles Deleuze and Felix Guattari, Ernesto Laclau and Chantal Mouffe, Antonio Negri and Michael Hardt – whose work enables a critical interrogation of the settled concepts and boundaries of IPE. Below, I discuss three themes that may be thought of as poststructuralist, and that are central to the dialogue in this volume. These themes should certainly not be seen as a coherent poststructural agenda. Rather, they have been articulated to introduce the reader to the promises of poststructuralism for the study of the global political economy. I will discuss, first, an emphasis on the politics of representation; second, a reconceptualization of power and agency; and third, a rethinking of the politics of resistance.

Politics of representation

First, poststructural analysis brings to the fore the importance of discourse and representation for political and economic practice. As Ashley (1996: 245) puts it, one contribution of poststructuralism to the study of world politics is 'the discovery of the centrality of the problem and paradox of representation to modern political life.' This involves not just the understanding that all political knowledge is discursively mediated, but also a recognition of the deeply discursive nature of the realms of politics and economics. This does not mean that the linguistic is to be prioritized over the material, but more precisely a 'moving beyond a simplistic consideration of objects by reconceptualizing materialism so it is understood as interwoven with cultural, social, and political networks' (Campbell 2005). However, the relation between the material and the discursive is a point of debate in this volume, and not all contributors – including, for example, the Jessop and Sum, and Davies chapters – are comfortable collapsing the distinction between the material and the discursive.

The questions of how certain meanings are fixed at the expense of others, how certain representations dominate alternatives, how the limits of political discourse are constituted, go to the heart of post-structural politics. As Spike Peterson summarizes this central question in her contribution to this volume: 'how does power operate...within specific contexts to stabilize – with a tendency to normalize and depoliticize – particular discourses and their effects?' Again, a politics of the limits is central to the task. As Judith Butler (2004: xvii) writes in her reflections on the public debate in the wake of 9/11: 'The public sphere is constituted in part by what cannot be said and what cannot be shown. The limits of the sayable, the limits of what can appear, circumscribe the domain in which political speech operates and certain kinds of subjects appear as viable actors.'

It should be clear that the agenda of the study of world politics shifts under the recognition of the politics of representation: from the (objective) study of material capabilities, national interests, and economic power, to the study of, for example, the practices of representation of danger, security and violence (Campbell 1998, Coward 2002; Weldes 1999; Luoma-aho 2004), to a critical assessment of the rationalist myths of political projects (Hansen and Williams 1999), to a rewriting of discourses of the discipline itself (George 1994). These authors have critically reexamined the central concepts of global politics, in order to expose the exclusions and marginalizations that enable their stabilization. Feminist analysis has been of particular importance to the destabilization of the conventional categories of IR and IPE, and broadening its field of study (see for example, Marchand and Runyan 2000; Hooper 2001; Ling 2002; Peterson 2003; Zalewski 2000). And despite what has been said above about IPE's resistance to poststructural intervention, a critical rethinking of IPE's core concepts and agenda in the light of the politics of discourse and representation is quietly underway (see for example, Aitken 2004; Amoore 1998; Deuchars 2004; Jessop and Sum 2001; Shapiro 1993; Rosamond 2002; Williams 1999).

What is perhaps most promising to IPE in this context, is the politicization of technical (economic, financial, political) knowledge that is made possible through rethinking the politics of representation. The move from the study of 'ideology' to the study of 'technologies of truth' in the work of Foucault is crucial here. While recognizing that historical transformations relating to the governance of the delinquent or the insane can have been 'economically advantageous and politically useful' to some, Foucault rejects the close and purposeful correspondence between dominant interests and historical change that is implied by the notion of ideology. Ideology implies an underlying *reality*, and a certain degree of plotting on the part of the dominant fraction to effect a distortion of reality by the subjected. Foucault, in contrast, leaves us with the realization that there is no reality (perceivable) outside of techniques of truth, and that techniques of truth are thus both less ideological and more political than assumed. 'I do not believe that what has taken place can be said to be ideological,' writes Foucault (1982: 102), 'It is both much more and much less than ideology. It is the production of effective instruments for the formation, and accumulation of knowledge – methods of observation, techniques of registration, procedures for investigation and research, apparatuses of control.' It is no longer to be assumed that *underneath* discursive representation a deeper truth is to be discovered, or that *underneath* ideology the real motivating forces of actors can be detected. As Shapiro (1996: xvii) puts it, 'discourse is always...a form of impoverishment, even as it affords value and access. All intelligible oral and textual articulations involve a temporary fix on a meaning at the expense of other possible structures of intelligibility.'

Understanding techniques of truth production as profoundly political is of crucial importance to the study of the IPE, for it opens up technical and depoliticized economic practice to political scrutiny. A burgeoning literature – not all of it taking its cue from Foucault – is critically examining economic truth techniques including credit rating (Sinclair 2005), accounting and auditing (Porter 1999; Power 1997), financial modelling and statistics (de Goede 2005; MacKenzie 2003b), debt restructuring standards (Soederberg 2003); and pensions calculations (Langley 2004). This involves getting *inside* the particular construction of numbers and statistics by developing an understanding of their normative assumptions, as well as a wider reading of the historical and institutional sedimentations that makes contestable numbers truth in the here and now. More broadly, 'cultural economy' is emerging as a field of study that takes seriously the discursivity and cultural contingency of current economic practice (see du Gay and Pryke 2002; Amin and Thrift 2003, also Shapiro this volume). As Don Slater (2002: 59) puts it, 'economic and cultural categories are logically and practically interdependent...In practice, social actors cannot actually define a market or a competitor, let alone act in relation to them, except through extensive forms of cultural knowledge.'

This understanding of discourse and cultural knowledge, rather than distracting from the study of material reality, enables it to be seen as profoundly political. In fact, it is in thinking about the political that IPE has a valuable contribution to make to the wider literature on cultural economy. For example, for Glyn Daly (2004: 5) it is precisely the discursivity of economy that makes possible a radical political economy: 'a *political* economy is one that...presupposes the essential discursivity of the economy. The reason for this is clear. The idea of an extra-discursive...is something that is wholly incompatible with that of the political' (emphasis in original, see also Daly this volume). There is then political potential – if not a political agenda – in the effort to show how economic truth techniques are particular and contestable representations of reality, rather than immutable facts. In this volume, Zalewski explores the politics of representation and (economic) survival, and concludes that 'survival and representation occur *in and through one another*' (emphasis in original).

At the same time, the move from the study of ideology to the study of truth techniques, makes visible a sharp difference between poststructuralism and constructivist work, that forms an important theme in this volume (as well as an important theme in current IR debates, see for example, Campbell 2001, Doty 2000; Zehfuss 2002). First, a constructivist reading is more likely to 'posit a limit to the limit-attitude' by carving out an extra-discursive domain (Campbell 1998: 224). For example, in this volume, Magnus Ryner argues for maintaining an extra-discursive realm that limits 'the extent to which discursive practices can construct commodities and their relations.'[2] While it should by now be clear that poststructuralists do *not* take the politics of representation to mean that anything-at-will can be constructed to be true, neither do they envision an extra-discursive realm through which such limits are imposed. They are more likely to understand the particular forms that socially constructed truth takes through cultural and institutional practice and historical sedimentation (see for example, Cameron and Palan 2004; Latour 1999). In this volume, Michael Shapiro argues, through rereading the work of Adam Smith, that 'the way value is deployed in the dynamics of political economy cannot be derived from...the way an object's materiality satisfies a need or want,' but that economic value emerges through complex cultural codes and historically contingent practices of valuation.

Secondly, and related, a constructivist reading is more likely to understand the social construction of truth to be purposefully in the interest of particular social actors. This may result in the (implicit) suggestion that 'social discourses are controlled and promoted...by socio-economic classes, gender groups, racial groups, powerful faiths and so on' (Cameron and Palan 2004: 48). But this reading fails to problematize the agent (and interest) behind the construction of discourse, and moreover fails to recognize the complexity of discursive constellations that 'are not easily manipulated' (Ricoeur, quoted in Cameron and Palan 2004: 48). Quoting Butler, Campbell (1998: 224) understands the construction of truth (in foreign policy) less as an '"act," singular and deliberate...than as a nexus of power and discourse that repeats and mines the discursive gestures of power.' In this volume, Aitken offers a similar understanding of the financial economy, not as an exploitative system designed by particular interest, but as a performative practice, the reiteration of which in the space of everyday life makes capital possible.

Power and agency

Problematizing interest and agency, then, forms a second theme to be highlighted here. According to Campbell (1996: 18), a critical questioning of the 'sovereignty problematic' in international politics involves challenging the concomitant 'economistic conception of power, whereby power is regarded as a commodity to be wielded by agents.' Instead of assuming a prior political agent that (individually or collectively) wields power (and discourse!) to serve its particular interests, it becomes imperative to enquire into the discursive constitution of agency and interest themselves. It becomes imperative, in Butler's (2004: 16) words, to 'rethink the relations between conditions and acts. Our acts are not self-generated, but conditioned.' In this volume, Gammon and Palan offer libinal political economy as a way of decentring the rational subject of political economy and replacing it with a Freudian subject who 'does not enjoy complete sovereignty, but is fragmented by an internal conflictual dynamic as it seeks to stabilize its object relations.' Although different from libinal political economy in many ways, Butler's work also draws upon a Freudian subject, and offers an understanding of human agency as not a singular starting point of political acts, but as always simultaneously enabled and constrained by (gender) discourses. By being called a name ('It's a boy!'), according to Butler (1997: 2), 'one is also, paradoxically, given a certain possibility for social existence, initiated into a temporal life of language that exceeds the prior purposes that animate that call' (see also Zalewski this volume). However, the rituals that exist before us and bring us into being, do not fully determine our possibilities: 'being acted upon is not fully continuous with acting, and in this way the forces that act upon us are not finally responsible for what we do.' Butler (2004: 16) concludes, 'We are at once acted upon and acting, and our "responsibility" lies in the conjunction between the two.'

One of the ways in which Butler's rethinking of agency speaks to the study of the global political economy and the concerns of this volume is by challenging the representation of capital as a coherent logic driven by class interests. There is no singular and purposeful political act or actor behind capitalist logic, but a circulating operation of power that constitutes agents and their interests. For Foucault, the panopticon did not imply a singular and all-seeing eye at the center of penal surveillance. Instead, Foucault (1979: 176–7) understands the 'disciplinary power' of the panopticon as

> organised as a multiple, automatic and anonymous power; for although surveillance rests on individuals, its functioning is that of a network of relations from top to bottom, but also to a certain extent from bottom to top and laterally; this network 'holds' the whole together and traverses it in its entirety with effects of power that derive from one another: *supervisors, perpetually supervised*. The power in the hierarchized surveillance of the disciplines is not possessed as a thing, or transferred as a property....And, although it is true that its pyramidal organisation gives it a 'head,' it is the apparatus as a whole that produces 'power' and distributes individuals in this permanent and continuous field (emphasis added).

The command center of the panopticon, put simply, is not manned by the all-seeing capitalist with a firm grip on the process, but by a supervisor – or these days, more likely an auditor – who is in turn supervised and who understands his agency, interests and responsibility in particular and historically contingent ways. Put differently, economic agents do not act purposefully and deliberately in the service of particular class interests, but emerge within a domain of explicit and implicit norms, which regulate the limits of the sayable for legitimate participation in economic practice.

In fact, theories of performativity, as developed by Butler and others in order to problematize the purposeful agent behind the political act, are becoming quite influential within the study of finance and economics from geographical and sociological perspectives, although the precise meaning and significance of performativity is under debate (see Callon 1998; Clark, Thrift and Tickell 2004; de Goede 2005a: 5–13; MacKenzie 2003a; Thrift 2002). In discourse theory, a performative is that which enacts or brings about what it names – the quintessential example being the priest whose words 'hereby I thee wed' enact the marriage (Butler 1993: 13; Austin 1962: 4–7). Understanding finance as a performative practice suggests that processes of knowledge and interpretation do not exist in addition to, or are of secondary importance to, 'real' material financial structures, but are precisely the way in which 'finance' *materializes*. For Michel Callon, for example, financial discourse is performative because it constitutes the reality it merely purports to describe. Economic measuring tools 'do not merely record a reality independent of themselves; they contribute powerfully to shaping, simply by measuring it, the reality that they measure,' according to Callon (1998: 23). In this volume, Martin Coward draws on Hardt and Negri's notion of Empire and understands 'the various thresholds of imperial power' to be 'performatively reasserted': 'The normalization of certain notions of life, community, and safety is never fully secured, but must rather be performatively re-iterated.'

Is it 'dangerous' to problematize the class agent behind economic discourse? This is certainly one of the strands of debate in this volume. Jessop and Sum wish to supplement Foucault's theorization of power with a coherent theory of capitalism. For Matt Davies, moreover, the Foucauldian theorization of power as a network results in an inability to theorize resistance, as it seems to extinguish agency. In contrast however, for Wendy Larner, it is liberating to see power as not emanating from one clear center, but operating as a practice of governmentality that constitutes agency and identity. Precisely through this theoretical move, the gaps and insecurities of neo-liberal governance become visible, and multiple sites of resistance may be thought possible.

Politics of resistance

This brings us to the third theme that needs to be drawn out for the purposes of this introduction. It is the rethinking of the politics of dissent and resistance that currently forms perhaps the most controversial, but perhaps also the most promising, poststructural intervention in the study of the global political economy. The rethinking of dissent through poststructural lens is sometimes seen as very problematic for left-wing politics, most recently for example, by Richard Wolin (2004), who argues that emphasizing the cultural and historical contingency of 'truth' deprives left-wing politics of sorely needed normative ground (for a counter-argument see the contributions to Butler, Guillory and Thomas 2000; also Rorty 2004). In feminist thought, for example, as Zalewski points out in this volume, the decentring of the subject 'woman' has 'seemingly threatened the capacity to answer – or ask – simple questions about important material issues such as why women are poorer than men with all the attendant suffering/violences that this incurs over lifetimes.' In addition, the understanding of capitalism as a performative practice 'increasingly resembles capitalism's description of itself' (Thrift 2005: 4; cf. Laffey 2000). These theoretical positions seem to raise insurmountable problems for the politics of resistance. If it is rendered problematic to speak in the name of a coherent political subject (for example, woman, the working class), how is emancipatory action possible? If critical theoretical discourse is dangerously close to capitalism's self-representation, how can it engage in effective resistance?

To the heart of these concerns of dissent and resistance goes a new realization of the ambiguities of the contemporary political economy and practices of dissent. For Thrift (2005: 4), it is clear that 'we have reached a point in which...capitalists and anti-capitalists...are not easily separated linguistically and, in some cases, even practically.' In her contribution to this volume, Louise Amoore points to the manifold contradictions in the global political economy within which we all find ourselves, and asks, 'how do we understand the Amnesty International Visa cardholder who stands opposed to the human rights abuses that characterize much of contemporary world politics, but whose debt is bundled up and sold in the global financial markets?' (see also Amoore and Langley 2004). For Amoore it is precisely these contradictions, however, that have the ability to become 'points of politicization,' as they contain 'the potential for a recognition of the intimate connections between "our" world and "theirs."' For Amoore, the realization of the ambiguous divide between the rulers and the ruled finds dissent in unexpected places. If capitalism lacks a singular center of power, it also lacks a singular center of resistance. In Foucault's (1998: 95–96) words, that inspired the title of Amoore's chapter, 'there is no single locus of great Refusal,' but instead a 'plurality of resistances...[M]ore often one is dealing with mobile and transitory points of resistance, producing cleavages in a society that shift about, fracturing unities and effecting regroupings, furrowing across individuals themselves, cutting them up and remoulding them.'

Paradoxically, then, a representation of agency as both constrained and produced in the social field of power may open up multiple possibilities for change. In this volume, Aitken offers an understanding of capital not as a monolithic and united force, but as 'something de-centered and something made, and potentially re-made, in the diverse and sometimes incoherent space of everyday life.' This understanding – of capital as a performative practice in need of constant articulation and reiteration – makes it vulnerable at the moment of enunciation: 'If...a structure is dependent upon its enunciation for its continuation,' writes Butler (1997: 19), 'then *it is at the site of enunciation that the question of its continuity is to be posed*' (emphasis added). In other words, despite the rigorous training and education economic agents are initiated by, their performances do not flawlessly reproduce previous formulations, but may reformulate, rearticulate, transform, and even fundamentally question orthodoxies. While Stephen Gill (1995: 2), for example, reads the theory of the panopticon as reducing the individual to a 'manipulable and relatively inert commodity,' for Butler discursive power is not always so felicitous. In its daily life, the gaps, disjunctures, contradictions and political openings of global capitalism may be rendered visible (cf. Gibson-Graham 1996). In this volume, Larner emphasizes the contingencies and 'messy actualities' of neoliberalism and reveals at work a 'complex and hybrid political imaginary,' instead of a coherent policy program or ideology.

In this context of capital as made and remade in mundane spaces, everyday life comes to be seen as an important site of power and resistance. In this volume, Jessop and Sum discuss how exploiting the 'affordances of mundane products and routine circumstances' in everyday life is able to subvert their disciplinary logic. At the same time however, Matt Davies warns that we should not interpret any nonelite gesture automatically as an act of resistance, but instead we should come to a *critique* of how capitalist practice transforms everyday life in order to theorize resistance and the everyday. Both chapters contribute to the increasingly important theorizing of everyday practice as an important site of power and resistance in the global political economy (see also, for example, Campbell 1996; Langley 2002; Sinclair 1999).

Moreover, the effects of resistance are themselves ambiguous and can never be securely known to produce the 'mimetic reflection of an a priori political principle' (Bhabha 1994: 25). For Homi Bhabha (1994: 28, 25), political resistance is to be understood as a *negotiation* rather than a negation, in order to recognize the unpredictable 'hybrid moment of political change,' in which emerges 'a political object that is new, *neither the one nor the other*' (emphasis in original; cf. Derrida 1981: 42–43). The outcome of the contingent process of negotiation that is political resistance cannot be known before one engages. As Daly (2004: 4) puts it, 'the effects of the political cannot be known in advance.'

Bhabha's intervention makes dissent unpredictable and ambiguous but also arguably more *political*. The insecurity of political positioning envisions a constant self-reflection and reexamination of one's politics. Political positioning becomes mobile, unfinished, tactical, and dependent upon context – instead of something to be decided before the battle starts. To give an example relevant to Dutch politics at the time of writing, political positioning may entail resisting the breakdown of the social welfare state – but that positioning needs to remain mobile and self-critical when it becomes clear that anti-migrant sentiment is central to much of the current protest against the breakdown of the welfare state. Simultaneously, social movements need to engage in a politics of strategic alliance and selective collaboration (Appadurai 2002; Shaw 2003). As Butler (2004: 48) writes: 'various routes lead us into politics, various stories bring us onto the street, various kind of reasoning and belief.' In this volume, Bice Maiguashca draws on Gramscian and poststructural theory to come to an understanding of the multifaceted strategies and tactics of social movements.

For Bhabha (1994: 20), culture forms a privileged site of dissent: 'Forms of popular rebellion and mobilization are often most subversive and transgressive when they are created through oppositional *cultural* practices' (emphasis in original). While it is clear that culture historically has played an important role in sustaining and reproducing dominant practices or repressive politics (Jenkins 2003), an increasing strand of literature relevant to IPE examines cultural practice as a site of dissent (see Amoore 2005, part 4; also Bleiker 2000; Campbell 2003; Shapiro 2002). For Amoore (2005: 358), 'playful resistance and celebratory festivals become a potential means to temporarily interrupt the pressures of everyday life and to suggest alternative ways of life' (see also Amoore this volume). In my own work, I have argued that comedy and carnival are particularly important in economic and financial criticism, because the authority and legitimacy of financial practices is underpinned by their rationality and differentiation from emotion (de Goede 2005b; also de Goede 2005a). Finally, for Edkins (1999: 142, 140), the task of repoliticization involves rendering visible the 'contingent, provisional nature' of the symbolic order, which may be helped by 'disrupting [the] claim to seriousness.'

If the dissenting task of poststructural criticism is to repoliticize that which appears as apolitical in modern life (and contemporary economics and finance do so *par excellance*), then art and culture can be important sites of disturbing, challenging, disrupting, making strange – in effect *repoliticizing* – these practices. This certainly does not mean, in Roland Bleiker's (2003: 417) words, that 'we should turn our eyes away from the key challenges of world politics, from war to inequality and hunger, to devote ourselves to reading poetry and gazing at art.' But it does mean encouraging multiple sites of dissent, and drawing 'upon the innovative nature of the aesthetic to rethink deeply entrenched and often narrowly conceived approaches to understanding and solving world political problems' (Bleiker 2003: 417). It moreover means facing up to the realization that the seriousness and coherence of global capitalism is constituted, in part, through the very discourses that seek to challenge it (Gibson-Graham 1996; see also Larner this volume).

And despite the debates cutting across these chapters – economy as discursive or material, power as network or resource, capitalism as coherent or vulnerable and diffuse, it is important to remind ourselves, as Amoore does at the very end of this volume with the words of Butler (2004: 48), that 'We could disagree on the status and character of modernity and yet find ourselves joined' in a politics of dissent.

Volume structure

The three themes set out here – the politics of representation, the problem of agency and the politics of resistance – run as a red thread through the present volume. The volume is divided into three parts, each with its own introduction in which a detailed description of the chapters can be found. First, the section titled 'poststructural interventions' offers a number of ways of thinking through the promise of poststructuralism in the study of the global political economy. If poststructuralism sees its work as an interpretative analysis with political effects – rather than the accumulation of objective knowledge – poststructural political interventions are already being made in both the theory and the practice of IPE, from a cultural reading of the work of Adam Smith in order to destabilize his conceptual apparatus that has been so influential on modern economics (Shapiro), to thinking about financial performativity (Aitken), to seeing power at work in Empire (Coward).

Section II engages explicitly with one of the most explosive issues in the debate on IPE and poststructural politics – the question of discourse and materiality. As will be clear from this introduction, this question is at the heart of some theoretical resistance to poststructuralism. This section does not pretend to resolve this thorny question once and for all – if anything, it becomes clear that one's position in the debate rests upon an act of faith more than a realization of the 'truth' – but offers a diversity of points of view that students of IPE may identify with.

Section III thinks through the question of ambiguity, dissent and social movements. As discussed in this introduction, some poststructural theoretical positions seem to problematize emancipatory politics, but also promise rich new ways of thinking about dissent. The readings in this section grapple with the politics of dissent in different ways, from emphasizing the politics of everyday life, to rethinking the politics of social movements, to exploring culture as a site of dissent.

Notes

1 However, in contrast to Harvey, Devetak (2001: 181) uses the term postmodernism to denote all (IR) authors who 'regard their own writing as either postmodern, poststructuralist or deconstructive.' An alternative term used in some IR literature is postpositivism (see Lapid 1989). Palan (2000) uses the term postrationalism in the context of IPE, to denote a break with traditional economic assumptions of rational economic actors.

2 Ryner sees his point about the extra-discursive supported by my exploration of discourses of scientific finance that led to the rise and fall of the hedge fund LTCM (de Goede 2005a, Chapter 5). The reason the fund failed, Ryner seems to imply, is that it came up against an extra-discursive realm of 'reality' that limited the constructive power of the discourses of scientific finance. However, it should be clear that I do not subscribe to this interpretation. My discussion of the LTCM case, while critical of discourses of scientific finance, does not base this criticism on the assumption that these discourses somehow *distort* reality, and can be exposed to be 'false' with reference to an underlying truth (as an ideology-critique might do). Instead, I read these discourses in the sense of truth-techniques as theorized by Foucault and discussed above, that have particular effects of power, and that are historically and socially contingent, but not necessarily *false* or unrealistic. For a discussion of the differences between ideology-critique and poststructuralism, see George and Campbell 1990.

References

Aitken, R. (2004) '"A Direct Personal Stake": Cultural Economy, Mass Investment and the New York Stock Exchange,' *Review of International Political Economy* 12 (2): 334–63.

Amin, A. and Palan, R. (2001) 'Towards a Non-Rationalist International Political Economy,' *Review of International Political Economy* 8 (4): 559–77.

Amin, A. and Thrift, N. (eds) (2003) *The Cultural Economy Reader*. Oxford: Blackwell.

Amoore, L. (1998) 'Globalisation, the Industrial Society and Labour Flexibility: a Sense of Déjà Vu?,' *Global Society* 12 (1): 49–74.

Amoore, L. (ed.) (2005) *Global Resistance Reader*. London: Routledge.

Amoore, L. and de Goede, M. (2005) 'Governance, Risk and Dataveillance in the War on Terror,' *Crime, Law and Social Change* 43 (2): 149–73.

Amoore, L. and Langley, P. (2004) 'Ambiguities of Global Civil Society,' *Review of International Studies* 30 (1): 89–110.

Appadurai, A. (2002) 'Deep Democracy: Urban Governmentality and the Horizon of Politics,' *Public Culture* 14 (1): 21–47.

Ashley, R. K. (1996) 'The Achievements of Post-Structuralism,' in Smith, S., Booth, K. and Zalewski, M. (eds) *International Theory: Positivism & Beyond*. Cambridge: Cambridge University Press.

Ashley, R. K. and Walker, R. B. J. (1990) 'Speaking the Language of Exile: Dissident Thought in International Studies,' *International Studies Quarterly* 34: 259–68.

Austin, J. L. (1962) *How To Do Things with Words*. Cambridge MA: Harvard University Press.

Balibar, E. (1999) 'At the Borders of Europe,' Lecture, Department of Philosophy, Aristotle University of Thessaloníki, October 4. http://www.makeworlds.org/node/80

Bhabha, H. (1994) *The Location of Culture*. Routledge: 1994.

Bleiker, R. (2000) *Popular Dissent, Human Agency and Global Politics*. Cambridge: Cambridge University Press.

Bleiker, R. (2003) 'Learning from Art,' *Global Society* 17 (4): 415–28.

Butler, J. (1993) *Bodies that Matter: On the Discursive Limits of 'Sex.'* London: Routledge.

Butler, J. (1997) *Excitable Speech: Contemporary Scenes of Politics*. London: Routledge.

Butler, J. (2004) *Precarious Life: The Power of Mourning and Violence*. London: Verso.

Butler, J. Guillory, J. and Thomas, K. (eds) (2000) *What's Left of Theory?* New York: Routledge.

Callon, M. (1998) 'Introduction: the Embeddedness of Economic Markets in Economics,' in Callon, M. (ed.) *The Laws of the Markets*. Oxford: Blackwell.

Cameron, A. and Palan, R. (2004) *The Imagined Economies of Globalization*. London: Sage.

Campbell, D. (1996) 'Political Prosaics, Transversal Politics, and the Anarchical World,' in Shapiro, M. J. and Alker, H. R. (eds) *Challenging Boundaries: Global Flows, Territorial Identities*. Minneapolis: University of Minnesota Press.

Campbell, D. (1998) *Writing Security: United States Foreign Policy and the Politics of Identity*, second edn. Minneapolis: University of Minnesota Press.

Campbell, D. (2001) 'International Engagements: the Politics of North American International Relations Theory,' *Political Theory* 29 (3): 432–48.

Campbell, D. (2003) 'Cultural Governance and Pictorial Resistance: Reflections on the Imaging of War,' *Review of International Studies* 29: 57–73.

Campbell, D. (2005) 'The Biopolitics of Security: Oil, Empire and the Sports Utility Vehicle,' *American Quarterly* 57 (3): 943–72.

Clark, G. L., Thrift, N. and Tickell, A. (2004) 'Performing Finance: the Industry, the Media and Its Image,' *Review of International Political Economy* 11 (2): 289–331.

Coward, M. (2002) 'Community as Heterogeneous Ensemble,' *Alternatives* 27: 29–66.

Daly, G. (2004) 'Radical(ly) Political Economy: Luhmann, Postmarxism and Globalization,' *Review of International Political Economy* 11 (1): 1–32.

de Goede, M. (2003) 'Beyond Economism in International Political Economy,' *Review of International Studies* 29 (1): 79–97.

de Goede, M. (2005a) *Virtue, Fortune and Faith: a Genealogy of Finance*. Minneapolis: University of Minnesota Press.

de Goede, M. (2005b) 'Carnival of Money: Politics of Dissent in an Era of Globalising Finance,' in Amoore, L. (ed.) *Global Resistance Reader*. London: Routledge.
Derrida, J. (1981) *Positions*, translated by Alan Bass. Chicago: University of Chicago Press.
Deuchars, R. (2004) *The International Political Economy of Risk: Rationalism, Calculation and Power*. Aldershot: Ashgate.
Devetak, R. (2001) 'Postmodernism,' in Burchill, S. *et al.* (eds) *Theories of International Relations*, second edn. London: Palgrave.
Doty, R. L. (2000) 'Desire all the Way Down,' *Review of International Studies* 26 (1): 137–9.
Dreyfus, H. L. and Rabinow, P. (1982) *Michel Foucault: Beyond Structuralism and Hermeneutics*. Chicago: University of Chicago Press.
du Gay, P. and Michael Pryke, M. (eds) (2002) *Cultural Economy*. London: Sage.
Edkins, J. (1999) *Poststructuralism and International Relations: Bringing the Political Back In*. London: Lynne Rienner.
Foucault, M. (1979) [1977] *Discipline & Punish: the Birth of the Prison*. New York: Vintage.
Foucault, M. (1982) 'Afterword: The Subject and Power,' in Dreyfus, H. L. and Rabinow, P., *Michel Foucault: Beyond Structuralism and Hermeneutics*. Chicago: University of Chicago Press.
Foucault, M. (1998) [1976] *The Will to Knowledge: The History of Sexuality, Volume 1*. London: Penguin.
George, J. (1994) *Discourses of Global Politics*. Boulder CO: Lynne Rienner.
George, J. and Campbell, D. (1990) 'Patterns of Dissent and the Celebration of Difference: Critical Social Theory and International Relations,' *International Studies Quarterly* 34: 269–94.
Gibson-Graham, J. K. (1996) *The End of Capitalism (As We Knew It)*, Oxford: Blackwell.
Gill, S. (1995) 'The Global Panopticon? The Neoliberal State, Economic Life, and Democratic Surveillance,' *Alternatives* 20 (1): 1–49.
Gills, B. K. (2001) 'Re-Orienting the New (International) Political Economy,' *New Political Economy* 6 (2): 233–45.
Hansen, L. and Williams, M. (1999) 'The Myths of Europe: Community and the Crisis of the EU,' *Journal of Common Market Studies* 37 (2): 233–49.
Harvey, D. (2001) *Spaces of Capital*. Edinburgh: Edinburgh University Press.
Hooper, C. (2001) *Manly States: Masculinities, International Relations and Gender Politics*. New York: Columbia University Press.
Jenkins, B. (2003) 'Creating Global Hegemony: Culture and the Market,' in Tétreault, M. A. *et al.* (eds) *Rethinking Global Political Economy*. London: Routledge.
Jessop, B. and Sum N.-L. (2001) 'Pre-Disciplinary and Post-Disciplinary Perspectives,' *New Political Economy* 6 (1): 89–101.
Krasner, S. D. (1996) 'The Accomplishments of International Political Economy,' in Smith, S., Booth, K. and Zalewski, M. (eds) *International Theory: Positivism & Beyond*. Cambridge: Cambridge University Press.
Laffey, M. (2000) 'Locating Identity: Performativity, Foreign Policy and State Action,' *Review of International Studies* 26 (3): 429–44.
Laffey, M. (2004) 'The Red Herring of Economism,' *Review of International Studies* 30: 459–68.

Langley, P. (2002) *The Everyday Life of Global Finance*, IPEG Papers in Global Political Economy, www.bisa.ac.uk/groups/ipeg/ipegpapers.htm

Langley, P. (2004) 'In the Eye of the "Perfect Storm": the Final Salary Pension Crisis and Financialisation of Anglo-American Capitalism,' *New Political Economy* 9 (4): 539–58.

Lapid, J. (1989) 'The Third Debate,' *International Studies Quarterly* 33: 235–54.

Latour, B. (1999) *Pandora's Hope: Essays on the Reality of Science Studies*. Cambridge: Harvard University Press.

Ling, L. H. M. (2002) 'Cultural Chauvinism and the Liberal International Order: "West" versus "Rest" in Asia's Financial Crisis,' in Chowdhry, G. and Nair, S. (eds) *Power, Postcolonialism and International Relations*. London: Routledge.

Luoma-aho, M. (2004) 'Arm Versus Pillar: the Politics of Metaphors of the Western European Union,' *Journal of European Public Policy* 11 (1): 106–27.

MacKenzie, D. (2003a) 'An Equation and Its Worlds: Bricolage, Exemplars, Disunity and Performativity in Financial Economics,' *Social Studies of Science* 33 (6): 831–68.

MacKenzie, D. (2003b) 'Long-Term Capital Management and the Sociology of Arbitrage,' *Economy & Society* 32 (3): 349–80.

Marchand, M. and Runyan, A. S. (2000) 'Introduction: Feminist Sightings of Global Restructuring,' in Marchand, M. and Runyan, A. S. (eds) *Gender and Global Restructuring: Sightings, Sites and Resistances*. London: Routledge.

Palan, R. (2000) 'New Trends in Global Political Economy,' in Palan, R. (ed.) *Global Political Economy: Contemporary Theories*. London: Routledge.

Patomäki, H. and Wight, C. (2000) 'After Postpositivism? The Promises of Critical Realism,' *International Studies Quarterly* 44 (2): 213–37.

Peterson, V. S. (2003) *A Critical Rewriting of Global Political Economy: Integrating Reproductive, Productive, and Virtual Economies*. London: Routledge.

Porter, T. (1999) 'The Late-Modern Knowledge Structure and World Politics,' in Hewson, M. and Sinclair, T. J. (eds) *Approaches to Global Governance Theory*. New York: State University of New York Press.

Power, M. (1997) *The Audit Society: Rituals of Verification*. Oxford: Oxford University Press.

Rorty, R. (2004) 'Philosophical Convictions,' *The Nation*, June 14, http://www.thenation.com/doc.mhtml%3Fi=20040614&s=rorty

Rosamond, B. (2002) 'Imagining the European Economy: Competitiveness and the Social Construction of Europe as an Economic Space,' *New Political Economy* 7 (2): 157–77.

Shapiro, M. J. (1993) *Reading 'Adam Smith': Desire, History, and Value*. London: Sage.

Shapiro, M. J. (1996) 'Introduction,' in Shapiro, M. J. and Alker, H. R. (eds) *Challenging Boundaries: Global Flows, Territorial Identities*. Minneapolis: University of Minnesota Press.

Shapiro, M. J. (2002) 'The State, Bourdieu and Method,' *Review of International Political Economy* 9 (4): 610–8.

Shaw, K. (2003) 'Whose Knowledge for What Politics?,' *Review of International Studies* 29: 199–221.

Sinclair, T. J. (1999) 'Synchronic Global Governance and the International Political Economy of the Commonplace,' in Hewson, M. and Sinclair, T. J. (eds) *Approaches to Global Governance Theory*. New York: State University of New York Press.

Sinclair, T. J. (2005) *The New Masters of Capital: American Bond Rating Agencies and the Politics of Creditworthiness*. Ithaca, NY: Cornell University Press.
Slater, D. (2002) 'Capturing Markets from the Economists,' in du Gay, P. and Pryke, M. (eds) *Cultural Economy*. London: Sage.
Soederberg, S. (2003) 'The Promotion of "Anglo-American" Corporate Governance in the South,' *Third World Quarterly* 24 (1): 7–27.
Thrift, N. (2002) 'Performing Cultures in the New Economy,' in du Gay, P. and Pryke, M. (eds) *Cultural Economy*. London: Sage.
Thrift, N. (2005) *Knowing Capitalism*. London: Sage.
Weldes, J. (1999) *Constructing National Interests: The United States and the Cuban Missile Crisis*. Minneapolis: University of Minnesota Press.
Williams, D. (1999) 'Constructing the Economic Space: The World Bank and the Making of *Homo Oeconomicus*,' *Millennium* 28 (1): 79–99.
Wolin, R. (2004) *The Seduction of Unreason*. Princeton: Princeton University Press.
Zalewski, M. (2000) *Feminism After Postmodernism: Theorising Through Practice*. London: Routledge.
Zehfuss, M. (2002) *Constructivism in International Relations: the Politics of Reality*. Cambridge: Cambridge University Press.

Part I
Poststructural Interventions

In this part, five poststructural 'interventions' into thinking about the global political economy are offered. According to Campbell (1998: 221–2), 'poststructuralists and their allies see their works as *interpretative interventions that have political effects*, whereas the mainstream (in both its orthodox and relatively progressive guises) perceives itself as engaged in the objective pursuit of cumulative knowledge' (emphasis added). What follows in this section, then, are five interventions that can be seen to have political effects and that enable thinking about IPE differently from its traditional pursuit of the objective accumulation of knowledge. These interventions, in different ways, offer cues for studying political economy culturally, historically, and discursively. Taken together, they introduce a broad scala of poststructural thought to the discipline of IPE, thus demonstrating the promise of poststructuralism in the study of the political economy.

To start, Marysia Zalewski offers a performative reading of a Kath Weston story in order to think through the complex interweaving of survival and representation. In Weston's story a beggar hails passers-by on the streets of the campus of an East Coast University. Zalewski reads the story to show that the (self)representation of the beggar and the historically contingent representation of vagrancy more generally, are crucial to survival. Gender plays an important part in this story, and Zalewski thus engages with the debates on feminism/poststructuralism that center on the question of whether political projects in the name of a 'decidable subject,' are undermined by poststructural analysis. For Zalewski, however, politics emerges elsewhere – not through a clear program for feminist reform, but through a decentring and political questioning of categories and identities we use unproblematically in daily life. In conclusion, Zalewski shows the interweaving of representation, materiality and survival, by developing the point that representation (as beggar, as woman, as Jew) is the 'thing to be survived.' Zalewski thus places representation squarely within the central problematic of IPE.

In the second chapter, Michael Shapiro reads the work of Adam Smith as an important nodal point that helped constitute the way we think about (political) economy today. Smith's influence is constituted through what Shapiro (1993: xxvii) calls 'the Smith effect,' 'a set of ways of scripting the self, for imagining spaces such as the state, and for constructing the dynamics of such selves within various spaces...All of these dimensions of the Smith Effect bear on understandings that are integral to modern capitalist political economy and the construction of the "social," "political," and "moral" within which such a political economy operates.' In Smith's story, value arises from the encounter between the body and the object, and the ability of the object to satisfy needs. In contrast, Shapiro offers a reading of value that emphasizes its discursive and culturally contingent construction, in which value is 'less an individual choice than an enactment of a social code.' This reading leads to an examination of the cultural history of taste. Shapiro concludes that in the study of political economy, 'those disciplines that theorize the collective and interpersonal webs within which desire is evoked become more crucial than those that address the production and exchange of commodities.'

In the third chapter, Martin Coward explores the currently developing literature on Empire as a terrain on which IPE and poststructuralism are fruitfully engaging. Coward outlines the central logic of the literature on IPE and globalization to be one of an 'either/or decision' between territorial sovereignty and supra-territorial globality. Thinking through the operation of power in Empire breaks with this 'either/or' distinction, and is able to conceptualize transversal power in conjunction with the ways in which limits and boundaries continue to be central to contemporary politics. Coward shows the importance of biopolitical power in the contemporary global political economy, that is, the power that determines the 'nature of human life itself.' This political constitution of what it is to be human establishes the conditions for hegemonic rule and capitalist accumulation. At the heart of the global political economy, then, for Coward, is a logic of security that seeks to establish the threshold of who counts as human, and what counts as legitimate and righteous. It is through an examination of these various logics of security that a poststructural IPE may open new political horizons and critically question the contemporary global conjuncture.

In the fourth chapter, Rob Aitken reconceptualizes capital not as a overarching or self-expanding force, but as a practice that is performed in the space of everyday life 'in the name of pursuit of freedom, security, ethical choice or some other objective.' For Aitken, it is not just that global capital manifests itself in everyday life, but more precisely that capital is 'possible only when it occupies the space of everyday life or when it is created by and through everyday working class populations.' Through an analysis of the ways in which financial advertising campaigns visualize good economic citizenship in direct relation to national security, Aitken traces not a linear narrative to contemporary capital, but a history of 'assertions and slippages' which articulate particular and historically contingent financial identities. This history challenges IPE's conventional account of the linear process of increasing globalization. Like Coward, Aitken collapses the IR/IPE distinction by showing the mutual constitution of discourses of individual and national security and their joint denial of the savage and the racialized other.

Finally, in Chapter 5, Gammon and Palan offer a different vision of the possibilities for poststructural IPE, by developing libidinal political economy as an approach that breaks with political economy's orthodox view of the rational subject. Because of its presupposition of the rational subject, according to Gammon and Palan political economy 'fails to comprehend an important dimension of its own economy.' The approach offered in this chapter 'refuses to take capital in its own words,' and seeks to problematize political economy's concepts including 'capital,' 'savings' and 'investments,' through theorizing the economy of desire. An almost anthropological reading of currently depoliticized economic concepts becomes possible. Gammon and Palan compare the recent loss of trillions of dollars in stock market value in the US and UK with the premodern cultural economy of the Trobiand Islanders that left unconsumed food to rot, which was interpreted as a sign of barbarism by the anthropologist Malinowski. In this manner, the chapter opens political possibilities by questioning the naturalness, rationality and presupposed superiority of current political economy and stock market investing.

References

Campbell, D. (1998) *Writing Security: United States Foreign Policy and the Politics of Identity*, second edn. Minneapolis: University of Minnesota Press.

Shapiro, M. J. (1993) *Reading 'Adam Smith': Desire, History, and Value*. London: Sage.

1
Survival/Representation

Marysia Zalewski

A 'real world' anecdote

Across the campus of an East Coast University, where money walks the corridors like ivy covers the walls, a woman sits on the pavement. To all appearances she is white. Day after day, her garments accented with frost or sweat, she calls to passers-by and gestures toward her cup. 'Spare change, sir?' she intones, with a rising inflection that suggests expectation. 'Ma'am, spare change?' Always a gendered appeal. In another year and a shorter haircut[1] *I eddied in the wake of a stream of commuters that channeled out of the subway to flow directly past her post. 'Spare change, ma'am? Spare change, sir?' When she got to me, her cadence held. 'Spare change, sir-ma'am-sir?' For that gift alone I offered up my coins.*

In this twenty-first-century vignette, a woman's survival depends upon calling people into classification. They will be stirred (she hopes) to action through a gendered form of address that in its application invokes class, age, and race as well as gender. Against a moving backdrop of T-shirts and knapsacks, cameras and skateboards, the formality of the language positions the speaker as supplicant. In this context, 'ma'am' and 'sir' cannot help but carry the inflection of centuries of subordination. These are the terms in which a street theorist hails her walking public. Kath Weston (2002), *Gender in Real Time.*

Introduction

A tenacious anxiety appears to still haunt contemporary theorizing in international political economy (IPE). This concerns the use value of poststructural ideas in the context of 'real' world issues and problems. A typical claim is that approaches which favor deconstruction and postfoundationalist/poststructural ways of thinking are of little or indeed no use in helping to either understand the material problematics that grip the world in the twenty-first century, or to alleviate them. For some therefore, this signifies that 'postmodern culture ... constitutes a crisis of representation because it is associated with a detachment of sign from the referent, the signifier from the signified, representation from reality, image from truth' (McGuigan 1999: 55). Simultaneously, and perhaps paradoxically, a major claim attributed to poststructuralists, is that more conventional theorizing *also* fails in similar ways. For example, it is suggested that traditional theorizing may be, in part, responsible for the apparent entrenchment of global inequalities and injustices. At the very least doubt is cast upon retaining confidence in progress narratives (such as those associated with western forms of liberal individualism) when their credibility has been called into question (Brown 2001: 15). Yet, however we think or theorize, we are surely faced with a scenario in which poverty, massive social injustices and sheer relentless violence in many of the richest countries in the world, let alone the poorest, appear all too familiar. One might wonder why (or how), as Slavoj Žižek muses, 'we are prepared, step by step, to accept as familiar a bizarre and morbid situation' (2002: 32). As scholars and students we might also question why so many conventional academic books on international politics and international political economy impart a sense of inevitability and intractability to deeply iniquitous situations. As Cynthia Enloe urges, 'a book about international politics ought to leave one with a sense that "I can do something." A lot of books about international politics don't' (2000: 17).

Feminist scholars are no strangers to the antagonisms that breathe life into these reputedly opposing camps of theorizing (Flax 1993; Butler and Scott 1992; Barrett and Phillips 1992; Felski 2000; Zalewski 2000; Bronfen and Kavka 2001). Innumerable criticisms have been heaped upon scholarship working in the areas of feminism, sex/uality and gender which, for example, employ poststructural understandings of the subject as undecideable, the persistent claim being that this kind of work is inevitably unable to support any political projects or demands made in the name of a decidable subject, namely woman. Alternatively, feminists who advocate more traditional interpretations of the subject and associated methodologies have been accused of anachronistic and melancholic attachments to an epistemology and ensuing politics which ensconces the oppressions and injustices it purports to liberate (Barrett and Phillips 1992; Brown 2001). As Robyn

Wiegman puts it, 'at the beginning of the twenty-first century, feminist theory is torn between a modernist and postmodernist political interpretation – between a desire for a materialist articulation of bodies and their liberation in indeterminate and/or multiple resignification' (2001: 379; also Weeks 1998: 2).

In this chapter, I want to take the opportunity to reflect upon some of the issues invoked by these debates and to do this the chapter will consist of three main sections. First I will further clarify some of the issues that animate this volume. Second I will reflect on some of the political possibilities of feminist poststructuralism.[2] In the final section, I will return to the themes raised in the introduction and reconsider the difficulties around questions about subjectivity and representation. I will focus mostly on the uses (or otherwise) of deconstruction in the study of international political economy in the discipline of International Relations/International Political Economy (IR/IPE). As a corollary, I will make some comments about disciplinary battles in IR/IPE by briefly ruminating on the contemporary managerial-bureaucratic westernized university and the challenges this has engendered.

What's the problem?

> Reality must appear to be *found* not *produced*
>
> Slavoj Žižek (2002), *Looking Awry*

> If we would have new knowledge, we must get a whole world of new questions
>
> S. K. Langer (1942), *Philosophy in a New Key*

Material issues often seem to be at the heart of feminist inquiry. Perhaps at its most simple, yet also most profound, the question 'why are women generally poorer, or paid less than men?' is regularly asked. The differential still seems to be hugely widespread, for example, ranging from the gender gap in academic salaries,[3] to women constituting 70 percent of the world's poor (Seager 2003: 88), to the figure that 65 percent of the world's women total work time is spent doing unpaid work (Seager 2003: 71). Yet answers to these questions about women – or indeed the ability to formulate them in the first place – implies the necessity of being able to recognizably classify the (sexual) *difference* that makes a *difference*. Alternatively phrased, feminists have consistently been aware of the political need to work with sexed subjectivity and identity – in this case related to women – in order to exact rights and justice for and on behalf of this group. This work on (sexual) identity and subjectivity is frequently understood to have facilitated the ability to make legitimate and acceptable knowledge claims about groups and individuals, some of whom we might identify as men and others as women. To make claims about women, feminists have drawn heavily on modernist epistemological and ontological methodologies, both implicitly and explicitly, sometimes and sometimes not, explicitly espousing allegiance to liberal, radical or socialist inspired politics.[4] In this way feminists have been clear about who women are and how we might judge how fair their lives are compared to those of men. Yet the incursion of poststructural work over the last few decades has potentially undermined the foundations upon which such traditional feminist theorizing and political practices have rested.[5] Jim McGuigan locates these incursions thus:

> There have been several different theoretical currents at work to deconstruct the modern subject and essential identity: the philosophical attack on the Cartesian subject of knowledgability, the Lacanian stress on the splitting and decentering of the psychological subject ... Foucauldian genealogies of the discursive techniques of selfhood, the performativity of queer theory, and the various critiques of essentialisms (1999: 87).

The casting of the subject of woman as undecideable; the deauthorizing of the epistemological promise of knowledge/truth claims; the annihilation of credible claims to authentically represent (anything) – have all seemingly threatened the capacity to answer – or ask – simple questions about important material issues such as why are women poorer than men with all the attendant suffering/violences this incurs over lifetimes.

Let me return to the anecdote told at the beginning of this introduction, a story I will revisit several times in this chapter to illustrate the discussion and to clarify what the problems are. How we are to interpret/tell the story told by Kath Weston? What explanations might be offered? What is going on? There are many ways in which these questions might be answered. For example, one could surely mine the jewels of Marxism to offer reasons for this act of begging in the richest country in the world, minimally invoking theorizations of the construction of valued and non-valued work and the brutalities of capitalism. Alternatively, the glittering legacy of feminist scholarship might be excavated to supply explanations for the specific poverty experienced by women.[6] To be sure, these Marxist and/or feminist-inspired arguments are not inevitably defined as *wrong* through the use of poststructural work. Indeed, a poststructuralist might argue that the worst of liberal individualism might be curtailed by the political acknowledgement of structural constraints on the conduct of lives and the dictates of life chances.

Yet a poststructuralist might also reflect on what facilitates or methodologically supports these more structurally inclined interpretations briefly gestured towards above. One suggestion is that more traditionally constituted Marxist or feminist analyses are structured by bounded and therefore potentially restrained understandings of the subject, identity, representation and the associated relationships between subjects and their representation, and theory and practice. The implication is that these bounded perceptions cast a fine but sturdy net over the manifold ways of understanding the relationships just mentioned. This has traditionally meant that subjects are perceived to precede their representation and that practice comes before theory. To return to the anecdote to illustrate further – significance is surely implied by the gender of the person – the subject (who is taken for granted) – asking for money. And it seems to matter that she is a woman – we would generally not doubt this. Consequently, a feminist researcher might trace the story of this woman's life to discover the gendered reasons for her current situation. Why is she begging on the street? Why doesn't she have money of her own (or not enough, or so we assume) either through paid employment or support from her family or someone else? (The years invoked by the changing seasons in the story seem to indicate that she is a 'genuine' beggar – not a journalist or researcher 'playing the part'). And more specifically why is this a *woman* begging on the street, as in the 'first' world it is still probably the case that most of the people begging for money are men. What happened in this woman's life? Numerous explanations might be offered for this woman's street life-style, ranging from those which apportion individual blame (she did not work hard enough, she lost her job, she left – or was left by – her husband/partner not to mention her parents – we don't have a sense of her age); to more structurally influenced interpretations which are more likely to assign responsibility to unfair and unjust systems of domination and oppression such as patriarchy and/or capitalism, concomitantly demanding state intervention to redress this inequitable situation.

A crucial question is evident and one that exercises social theorists persistently and this is – how are we to know what the truth is? How is it genuinely possible to make judgments about the truth of this woman's life? To claim to have the truth of her story is vital for many reasons not least because the truth(s) deemed legitimate and authoritative will impact significantly upon her. Historically, vagrancy – perceived as individual failing – has been subject to punitive legislative sanctions; in a different time or place this woman's life may be subject to extreme state violence (not to mention other forms of violence). Currently, in the west, itinerant life-styles are still the focus of official regulatory surveillance and under constant threat of disciplinary action as well as from 'random' aggression. Scholars who protest against the use of poststructuralist ideas to make sense of what really happens 'on the ground,' or in the 'real world,' or simply to be able to say 'what is,' propose that the hardships that this woman suffers – by virtue of her need to ask strangers for money and the possibility of violent acts visited on her (minimally) – surely verifies the need for concrete analyses, answers and solutions to this concrete example. What is the use – political or otherwise – in offering a poststructurally inspired deconstructive reading of this tale? What we need is the truth. The alleged poststructural focus on identity, subjectivity and representation is imagined as distracting us from important questions about the truth in the context of material structures and distributive justice plainly gestured towards in this story. Or to recall an example raised in the introduction to his volume – as Stephen Krasner ardently suggests, 'the achievements of international political economy have been generated by an epistemology that conforms with the western tradition ... not with ... postmodernism' (1996: 122). Krasner's (1996: 124–5) concern is that the loss of conventional epistemology and associated methodologies would 'strip social science of the most important contribution that it can make to the betterment of human society: that contribution is to discipline power with truth.' Passionate words indeed.

Who's there?[7] Am I that name?[8]

Rather than offer comprehensive descriptions and evaluations of either conventional, structural, poststructural and/or feminist approaches, my aim in this chapter is to explore, by performative example, what poststructurally inspired feminism has to offer. To do this I want to stay with the anecdote I started this chapter with to keep thinking through some of the ideas and assumptions littering the reading/telling of it. However at this point it might be helpful to consider a little more closely some of the ways poststructurally inflected approaches work, both to allow a better sense of what it might mean to 'do' poststructuralism and perhaps also to get a clearer understanding of what fuels the persistent concerns about the political utility of this work.

Largely drawing on some of Derrida's work I will start by discussing the concept/activity of *decentering* to impart a flavor of poststructuralism. This activity is crucial to poststructuralism as it invokes the decentering of the subject, of institutions and of the *logos* – the latter being ancient Greek for 'word,' with all its connotations of the authority of the 'truth' (Royle 2003: 15). Why do this? What is the point of decentering anything? If the idea is to expose how power works, or to show where power lies, what makes poststructuralists importantly different from Marxists or feminists? The latter is an especially pertinent question in the light of Seidman and Alexander's suggestion that the political work of poststructuralism lies in the attempt to show how 'claims to textual coherence or closure are linked to social power and inequality' (2001: 7). Surely more conventional structurally inclined scholars are similarly concerned with social power and inequality? And if these scholars share comparable concerns, what accounts for the animosity between them, an enmity which partly instigated the production of this volume?

Briefly stated, decentering, as a practice of deconstruction, evinces a profound wariness of 'proper names.' As such, one of the aims of decentering is to illustrate how 'proper names,' for example, 'woman,' 'fact,' 'reason,' 'beggar,' 'white'– the list is, literally, inexhaustible – come to assume a coherency and unity which is unwarranted (implying that quotation marks *always* hover whether explicitly marked or not, see also Peterson this volume). They are unwarranted, claim poststructuralists, because unity, coherence, univocality are effects produced out of division and divisibility (Barry 2002). Thus, for example, feminists have made claims on behalf of the subject of woman, yet, for poststructuralists, that subject does not exist – at least not as a coherent, immutable, essence, which might be recognized as such and agreed upon by all. Is a woman to be identified by her genes, her chromosomes, her femininity, her hormones, her frailty, her strength, her fertility? All of these things (and many more) have been used as markers or signifiers of what woman is – yet all of these things have also acted as *disputed* markers of what woman is – or some women ... were black slave women – women? What is to decide the final and ultimate resting place of the 'truth' of woman – or what methods might be used to decide this?

This does not simply mean that asking endless questions is all that poststructuralism offers, rather that the process of persistent questioning and a related refusal to stop deconstructing (not that 'stopping' is achievable), has the capacity to (begin to, but never get to the 'end') make sense of claims made by poststructuralists that coherency is an effect produced out of division and divisibility. As Judith Butler suggests, this questioning is not about 'debunking' but rather to 'revitalize.' 'If one calls ... terms into question, does this mean they cannot be used anymore?' (Butler 2001: 418). Consequently, intensively concentrating on a single passage or some apparently small (insignificant?) aspect is employed in the service of illustrating the impossibility of sustaining a univocal reading.

At the same time, paying attention to 'distractions' – the things that seem irrelevant, trivial, peripheral but yet refuse to go away – emerges as an important activity (Zalewski forthcoming). For example, in her introduction to *Bodies That Matter* (1993), Judith Butler remarks that the more she thought about the materiality of the body (the subject of her book), the more she found she kept thinking of other things and in other domains. Despite urging herself to be more 'disciplined' and to keep focused, she kept 'losing track' of the subject. This eventually led her to suppose that 'resistance to fixing the subject [might be] essential to the matter in hand' (Butler 1993: ix).

'Keeping on track' is perhaps precisely what decentering – and the questioning/destabilizing strategy inhabiting it attempts to avoid. The 'track' is the problem, or perhaps constitutes the problem especially if we bear in mind Cynthia Enloe's point that 'for an explanation to be *useful*, a great deal ... has to be left on the cutting room floor' (1996: 188, my emphasis). Enloe's editing/film analogy is helpful as it is clear that different editing choices can result in vastly differing 'end products.' This is not about a simple choice of which particular *'facts'* to emphasize, but relates to deeper issues of the constitution of legitimate and authoritative narratives and authentic representation. Let me, once again, return to the anecdote to clarify.

In the first iteration my telling of the story conveyed a tale of a woman asking for money – which I suggested was an act of begging, which I further suggested was in need of explanation, and yet further, I gestured toward ways in which we might start to explain this act. Yet on what basis did I decide which aspects were the central/important part of the story? On what basis might I decide if the person's sex/gender is relevant to any discussion? Recall that one of the ruses of deconstruction, specifically if not exclusively through decentering, is to insistently keep reading a text against the grain (off the track) in order to illustrate how instability takes on the mantle of stability, in order to dishevel some of the parameters which keep the telling of the story encircled/imprisoned.

For example, the tale begins with an 'East Coast University.' Which east coast of which country? To be sure, we perhaps assume the US east coast especially if we know more about the author of the piece (a professor at Harvard University in the US). Yet, there is surely a sense that it is obvious which east coast is being referred to. Does this matter? Does it raise the specter of US hegemony? Is this an overstatement? Trivial? Peripheral? How might we judge if this point is relevant? A white woman is sitting on a pavement. Is she sick? Did she fall? Is she resting? Does her 'whiteness' or 'womanness' have any significant function? And further, how might we judge that this is a woman and that she is white? Why does it matter that she is a woman, or white, she may or may not be – how do we know – what is it that would make us finally agree?

Kath Weston's telling of the story helps us in the quest to undo the sense of the story (as opposed to make sense of it). She does tell us that this is a woman – yet her narration suggests that this might not be relevant. Or more expressly we might think about the woman's sex/gender in a rather different register than that usually employed by more structurally inclined scholars. Thus rather than focus on the subject of woman *per se* and therefore this woman's embodied and (en)gendered sex, theories around gender/sex are used to think through some of the complex relations between subjectivity, division and domination (Kay 2004: 83). For instance, we might move from a methodological position which works around and on the basis of the stability of the subject of woman and consequently ask questions about this woman and her place in structured systems of gendered discrimination, and instead think about the functions of gender as they are expressed in this anecdote. For example, Weston subtly notes that the woman's request for money is 'always a gendered appeal. They (passers-by) will be stirred (she hopes) to action through a gendered form of address that in its application invokes class, age, and race as well as gender.' As such, our questions about gender focus not on the embodied sex and/or gendered subordination of this individual in the context of structurally gendered subordination, but rather on how ideas and beliefs about gender/sex materialize in and through the street practice of asking strangers for money. And this surely will tell us something about the integral relationship between subjectivity, representation and 'material reality.' These are points to which I will return.

As such there *is* a history to this story, though perhaps not an essentialist and linear one, but one layered through with innumerable ideas around gender, sex, race, class (I hesitate to add 'etc'). This is clearly demonstrated by Weston's comment, 'in this context "ma'am" and "sir" cannot help but carry the inflection of centuries of subordination.'

> In their split-second decisions to contribute or pass on, the commuters respond to petitions that exceed words. Hailed as bourgeois, they peer at her through histories of propriety and suspicion: Is this beggar shamming? What legitimate circumstances could lead a 'good woman' to the streets? (Weston 2002: 20).

As such, the purpose of a decentered reading/telling is not to work towards finding or building a perfect methodology in order to reach the truth, or indeed to discipline power with truth. Rather a poststructuralist inclined approach prefers to focus on how categories or representative forms function and gain authority (or are resisted) through incremental accretions (or refusals) of credibility. As such, our attention might be turned to how the person on the street employs and is employed by understandings of gender/sex. As Weston eloquently articulates, this woman is a 'street theorist hailing her walking public.' As a street theorist this woman is already and always epistemologically and ontologically imbued with and by an unending cache of meanings. These she uses (like all of us) to make meaningful, hopefully effective requests. The passers-by are similarly marked – decisions (split-second ones) to give money may well depend on what is perceived to be 'appropriate' behavior exhibited by the person asking for money. The poststructural insinuation is not that any of these meanings are predetermined or that they are irretrievably bounded, indeed quite the opposite. Imagining categories such as sex or beggar to have – *somewhere* – an essential unchangeable meaning is at best unhelpful, and at worst reifies the category and its attendant harms. Yet meanings *do* become attached – and have effects.

It is not happenstance that the work gender might be doing becomes easier to notice *via* its own decentering – a decentering enacted by the street theorist herself through the form of address she chooses (decides upon) when faced with gender/sexed ambiguity – 'sir-ma'am-sir.'

> In another year and a shorter haircut I eddied in the wake of a stream of commuters that channeled out of the subway to flow directly past her post. 'Spare change, ma'am? Spare change, sir?' When she got to me, her cadence held. 'Spare change, sir-ma'am-sir?' For that gift alone I offered up my coins.[9]

Why did I include a (footnoted) explanation about the narrator's appearance? The gender/sex uncertainty implied by the 'shorter haircut' of the author (we assume from her [assumed female] name and self-perceived need to make this remark about her hair) ruptures a usually clear (we think/assume) boundary – one which the 'street theorist' deals with (in a split second) by including all currently culturally available options – 'sir-ma'am-sir.'

> Her invocations runs back and forth – creatively – between culturally fixed possibilities. As with 'sir' and 'ma'am' rests on a conception of gender that permits only dual options, which may or may not find resonance in the bodies passing by (Weston 2002: 19).

Does my *footnoted* explanation in the conventions of academic writing indicate a remark or clarification of less significance or value than the discussion included in the main text of this chapter? This surely tells us something about the parameters or boundedness about what counts as appropriate to invoke when making a judgment about what *matters* in the story, or what is of central importance to make sense of the story. But it is evident that ideas and beliefs related to elitism, race, gender, sexuality, class (yet another 'not exhaustive list') are all functioning in the reading, telling, narrating and understanding what is going on in this brief anecdote. This well highlights Enloe's (1996) point mentioned earlier about explanation only emerging as *useful*, if a great deal is left on the cutting room floor. Useful to whom, with what effect and to what end? What story (or stories) would emerge if the 'bits on the cutting room floor' were weaved back into the telling?

Making undecideable decisions

> Decisions are moments of non-knowledge
>
> Nicholas Royle (2003), *Jacques Derrida*

Poststructurally influenced work focuses less on what appears to be obviously relevant (indeed on what *appears*), or significant or important and instead concentrates on 'the gaps that haunt our speech' (Kay 2003), the 'whispered priorities' (Vaughan-Williams forthcoming), the 'epistemological conceits' (Campbell 1998: xi). Differently configured, poststructuralist work revisits *common-sense* (what *appears*) partly to illustrate how in the 'name of common-sense laziness is promoted to the rank of rigor' (Belsey 2002: 26). Or as Hunt suggests,

> the languages used to preserve domination are complex and sometimes contradictory. Much of how they operate to anesthetize desire

> and resistance is invisible; they are wedded to our *common-sense*; they are formulaic without being intrusive, entirely natural – 'no marks on the body at all' (1990: 199, my emphasis).

And recall that a crucial/significant purpose is to illustrate the instability and incoherence of what appears to be stable and coherent. Let me turn the discussion briefly to the issue of undecidability to clarify further.

Poststructural work on undecidability suggests that each decision, any decision, could always have been made otherwise. This is not a statement about individual choice and/or agency, but rather gestures towards the sedimented deposits of beliefs, prejudices, hatreds, jealousies, altruisms, kindnesses, tiredness, greed, fears (yes – another unending list) that structure/haunt and give meaning/life to the meanings which give meanings to meanings. Nothing is ever unread, or as Jameson puts it, 'texts come before us as the always-already-read; we apprehend them through sedimented layers of previous interpretations' (2001: 101). We can surely see this happening in my own closing of the decisions around naming the woman on the street in the anecdote which I started this chapter with. What else might I have chosen to name her? A beggar? A tramp? A homeless person/woman? A wastrel? A scrounger? A poor soul? A survivor? A free spirit? A victim? An escapee? Another unending list. In making any of these decisions, or in the decisions that the 'street theorist' makes, or the 'passers-by' make – flowing in and out of each nano/meta decision are innumerable, untidy, ragged but often very robust tiers of beliefs, prejudices, feelings and emotions. *Yet we tend not to act as if any of this messiness happens*. We tend to act as if all decisions are 'foregone conclusions' (Lucy 2004: 148). This *is* a woman; this *is* a white woman. But (unseen) question/quotation marks inhabiting all these decisions always haunts. The idea of undecidability opens every decision (and keeps it open) to the possibility of being otherwise (Lucy 2004: 151). And for poststructuralists, political possibilities exist in this space of undecidability. Yet this space can appear as an abyss, as unacceptable, as apolitical, as not useful and as a reprehensible chasm for those who would claim that a focus on deconstruction is inappropriate for matters relating to the material realm.

There is a scene in the film *Schindler's List* (1993) in which the Nazi officer (Goeth, played by Ralph Fiennes) visits the basement where his maid-servant (one of the prisoners Helen Hirsch played by Embeth Davidtz) lives/works. In a previous scene, we witness this young woman pouring her heart out to Oskar Schindler (played by Liam

Neeson) describing how she tries to do the right thing, to do exactly what Goeth wants, to follow all his orders. But she cannot. She cannot because he keeps changing the rules. Indeed, there are no rules – he makes arbitrary decisions. The woman has no choice but to take whatever will happen to her. There is no right thing. 'There are no set rules you can live by ... and be safe.'

With this in our minds, the inevitability of the brutality visited upon the woman by Goeth is all the more terrifying because we know she is right. On his arrival in the basement Goeth appears almost 'kindly' and asks Helen if she is lonely saying that he would like to 'touch out to her in her loneliness.' She remains silent even though he gives her permission to answer. 'You can answer,' then saying he knows what she is thinking and why she is silent – 'what *is* the right answer?' 'What will please him?' To which he 'replies,' 'the truth, Helen, is always the right answer.' Carrying on the 'conversation' – he asking his own questions and 'answering' for Helen's imagined/imposed questions – Goeth muses vaguely about the possibility of the 'us' that he and Helen might be. The sexual character of Goeth's interest in Hirsch has been incrementally established in the film. Wondering aloud about the idea that people 'like Helen' are more like vermin and lice and not people 'in the strictest sense,' Goeth moves closer and closer to Helen – moving finally as if to touch her breast and kiss her on the lips. All through this, Hirsch is standing wearing only a flimsy under-slip, she is silent and she is petrified. A spilt-second before the threatened delivery of the kiss, Goeth draws away saying, 'no I don't think so, Jewish bitch. You nearly talked me into it didn't you?' And then the moment that Hirsch was waiting for arrives – Goeth brutally beats her.[10]

It is, perhaps, precisely this kind of terrorizing activity understood as the brutal and arbitrary exercise of power that has consistently provided fuel for the idea that there have to be sure, incontrovertible grounds for adjudicating knowledge claims and to discipline power with truth. The sense is that a primary purpose of social science/theory broadly conceived[11] is to play a (surely very small) role in the generic modernist project of understanding and ameliorating injustices in the service of facilitating conditions which induce fairness and equality and progress – progress towards making Goeth's behavior (as an example of Nazism rather than individual pathology) impossible. My reasons for thinking about this scene – albeit briefly – is not to deny (or affirm) the purpose of social science/theory. Nor is it to say that a decision cannot or should not be made about Goeth's behavior (or Nazi ideology). Hirsch survives Goeth's brutal assault on her – at least physically as far as we know. But what is it that Hirsch survives if not (her) representation as a woman, as a Jewish woman in a prison/death camp in the Second World War? What is it that the 'white woman on the pavement' is constantly surviving if not (her) representation – a representation(s) made real many times over?

The concern that poststructural deconstruction – decentering identity, destabilizing subjectivity and representation – is oppositional or antagonistic to focusing on material structures and violences surely misses the point. Weston's telling of the story that opened this chapter poignantly illustrates the ways in which survival and representation occur *in and through one another*. Or to put this another way, 'representation becomes both a means to survival and the thing to be survived' (Weston 2002: 19). Living within the representational sphere of 'polite beggar' perhaps works to persuade passers-by to part with their 'spare change' – as such representation is also undoubtedly a means to survival. Yet simultaneously this representation is the 'thing to be survived' – day after day sitting on the pavement come rain or shine, come blows or kindness.

Hirsch's identity as a 'Jewish bitch' is clearly not a simple figment of Goeth's individual imagination or cruel persona. The incremental and deadly accretion of debased values to 'Jewishness' by Nazi ideology in this instance is surely a form of representation that is the 'thing to be survived' – though Hirsch's agency in this instance to survive is undeniably constrained. But it is not an accident, or 'mere' coincidence – the director's intentionality notwithstanding – that the scene in which Goeth beats Hirsch is spliced through with a rather different display of heterosexual masculinity.[12] Oskar Schindler's emotional manipulation of Hirsch in an earlier scene is surely preferable to Goeth's violence; nevertheless this juxtaposition of masculinities provides another example of the complex layering and sedimentations that work to (re)constitute subjectivities and identities. Deconstruction is not intended to shatter something that is coherent and solid. Rather it is to illustrate how fluidity and incoherence becomes weaved into seemingly unyielding forms.

Closing thoughts

> Nothing escapes invention
>
> Zillah Eisenstein (2004), *Against Empire*

> The university professes the truth, and that is its profession
> Jacques Derrida (1994), *Specters of Marx*

This book is primarily written for a university audience and specifically IPE/IR students and scholars. Yet all is not well in this 'tormented' (Derrida 2002: 207) institution. Imposed changes over the last few decades have propelled universities ever more deeply into the business of the commercial production of knowledge – as my inter-library-loan cover sheet enthusiastically proclaims 'delivering the world's knowledge.' But disputes as to appropriate methods of research within disciplines rage and indeed draw attention from some of the self-appointed popular guardians of higher education. If 'the postmodern condition is fundamentally an epistemological condition to do with the production and legitimation of knowledge' (McGuigan 1999: 11) it is perhaps not surprising that battles over appropriate methodologies constantly recur. This is especially the case in relation to the extent to which the 'organization of research and teaching has to be supported ... let us euphemistically say "sponsored" by commercial and industrial interests' (Derrida 2002: 206). Researchers of more apparently policy or 'real world' issues which are typically the focus of IPE may have much to fear from a presumed disassociation with 'real' research and the production of truth, or indeed appropriate ways to study material issues. Falling prey to the seemingly inappropriate practices of deconstruction – especially feminist – which may not readily appear to fulfill the criteria of excellence/truth does indeed raise problems for such researchers.

But the question has been posed. What use is a focus on subjectivity/representation especially when considered in a context of undecidability illustrated and enacted through the activities of decentering and deconstruction? One implication is that this approach is unhelpful and unworthy. Unworthy because it seems frivolous to insistently 'worry away' at issues/facts which seem (to some) obvious and unquestionable or if questionable, only in a trivial sense. Unhelpful because it won't tell us *what to do*. As such the more specific question might be asked – what help is 'spending years on a sentence' (Royle 2003: 1) in knowing what to do about the woman asking strangers for money on the street of a (US) east coast campus? Or the Jewish woman being brutalized by a Nazi officer?

We (academics/students?) tend to like fully rounded, satisfying neat conclusions with clear answers to the questions asked – well, perhaps not all of us. 'Conclusions shouldn't sound too satisfied, all the edges rounded off' (Interview with Enloe 2001: 660). Yet as I suggested earlier, I am offering a performative example of the ways in which (one version or aspect) of feminist poststructuralism might work. This is not to suggest that decisions cannot, should not, or will not be made. Money might be offered to the 'white woman sitting on the pavement.' A 'passer-by' might offer shelter, help, support. Another might be inspired into action by her plight, which might mean inquiring into her personal story, or in some other way. But question marks litter and splinter through Kath Weston's telling of the story. A white woman sitting on a pavement. There are no simple conclusions or answers. Attempting to weave some of the 'bits off the cutting room floor' into any narrative is always messy and awkward – but surely necessary. If representation is all there is – then 'without representation there is no violence' (Weston 2002: 19).

Notes

1 From this comment we might conclude that the narrator presents herself as someone whose 'sex/gender' might be read as ambiguous.
2 What might be considered as 'feminist poststructuralism' is clearly broad as well as debatable. In this chapter I can only gesture towards something I regard as within the realm of feminist poststructuralism.
3 *The Guardian*, 'Women Paid Less at Every University,' 2 September 2004, http://education.guardian.co.uk/gendergap/story/0,7348,1296062,00.html, last accessed 25 April 2005; Melanie Ward, *Salary and the Gender Salary Gap in the Academic Profession*, Ideas discussion paper, 1999, http://ideas.repec.org/p/iza/izadps/dp64.html, last accessed 25 April 2005.
4 Clearly not an exhaustive list.
5 This is not to imply that criticisms of traditional western feminist theorizing only emanates from poststructuralist work.
6 Who might be defined as (traditional or neo) Marxist or (traditional) feminist work in IPE is clearly debatable. A selective sample of related work and helpful references in this area includes: Jessop 1994; Overbeek 2000; Rupert and Smith 2002; Kelly *et al.* 2001. See also Peterson 2003 for further bibliographic sources.
7 Derrida 1994.
8 Riley 1988.
9 From this comment we might conclude that the narrator represents herself as someone whose 'sex/gender' might be read as ambiguous.
10 Interspersed through this scene are shots of Schindler at a party surrounded by women. Indeed at the moment of the 'near kiss' between Goeth and Hirsch, Schindler is shown (passively) waiting to be embraced by a female singer at the party. As the blows rain down on Hirsch, Schindler showers kisses on many women in a raucous party atmosphere.
11 Here I am including the scholarly activities of International Relations and International Political Economy scholars under the rubric of 'social science/theory.'

12 Which I footnoted (fn 10) – yet another example of a decision which relegated a perhaps less apparent aspect of the narrative to a position of lesser significance or to the 'cutting room floor'....

References

Barrett, M. and Phillips, A. (eds) (1992) *Destabilizing Theory: Contemporary Feminist Debates*. Oxford: Polity Press.

Barry, P. (2002) *Beginning Theory*. Manchester: Manchester University Press.

Belsey, C. (2002) *Poststructuralism: A Very Short Introduction*. Oxford: Oxford University Press.

Bronfen, E. and Kavka, M. (eds) (2001) *Feminist Consequences: Theory for the New Century*. New York: Columbia University Press.

Brown, W. (2001) *Politics out of History*, Princeton: Princeton University Press.

Butler, J. (1993) *Bodies That Matter: On The Discursive Limits of 'Sex.'* New York and London: Routledge.

Butler, J. (2001) 'The End of Sexual Difference,' in Bronfen, E. and Kavka, M. (eds) *Feminist Consequences: Theory for the New Century*. New York: Columbia University Press.

Butler, J. and Scott, J. (1992) *Feminists Theorize the Political*. London: Routledge.

Campbell, D. (1998) *National Deconstruction Violence, Identity, and Justice in Bosnia*. Minneapolis: University of Minnesota Press.

Derrida, J. (1994) *Specters of Marx*, translated by Kamuf, P., New York and London: Routledge.

Derrida, J. (2002) *Without Alibi*, edited and translated by Kamuf, P., California: Stanford University Press.

Enloe, C. (1996) 'Margins, Silences and Bottom Rungs' in Smith, S., Booth, K. and Zalewski, M. (eds) *International Theory: Positivism and Beyond*. Cambridge: Cambridge University Press.

Enloe, C. (2000) *Bananas, Beaches and Bases: Making Feminist Sense of International Politics*. California: University of California Press.

Enloe, C. (2001) 'Interview with Professor Cynthia Enloe,' *Review of International Studies* 27 (4) 649–66.

Eisenstein, Z. (2004) *Against Empire: Feminism, Racism, and the West*. London: Zed Books.

Felski, R. (2000) *Doing Time: Feminist Theory and Postmodern Culture*. New York: New York University Press.

Flax, J. (1993) *Disputed Subjects*. London: Routledge.

Jameson, F. (2001) 'The Political Unconscious' in Seidman, S. and Alexander, J. (eds) *The New Social Theory Reader*. London: Routledge.

Hunt, E. (1990) 'Notes for an Oppositional Poetics' in Bernstein, C. (ed.) *The Politics of Poetic Form: Poetry and Public Policy*. New York: Roof Books.

Jessop, B. (1994) 'Post-Fordism and the State,' in Amin, A. (ed.) *Post-Fordism*. Oxford: Blackwell.

Kay, S. (2004) *Žižek: A Critical Introduction*. Cambridge: Polity Press.

Kelly, R. M. *et al.* (eds) (2001) *Gender, Globalization and Democratization*. Lanham, MD: Rowman and Littlefield.

Krasner, S. (1996) 'The Accomplishments of International Political Economy' in Smith, S., Booth, K. and Zalewski, M. (eds) *International Theory: Positivism and Beyond*. Cambridge: Cambridge University Press.

Langer, S. K. (1942) *Philosophy in a New Key*. Cambridge, Massachusetts: Harvard University Press, in Plummer, K. (ed.) (1995) *Telling Sexual Stories*. London: Routledge.

Lucy, N. (2004) *A Derrida Dictionary*. Oxford: Blackwell.

McGuigan, J. (1999) *Modernity and Postmodern Culture*. Buckingham, Philadelphia: Open University Press.

Overbeek, H. (2000) 'Transnational Historical Materialism,' in Palan, R. (ed.) *Global Political Economy: Contemporary Theories*. London and New York: Routledge.

Peterson, V. S. (2003) *A Critical Rewriting of Global Political Economy*. London: Routledge.

Riley, D. (1988) *'Am I That Name?' Feminism and the Category of 'Women' in History*. Basingstoke, Hampshire: The Macmillan Press Ltd.

Royle, N. (2003) *Jacques Derrida*. London: Routledge.

Rupert, M. and Smith, H. (eds) (2002) *Historical Materialism and Globalisation: Essays on Continuity and Change*. London: Routledge.

Seager, J. (2003) *The Atlas of Women: An Economic, Social and Political Survey*. London: The Women's Press.

Schindler's List (1993) Amblin Entertainment Production, Universal City Studios, Inc, Dir. Steven Spielberg.

Seidman, S. and Alexander, J. (eds) (2001) *The New Social Theory Reader*. London: Routledge.

Vaughan-Williams, N. (forthcoming) 'Towards a Problematisation of the Problematisations that Reduce Northern Ireland to a "Problem"' in Zalewski, M. and Barry, J. (eds) *Intervening in Northern Ireland: Critically Representing the Conflict and its Legacy*, special issue of *Critical Review of International Social and Political Philosophy*.

Weston, K. (2002) *Gender in Real Time: Power and Transcience in a Visual Age*. London and New York: Routledge.

Weeks, K. (1998) *Constituting Feminist Subjects*. Ithaca: Cornell University Press.

Wiegman, R. (2001) 'Object Lessons: Men, Masculinity, and the Sign *Women*,' *Signs: Journal of Women in Culture and Society* 26 (2): 355–88.

Zalewski, M. (2000) *Feminist Theory After Postmodernism: Theorising Through Practice*. London: Routledge.

Zalewski, M. (forthcoming) 'Distracted Reflections on the Production, Narration and Refusal of Feminist Knowledge in IR' in Ackerly, B., Stern, M. and True, J. (eds) *Feminist Methodologies for International Relations*. Cambridge: Cambridge University Press.

Žižek, S. (2002) *Looking Awry*. Cambridge, Massachusetts: The MIT Press.

2
Adam Smith: Desire, History and Value

Michael J. Shapiro

The fragment, reproduced from my *Reading 'Adam Smith'* (Shapiro 1993), which begins 'Smith and the Problem of Value,' is predicated on the central argument of the book: Smith's *Wealth of Nations* is best read as a spatio-temporal story. And insofar as the *Wealth's* narrativity shapes its perspective, what I refer to as Smith's 'theory of value' is located more in the way he develops a historical plot than in his explicit economic concepts. In Smith's writing, value emerges in the interface between his larger historical plot and his smaller, epistemological one. The former (elaborated in Smith's *Wealth*) treats his narrative of expanding exchange, while the latter (developed in many of his other writings) comprises his sensationalist account of how the world becomes intelligible to individual, perceiving subjects, as bodies encounter objects. Ultimately, after analyzing the failure of Smith's theory to account for how things become valued, I suggest, that an appreciation of the way value is deployed in the dynamics of political economy cannot be derived from an inspection of the way an object's materiality satisfies a need or want, even when, à la Smith, one focuses on the productive processes that make that object available. Rather, it is necessary to locate a drive towards satisfaction – this is, desire – within a complex set of evolving cultural codes. Among the implications of this argument is a shift in the intellectual terrain within which political economy is to be thought. Those disciplines that theorize the collective and interpersonal webs within which desire is evoked become more crucial than those that address the production and exchange of commodities.

Smith and the problem of value

Two dimensions of Smith's story must be understood to appreciate his approach to value. The first part is an epistemological narrative about the meeting of bodies and objects. The second is a social narration about the meeting of the individual body with the social body. Smith had an abiding ambivalence towards sensation. On the one hand, he thought of 'the external senses,' as he called them, as a bounty 'given us by nature' to tell us about the conditions of external bodies so that we can judge what might 'benefit or hurt us' (Smith 1982a: 168). On the other hand, sensation disturbs our tranquility. In his 'History of Astronomy,' Smith (1982b: 61) speaks of the mind's search for tranquility and harmony, which he posits as the motive for seeking parsimonious explanation. Moreover, he says that the excitement produced by novel objects is dreadful. 'How much we dread the effect of the more violent passions, when they come suddenly upon the mind, appears from the preparations which all men think necessary when going to inform anyone of what is capable of exciting them.' (Smith 1982b: 35).

Here Smith is thinking not only of calamities but also of good fortune, for he goes on to argue that too much sudden joy is even worse than news of misfortune. In general, then, he ascribes to humans the desire to 'deaden vivacity of both pain and pleasure' (Smith 1982b: 37).

For Smith, therefore, sensation is the primary source of value, and embodiment is represented as a screening mechanism to dampen one's relationship with objects. Smith operates, it seems, with a simple grammar of subject-object relations. Objects constitute initiating causes – for example, they 'excite our wonder,' and in general he uses the idea of excitement in a way that holds objects responsible for what is sensed (Smith 1982b: 40). The subject/perceiver reacts to the initiating impacts of the objects by attempting to dampen their more extreme effects on themselves and others. The formulation of experience and value for Smith is thus based on the encounters between an object's tendency to excite sensations and a subject's attempts to manage the effects. The implicit narrative of this epistemology should be evident: objects act prior to subjects. This narrative's relationship to value is also clear: value is generated from objects.

But more than sensationalism governs Smith's attempt to isolate materiality. His interest in exchange and his (Newtonian) scientific predilection combined to motivate him to find what was *common* to each instance of materiality. For Smith (1982b: 105), Newton's system was 'the greatest discovery that ever was made by man,' and what was integral to this was the system's ability 'to connect together the otherwise disjointed and discordant phaenomena of nature.'

The search for this material commonality was therefore to provide Smith with two coherences. The first was epistemic – it would satisfy his Newtonian emphasis on a unified and parsimonious explanation. The second was economic – it would provide a unit of measure that would free value from the purview of state authority and locate it in a broadly distributed way in the society. As Marx suggested, Smith was the Martin Luther of political economy.

The advantage of exchange was, for Smith, self-evident. It leads to enhanced levels of satisfaction. Instead of posing a fixed level of value for which states compete (the mercantilist view), for Smith 'wealth' as value increases with increased exchange. At the level of thought, the production of an unfettered level of exchange required a separation of the idea of the domain of economy from the political and moral crotchets of the state.

Smith's idea of value shifts uneasily back and forth between his interest in exchange and his emphasis on production. Siding with Quesnay, who located 'real wealth' in its creation, Smith focused on that which contributed to making objects available for satisfactions, but emphasized labor and paid less attention to land than Quesnay. The epistemological story remained in place. Objects satisfy senses, that is, their value derives from their material relationship to the body. But this epistemological narrative in which objects are primary is subsumed within a larger story, a story about the increased productivity that derives from the division of labor.

In the smaller epistemological story, objects (or materiality) lose some of their primacy inasmuch as Smith, as was the case subsequently with Marx, reduces objects to their subjective essence (even at times to the biological dimension of subjectivity). However, this is not the individual subjectivity or collective, cultural subjectivity that produces value through perspective. It is the subjectivity involved in making objects materially available for use in an economic way. The primary materialist narrative thus remains in place epistemologically for Smith, as it did for Marx (1977: 126), who insisted that the value of a commodity, in the sense of its 'use value' 'is conditioned by the physical properties of the commodity, and has no existence apart from the latter.'

In the larger story, Smith's fable is remarkably individualistic. He imagines a self-sufficient human supplying basic necessities with her/his own labor. The Smithian subject faces the world of objects alone, both as one with unproblematic needs and as a supplier. As Smith (1978: 487) put it in his *Lectures on Jurisprudence,* 'In general ... the necessities of man are not so great but that they can be supplied by the unassisted labor of the individual.'

Although Smith (1981: 454) occasionally turned his attention to the individual seeking 'the most advantageous employment for whatever capital he can command,' his story paid little heed to the social and economic organization of labor in firms. Rather, his story, like the exemplary stories in classical political economy and canonical political treatises of his time, was constructed on the basis of a juxtaposition between a state of nature in which an individual is responsible for satisfying his/her own needs and the present, 'real' condition in which various reciprocities obtain. Thus Smith (1981: 39) speaks of 'that early and rude state of society' in which a laborer keeps everything [he] produces, and contrasts this with the market system of exchange.

The language of Smith's historical fable is strikingly retrospective, for the primitive hunter to which Smith frequently refers is not a laborer in most senses, especially not in the sense in which people who work and people who manage work are interrelated in what Marxists call the 'relations of production.' Not surprisingly, Smith's discourse here is Lockian/individualist rather than Marxist. He was focused more on an origin myth in which work produces entitlement to value rather than on the value extractions involved in the social organization of work. For Smith, as for Locke, labor is not simply a concept used to understand economy; it is ontological, emerging from a form of philosophical naturalism.

As Louis Dumont (1977: 190) has pointed out, Smith's reliance on the 'early and rude state' origin myth is a 'natural law argument,' although Smith doubtless avoided a 'state of nature' expression because of his friend David Hume's effective and influential dismissal of the idea. So fixated was Smith on this preexchange condition story, in which he produces an individualistic relation between persons and work, that his explicit development of his position on value is highly vexed.

On the one hand, Smith (1981: 47) baldly states in Chapter 5 of *The Wealth of Nations* that 'labour is ... the real measure of the exchangeable value of all commodities,' and that 'the real price of everything, what everything really costs to the man who wants to acquire it, is the toil and trouble of acquiring it.' On the other hand, Smith's (1981: 73) exchange orientation takes him over, and he gets wrapped up in treating the actual or what he ends up calling the 'market price' of commodities, which he recognizes to be a function of other than labor contributions – the appropriation of land, the 'stock,' which involves capital for advances on wages and the materials for work, and the 'ordinary rate of profit in [the] neighborhood.'

Dumont has stated the vexation clearly. In his words, '*Labor and exchange* taken together are central to Adam Smith's thought. This pair runs like a red thread throughout the beginning of the *Wealth*' (Dumont 1977: 93). He goes on to trace Smith's heroic attempt to pull his notion of value constantly back towards the contribution of labor in order to maintain the identity with which he constructs economic reality, the identity between labor and value.

Yet Smith could not ultimately extract value from the process of exchange. His 'natural state,' in which he equates labor with value by noting that the primitive producer enjoys the fruits of his labors himself, simply would not travel into a market economy. Dumont has told the story of Smith's struggle well. Here a somewhat different problem is stressed. Smith's narration of the shift from the primitive condition to the market condition, his economic history, was vexed. But at another level, that of his smaller epistemological story, his history, as has been noted, is uncomplicated. Objects produce satisfactions because of their materiality, not, for example, because of the interpretive process in which they achieve their significance (as for example, in the case of a gift, whose 'value' is a function of the context of the exchange, especially the intersubjective bond it reinforces or creates).

The Smithian subject or body faces things alone, alone in the sense that there is no linguistic or cultural mediation between a person and the satisfaction of value. Smith's empiricist story of value, notwithstanding its vexations stemming from his ontological commitment to labor and his interest in exchange, is conceptually disenabling in that it neglects the contexts in which objects take on value, and politically disenabling in that part of the context is the interpretive struggle that determines what will control what 'value' is to mean.

A semiological alternative

If value is an interpretive imposition, the analysis must turn to the modalities of imposition. Accordingly, Smith's narrative style has been interrogated at two levels, the first or smaller story of the subject-object relation and the second or more general history of the emergence of value. It was shown, generally, that Smith's position on value cannot be separated from his sensationalist epistemology, built on an object-to-subject narrative in which an object's materiality excites a subject's sensations. This applies for Smith even in the case of an aesthetic object such as a work of art. As Smith would have it, the object excites passions and fulfills the subject's need for stimulation and novelty. Somehow, of course, genre must be intrinsic to objects as well, for Smith does not deal with the complex interpretive dynamics that determine whether, for example, a given object is food or an item of aesthetic appreciation at one or another moment.

To disrupt the Smithian view, it is necessary not only to shift the locus of value production away from objects but also to note *how* they become valued within a syntax that relates them to other things. To appreciate how objects support valuing, we must do more than posit an initiating subjectivity. We must be able to follow the twists and turns through which narrative structures position objects. Although there is a variety of analytic discourses within which this can be shown, not the least of which is psychoanalytic (see Gammon and Palan this volume), here the focus is on the semiological frame, for it has been used by A. J. Greimas to treat explicitly the narrative structure of valuing.

The first important step to take, according to Greimas, is to avoid confusing the notions of object and value. For him, the object is 'no more than a pretext, a locus of value investment' (Greimas 1987: 86). Here the semiotic model is close to the psychoanalytic approach to the object of desire which, even 'where it proposes itself in its nakedness,' is only the 'slag of a fantasy,' as Jacques Lacan (1989: 67) puts it. Greimas proposes the example of an automobile, which is a linguistic object that exists as a set of virtualities with respect to value. It takes part in value determinations as a means of transportation, as something related to prestige, and so on – only 'thanks to syntactic trajectories established outside discursive manifestation' (Greimas 1987: 86).

In separating the object from its place in a valuing process, Greimas effectively counters the empiricist/sensationalist approach of Adam Smith and others that organizes both traditional epistemology and classical political economy. Objects are not *knowable* in and of themselves; they are known by their 'determinations,' as Greimas puts it. From a narrative standpoint, determinations take the form of the 'syntactic trajectories' for which the objects serve as supports. Similarly, objects are not *valuable* in and of themselves. Their value emerges as the endpoint of a person's aim. The 'endpoint' imagery is especially important here, for the object's service as a locus of value investment operates within a syntactic and semantic structure. In the process of valuing, it serves as an end term in a relationship between the subject and the world, as 'the subject's intended project' in Greimas's (1987: 87) terms.

Although Greimas here appears to work within a simple subject-object grammar, which postulates a world within which subjects seek values, he recognizes that language is not owned by individual subjects; it takes on its ability to perform within both a structure and a temporal context. The narrativization of value of which he speaks is less an individual choice than an enactment of a social code, for he notes that the value of an object for a subject emerges within a linguistic act that is not only structural but also 'anchored in history' (Greimas 1990: 93).

Thus for example, to understand the 'hidden treasure problem' in the Pinocchio story – Pinocchio acquires, loses, and then finds again some gold coins with the help of a fairy – it is necessary, as Greimas points out, to place it historically in a Tuscan agricultural society at a time when the economy was static. There was a more-or-less 'closed universe of values ... such that for every instance of acquisition on the part of a member of the society there corresponds necessarily a loss on the part of another' (1987: 92). For example, to provide Pinocchio with a school primer, his maker/father, Geppetto, has to sell his coat. In this context a story of a found treasure is a story about the existence of value outside of the 'closed universe.' Of course, hidden treasure has meaning as an anti-type, for 'found treasures' are opposed to produced goods, and within the ontology of classical political economy, such non-work related experiences of value would, in Greimas's (1987: 93) terms, 'appear as anti-values or *negative values* having to do with an axiological anti-universe.'

What is important in this story for present purposes is that the juxtaposition is not one of economy versus myth but myth versus myth. The work-value story at the center of Adam Smith's position on value is represented materialistically by Smith but achieves its coherence only when complemented by an ontological commitment to the importance of work and a narrative that foregrounds work and makes it responsible for value, given its place in the dynamic that makes material things available for satisfactions.

The counternarration that Greimas discerns in the Pinocchio story, based on a different economic structure and a different corresponding 'axiological universe,' unfolds with some significantly different value producing interpretive impulses. In the static Tuscan economy, the human subjects exist within a two-tiered universe. There is the everyday, earthly place within which value shares are limited, static, and acquired through work-related activities constrained, of course, by the norms fixing subjects' identities and the meaning of their activities.

Then there is a transcendent universe that makes value possible. The finding of value places the finder not in a litigious relationship with another earthly possessor but in a spiritual relationship with a supernatural being (for example, the benevolent fairy) who, as Greimas (1987: 93) puts it, 'plays the role of mediator between the universe of transcendent values and the immanent universe into which the new values are introduced for circulation.'

The Tuscans of the Pinocchio story clearly live in an enchanted world, and such stories have the effect of legitimating the worldly economy by sacrilizing the human condition, that is, by leaving one's economic fate to divine intervention. The idea of divinely inspired luck serves no doubt to draw attention away from the more local forms of domination and control over value.

In the Pinocchio story, the ontology and ethic are predicated on a spatial orientation that is medieval/sacred in construction. By contrast it would appear at first inspection that the social setting of exchange operating in Adam Smith's imaginative cartography has been entirely disenchanted. Smith's implicit geography certainly departs from the more traditional medieval spatial arrangement, which Foucault (1986: 22) has summarized as follows:

> In the Middle Ages there was a hierarchical ensemble of places: sacred places and profane places; protected places and open, exposed places; urban places and rural places.... In cosmological theory, there were supercelestial places, as opposed to the celestial, and the celestial place was in turn opposed to the terrestrial place.

But there remain sacred moments in the Smithian space within which his value narrative unfolds. First, there is a sacred structure implied in Smith's history of economy inasmuch as he posits a transcendent, purposeful intent by a deity that guarantees harmonious results, even though the deity exists only in the form of mechanisms. Second, modernity's spatial arrangements, which were emerging as Smith wrote, retain elements of the sacred. As Foucault has noted, there has been a tendency to misperceive the normalizations and sanctifications of modern space because we have learned to resist only one form of sacrilization, the sacred cartography of the Middle Ages. Nevertheless, as he puts it,

> perhaps our life is still governed by a certain number of oppositions that remain inviolable, that our institutions and practices have not

> yet dared to break down. These are oppositions that we regard as simple givens: for example, between private space and public space, between family space and social space, between cultural space and useful space, between the space of leisure and that of work. All these are still nurtured by the hidden presence of the sacred (Foucault 1986: 23).

Adam Smith was unreflective about the normalizations of space that his writing reproduced. Not only did he set his 'economy' outside of the effectivity of social space – his social space held an economy rather than animating it – but also his substantive references to space constituted places as innocent arenas. For example, in his discussion of the difference between natural and market prices, he spoke of the average rate of rent in a 'neighborhood,' as if every place has something intrinsic to it rather than being shaped by various remote forces (Smith 1981: 73). Certainly, for example, the dynamics of political economy from Smith's age to the present have had effects on such spatial practices as being able to maintain a neighborhood, that is, a stable and relatively self-contained domain of residence and commerce. But Smith simply naturalizes places by ascribing such things as 'natural rates of wages' to each neighborhood as if the effectivity exists in the place rather than as forces shaping places.

Ultimately, Smith's neglect of the cultural, social, and political practices involved in constructing space, as well as of the other contextual dimensions of value, permitted him to maintain his view that objects have value for subjects by dint of their materiality. However, as it is put by Greimas, it is the 'determinations' of objects – the narrative and other meaning structures through which they are known – that have value, and, as has been shown, one of the significant aspects of the determination of objects is the imaginative cartography, the view of space within which they are recognized. The uncritical view of space found in Smith's writing can be dramatically juxtaposed to that of Foucault, whom Gilles Deleuze (1986: 23–44) has called a 'cartographer' precisely because he recodes and therefore remaps contemporary spaces. Foucault's writing operates within a radical rethinking of social space. For example, rather than naturalizing the existing spaces of modernity, he has collapsed the spaces of the prison, hospital, school, and the like, and placed them within the domain of practice he labels 'the carceral' (Foucault 1977: 293–308). What have existed in dominant social discourses as spaces innocent of the operation of power are repositioned in his writing as part of a structure of surveillance and control.

Toward a dematerialized political economy

The constructions of the body or subject, of space, and, more generally, of the interpretive impositions of meaning on bodies, things, and places are inextricably involved in what is valuable. All of these interpretive dimensions that establish value constitute the non- or dematerialized dimension of political economy. The semiotic contribution to understanding this aspect of value has been elaborated in the discussion of narrativity and value. There is another domain of contemporary theorizing that makes an important contribution to appreciating the indissolubly interpretive component of valuing, that is the anthropological domain.[1]

The contemporary anthropological contributions to dematerializing economy effectively begin with Marcel Mauss' treatment of the gift. Mauss showed that gift-giving is governed not by the material or intrinsic value of the objects exchanged but by the social positions of the giver and receiver. What is exchanged are signs, and the fact that gift-giving operates within a symbolic economy is repressed. As Mauss (1970: 1) puts it, 'The form usually taken is that of the gift generously offered, but accompanying behavior is formal pretense and social deception, while the transaction itself is based on obligation and economic self-interest.'

Since Mauss, various theorists have theorized society and culture as systems of sign exchange and thereby overcome the radical separation between culture and economy that obtains in both liberal/capitalist and Marxist formulations of political economy. For example, Pierre Bourdieu has emphasized how 'cultural capital' is deeply embedded in all forms of exchange and how 'symbolic interests' cannot be separated from economic ones. With the help of such conceptions, he is able to move from political economy to the analysis of power and authority, for the ability to hoard and control signs is at least as significant as the control over 'material wealth' in the dynamics of power (Bourdieu 1984: 99–168). Similarly, Jean Baudrillard (1981) bases his version of political economy on the sign and Georges Bataille (1988) on a model of ritual expenditure involved in processes of distinction in which the squandering of resources is central to a culturally embedded economy.

Where did culture sit for Adam Smith? It would appear that it was a mere nuisance from his point of view. He treated culture more or less the way he treated any domain of normativity (for example, in some respects, the state) that might mediate or impede exchange and the division of labor. For example, he noted that the norms of 'Indostan' and 'ancient Egypt,' which bind 'every man' to follow the occupation of his father, have the effect of lowering wages and 'the profits of stock below their natural rate' (Smith 1981: 80).

As has been noted, in the Smithian narrative, people generally sort themselves into occupational positions in a way that optimizes the production of wealth. And culture stands wholly outside of economy for Smith. The value of a product for persons is a function of bodies meeting things. It has also been noted, however, that Smith entertained a model of the meeting of individuals with the social body. Here, we encounter a paradox in Smith's thinking. In the domain of economy, the individual connects with the social in a strictly consequentialist way. Persons end up selecting occupational niches and engage in work strictly from the point of view of individual utilities. Insofar as consciousness enters this picture, it is consciousness of individual gain. The developing shape of the labor force in industrial society is innocent of cultural promptings. It emerges from a series of isolated individual strivings. This mythic, depoliticizing narrative not only contrasts markedly with the socially self-conscious orientation Smith has in *The Theory of Moral Sentiments* (1982c) but also contrasts markedly with some contemporary analyses of the historical shaping of the industrial work force.

For example, Raymond Williams is among those who tell a different story of the role that culture plays. Rather than standing in the way of labor docility and productivity, the emergence of what he calls a 'culture of production' helped to shape and deliver a working class. There are, as Williams (1977: 115) puts it, 'indissoluble connections between material production, political institutions and activity, and consciousness.' Williams, like Gramsci, has emphasized the significance of the forces at work that have ideationally shaped the social milieu into the cultural support for industrial development and that have continuously reproduced the bases for a class system that supplies the relationships behind the process of capital accumulation (see also Davies this volume).

E. P. Thompson's story is a more agonistic one. It emphasizes the shaping forces of antagonisms within both the ruling and working classes as well as between them. In his view, the class basis of work, as well as the structure of the work itself, has become shaped more by forms of domination and resistance than by the process of individuals striving to better themselves that Smith assumed. And contrary to the Smithian optimism about the prospects for self-improvement, Thompson's story is often one of the degradation of labor, for example, the decline of the Yorkshire woolen and worsted weavers who, like their counterparts in cotton, worked continuously longer hours for less pay as a result of being divided against themselves as manufacturers learned to manipulate the fact of their scattered venues (Thompson 1966: 280–1).

There have been many politically perspicuous contributions to the 'culture of production' story, but for present purposes the relationship of culture to economy inherent in the value of products rather than of production is more central to the value problematic under analysis. Since the development of the classical political economy of Adam Smith and others, economic thinking has gradually shifted its focus to a substantial concern with consumption. Once consumption came under scrutiny, it became increasingly recognized that contrary to the classical and Marxian view that the materiality of the object met the desires for need satisfaction of the consumer, it was desire itself that produced an interpretation or determination that lent value to objects. As one commentator on the shift has astutely put it, under the new emphasis on consumption 'economists increasingly understood that in their new science it was not that useful things were desired but that desired things were useful' (Birken 1988: 31).

Recall that for Marx, like Smith, the opposite position is asserted. For him, the materiality of the object, not its interpretive status, gives it value. As he put it in *Capital*, 'the usefulness of a thing makes it a use value. But this usefulness is conditioned by the physical properties of the commodity and has no existence apart from the latter' (Marx 1977: 126). Once the emphasis is shifted to desire or the motivated interpretations of subjects, the value of things belongs to a different account. And as was shown above, treatments of the cultural vagaries of interpretation are inextricably bound to issues of economy.

The production of taste

There is a variety of conceptions under which the interpretive dynamics lending value to objects can be discussed, but among the most readily available is the concept of *taste*. Insofar as taste is a biological metaphor, it appears deceptively simple as an account of the desire of persons for objects, but the complexities mount as one assesses all the historical and structural components involved in the vagaries of taste. Consider a product that was popular in the 1990s, the 'Swatch,' a line of relatively inexpensive Swiss-made watches that come in many different colors and designs and were produced in limited editions commemorating events, seasons, and other public codes. Given the relatively low cost and the combination of their coding and restriction in issue, Swatches have become collector's items, and crowds form at the Swatch counters of department stores as stamp collectors gather in anticipation of the latest issue. What, then, is a Swatch, and how does it achieve its value?

As a first approach to these questions, recall the now-anachronistic term, the *timepiece*. The dictionary eschews its social dimensions and baldly states that it is 'an instrument for measuring and registering the passage of time.' But even if we are restricted to this horologic aspect of a Swatch, its value cannot emerge from the facts of its ability to represent mechanically and electronically a conceptual model of temporality. To appreciate the value of a Swatch as a timepiece, one must locate the historical development of the monitoring of time. There are of course many developments related to the modern tendency to monitor time in ever more precise ways, but the practices behind this tendency effectively began in Adam Smith's century with the development of the transportation timetable. With the development of an industrial work force carried by transportation from residence to work place, it became necessary not only to order the process of moving a work force but also the responsibility of the individual to schedule precise arrivals and departures. This general development along with the growing administrative rationality of the modern state made the portable timepiece almost essential.

Therefore, to speak of a *timepiece* is to recognize implicitly many of the essential dimensions of the modern society and polity, which embodies 'space-time ordering devices' (Giddens 1985: 172–97) as the primary mechanisms through which work, governance, administration, and leisure are coordinated. The timepiece becomes valuable as such only in a society that closely coordinates such flows of people and things and that, accordingly, judges performance not simply on the basis of material accomplishments but also, and primarily, on *timeliness*.

Once the timepiece dimension of the Swatch is situated in the historically developing field of practices that summon timeliness as valuable, analysis of its value requires inquiry into social connections. It is important to note in a cursory way that the social is constructed not simply as a domain of functional coordination but also as a domain for the exchange of recognition. Thus, objects such as watches with functional significance also operate as signs in this exchange dynamic.

Considering first the emergence of the Swatch as a collector's item, it should be noted that collections can be understood as intimately involved in the identity dynamics through which people achieve recognition. As Susan Stewart (1984: 162) remarks about collection-identity relationships:

> When objects are defined in terms of their use value, they serve as extensions of the body onto the environment, but when objects are defined by the collection, such an extension is inverted, serving to subsume the environment to a scenario of the personal. The ultimate term in the series that marks the collection is the 'self,' the articulation of the collector's own identity.

Of course, in addition to the modern identity economy within which Swatches take on value as collector's items, one has to recognize aspects of the modern political economy that make it possible for some to collect things – differentials in income, storage and display space, and so on. Not the least of the conditions of possibility for collecting are all the historical dynamics associated with the violent triumph of sedentary, agriculturally-based groupings over nomadic hunter-gatherers. These latter groups also had objects with a primarily sign function value, but their ability to collect and store was inhibited by their tendency to be on the move.

The primary qualifications of a materialist reading of the tastes that lend value to a Swatch are in place. It is evident that almost everything involved in the emergence of the present, modern condition has a part in providing the interpretive context that lends value to these particular 'timepieces.' Perhaps the most important part of the context is spatial, the condition in which media space, ranging from the relatively static store window displays (by which Walter Benjamin marked the emergence of modernity) to the dynamic space-time venues of the printed periodical, radio, and television, where objects are presented for acquisition. It is in these 'spaces' that tastes are developed, modified, and connected with other dimensions of social life. They provide the most compelling domains in which to analyze the semiotic/interpretive aspects of political economy.

Although Adam Smith's approach to objects was primarily sensationalist rather than semiotic, he did have a place for culture in his approach to value. Although in many places, as has been noted, an object's materiality, refined and made available for use by labor and need-satisfying in its usable form, is predominant for Smith, in other places the object seems to be valuable because of the recognition it confers on the user. Thus, while he predicates his motivational model on individuals striving to better their condition, he ascribes to the striver a look at that 'condition' from the standpoint of an Other.

Certainly, throughout *The Theory of Moral Sentiments,* Smith notes that [men] seek wealth because of the approbation it affords them.

> Nature, when she formed man for society, endowed him with an original desire to please, and an original aversion to offend his brethren... She rendered their approbation most flattering and most agreeable to him for their own sake; and their disapprobation most mortifying and most offensive (Smith 1982c: 116).

However, the pursuit of gain creates the appeal of *action* choices for Smith in *The Wealth of Nations,* and however those actions may be viewed by the actor, who may be operating with an imagined peer or member of another class as observer, the objects themselves are still valued primarily as *things* that do not carry a complex cultural coding.

Smith well recognized that different types – that is, members of different classes – have an effective demand for different things. For example, 'a very poor man may be said in some sense to have a demand for a coach and six; he might like to have it; but his demand is not an effectual demand, as the commodity can never be brought to market to satisfy it' (Smith 1981: 73). But Smith offers no logic that allows one to see how things become coded and, indeed, how demands, whether they become 'effectual' or not, are summoned by the cultural coding – within which objects are interpreted.

Classical political economy from Smith onwards was robustly oriented towards the production of commodities and anemically elaborated with respect to the vagaries of consumption. With the modern recognition that the value of products to consumers is often primarily a function of the social codes within which objects have significance, value and social identity become intimately connected.

As a result, to situate the value of objects it is necessary to invoke a semiological context and heed Greimas' argument about how it is the structure of determination of objects, not the objects themselves, that gives rise to value. Baudrillard (1981: 38) has summarized it well, while adding the important neostructural concept of 'social logic':

> Thus objects, their syntax, and their rhetoric refer to social objectives and to a social logic. They speak to *us* not so much of the user and of technical practices, as of social pretension and recognition, of social mobility and inertia, of acculturation and enculturation, of stratification and of social classification.

Attuned to this social semiotic aspect of products, much of contemporary critical social theory concerned with political economy must articulate a logic of the social with a logic of the commodity. Bourdieu (1984: 230), who is among those who treat the semiotic sign exchange aspects of societies, has attempted just such an articulation in a treatment of 'the correspondence between goods production and taste production.' For Bourdieu, 'choosing according to one's tastes' is controlled by a social logic of differentiation that emerges from the entire social, political, and economic order. Accordingly, to understand the value of the product in this domain is to read or interpret it in a way that extends that reading to the structure and dynamic of power relations within the social field.

Conclusion

The main focus throughout this chapter has been on the relations between value and interpretation. It has been argued that, in general, how people 'value' comes about through interpretive mediation, that the person-object and interpersonal confrontations in which value emerges are mediated by how these confrontations achieve meaning. As a corollary to this general position, it has been argued specifically that Adam Smith's constructions of value turn on *his* interpretive mediations, which are most evident in his historical narratives.

Adam Smith and classical political economists as a whole tended to neglect the imbrication of culture and economy. When these two domains are brought together, the concept of taste achieves important recognition, and a contemporary political economy, one attuned to the conditions of the present, can be seen to revolve more around the production of taste than of things. What becomes important are the codes within which subjects are formed and interpret themselves in such a way that some 'things' have value. The ground for such interpretation is a social logic that allies certain users of signs with certain producers of them.

Note

1 Editor's note: In his book Shapiro (1993: 69–71) signals two domains at this point, the psychoanalytical and the anthropological. Here, I have retained only the latter, as the psychoanalytical domain is dealt with in the Gammon and Palan chapter.

References

Bataille, G. (1988) *The Accursed Share, Vol. I*, trans. Robert Hurley. New York: Zone Books.

Baudrillard, J. (1981) *For a Critique of the Political Economy of the Sign*, trans. Charles Levin. St. Louis, MO: Telos Press.

Birken, L. (1988) *Consuming Desires*. Ithaca, New York: Cornell University Press.

Bourdieu, P. (1984) *Distinction: A Social Critique of the Judgment of Taste*, trans. Nice, R. Cambridge, MA: Harvard University Press.

Deleuze, G. (1986) *Foucault*, ed. and trans. Sean Hand. Minneapolis: University of Minnesota Press.

Dumont, L. (1977) *From Mandeville to Marx*. Chicago: University of Chicago Press.

Foucault, M. (1977) *Discipline and Punish: The Birth of the Prison*, trans. Sheridan, A. New York: Pantheon.

Foucault, M. (1986) 'Of Other Spaces,' trans. Miscowiec, J. *Diacritics* 16, Spring.

Giddens, A. (1985) *The Nation-State and Violence*. Berkeley, CA: University of California Press.

Greimas, A. J. (1987) 'A Problem of Narrative Semiotics: Objects of Value,' in *On Meaning: Selected Writings in Semiotic Theory*. Minneapolis: University of Minnesota Press.

Greimas, A. J. (1990) 'Structure and History,' in *The Social Sciences: A Semiotic View*. Minneapolis: University of Minnesota Press.

Lacan, J. (1989) 'Kant with Sade,' trans. Swenson, J. B., Jr., *October* (Winter).

Marx, K. (1977) *Capital, Vol. 1*, trans. Fowkes, B. New York: Vintage.

Mauss, M. (1970) *The Gift*, trans. Cinnison, I. London: Cohen and West.

Shapiro, M. J. (1993) *Reading 'Adam Smith': Desire, History, and Value*. London: Sage.

Smith, A. (1978) *Lectures on Jurisprudence*, edited by Meek, R. L., Raphael, D. D. and Stein, P. G. Oxford: The Clarendon Press.

Smith, A. (1981) *An Inquiry into the Nature and Causes of the Wealth of Nations*. Indianapolis, IN: Liberty Classics.

Smith, A. (1982a) 'Of the External Senses,' in *Essays on Philosophical Subjects*. Indianapolis, IN: Liberty Classics

Smith, A. (1982b) 'The History of Astronomy,' in *Essays on Philosophical Subjects*. Indianapolis, IN: Liberty Classics.

Smith, A. (1982c) *The Theory of Moral Sentiments*, Glasgow Edition, edited by Raphael, D. D. and Macafie, A. L. Indianapolis, IN: Liberty Classics.

Stewart, S. (1984) *On Longing*. Baltimore: John Hopkins University Press.

Thompson, E. P. (1966) *The Making of the English Working Class*. New York: Vintage.

Williams, R. (1977) *Marxism and Literature*. Oxford: Oxford University Press.

3

Securing the Global (Bio)Political Economy: *Empire*, Poststructuralism and Political Economy[1]

Martin Coward

Introduction: thickening the analysis of politics on a global scale

In their discussion of Michael Hardt and Antonio Negri's *Empire* (2000), Tarak Barkawi and Mark Laffey (2002: 110) note that the discipline of International Relations (IR) has traditionally understood 'the international' to be a '"thin" space of strategic interaction,' a space that is 'spare compared to domestic spaces.' Barkawi and Laffey go on to argue that 'IR's central categories of sovereignty and the states-system generate a systematic occlusion' of a '"thick" set of social relations, consisting of social and cultural flows as well as political-military and economic interactions' (2002: 110). It would thus seem desirable that the thin schema of territorial sovereignty that dominates the disciplinary imaginary of IR is thickened in order that the social, cultural, political, military and economic relations occluded by such thin accounts might be discerned.

The motif of the thickening of the conceptual schemas deployed by IR scholars resonates with a number of so-called 'critical' understandings of global politics. Indeed, in general, those contributions to thinking about politics on a global scale that have been regarded as 'critical' of traditional IR scholarship have shared a concern to demonstrate the limitations of the classical territorially-bound international imaginary. International Political Economy (IPE) and so-called poststructuralism comprise two such accounts that might be said to provide thick accounts of politics on a global scale.

IPE – as the study of the relationship between politics and economics on a global scale – might be said to offer the possibility for an expanded study of world order beyond the narrower study of the interstate order (cf. O'Brien and Williams 2004: 11–36). IPE suggests that it is necessary to understand global politics as a 'thick' set of transversal forces that include, at the very least, patterns of trade, division(s) of labor, migration(s) of bodies, and movement(s) of goods/information as well as the types of power exercised by states and international organizations, which, at the global level, includes not only negotiation but the deployment of (military) force.

Similarly, so-called 'poststructuralist' IR scholarship seeks to broaden the study of global politics to comprise a delineation of the flows and relations wider than simple territorial sovereignty. For example, David Campbell (1996: 23–4), whose work is often taken to epitomize poststructuralist IR scholarship, has argued that the study of international politics should comprise a 'philosophical anthropology of everyday life on a global scale.' Such a wide-ranging study of the various connections, flows, relations and encounters occurring on a global scale contests the notion common to classical theories of IR that politics is restricted to the interactions of preconstituted, juridically sovereign states.

Given such a seemingly common concern, it would perhaps seem natural that poststructuralist IR theory and IPE would enjoy mutually interpenetrating conceptualizations of global politics. However, whilst there has been some engagement between IPE and poststructuralist IR theory, these have largely consisted of problematizations of conceptual terms. Thus, for example, Daly's (1991) conceptualization of the discursive constitution of the economy, and de Goede's (2003) rejection of the economism implicit in many understandings of IPE are oriented towards contesting the objectivity of the economic (see also Daly this volume). Whilst it would, therefore, be inaccurate to portray the possible domain of an encounter between poststructuralist IR theory and IPE as a blank canvass, it seems fair to argue, as de Goede (2003: 79) does, that engagement between the two has been sporadic and unsystematic (see also introduction). The question thus arises as to what form such an encounter between poststructuralism and IPE might take.

In this paper, I will argue that the concept of 'Empire,' as elaborated by Hardt and Negri (2000), offers an opportunity for an encounter between poststructuralism and IPE. Empire and imperialism – as Barkawi and Laffey (2002) note – demand that scholars recognize a complex pattern of flows and hierarchies productive of a set of power relations thicker than the simplistic territorial geographies that have traditionally underpinned IR's disciplinary imaginary. It is this thicker conceptual terrain that provides an ideal opportunity for an encounter between IPE's concern with the mutual constitution of the political and economic and poststructuralism's concern with the manner in which power and territoriality are discursively constituted. Hardt and Negri take advantage of this opportunity and stage an effective encounter between poststructuralism and IPE: producing an account of the global political-economic structures of the post-Cold War era that resonates with poststructuralist tropes of thought.

The argument is divided into four principal parts. In the first part, I will begin by demonstrating the manner in which the imperial constitutes an appropriate conceptual motif for the contemporary era. In the second part, I will outline the manner in which Hardt and Negri's *Empire* (2000) can illuminate the four central dimensions of the contemporary imperial experience. In the third part, I will delineate the central conceptual characteristic of Empire: its expansion *via* 'unstable dialectics of inclusion and exclusion' (Walker 1999: 173). Such dialectics of inclusion and exclusion rest upon the drawing of boundaries that I will characterize as the constitution of thresholds, or liminal limits. Furthermore, dialectics of inclusion and exclusion are predicated upon the constitution of an encounter, across a threshold, of self and other, identity and difference. Such a logic of encounter is, fundamentally, a logic of security (cf. Campbell 1998; Dillon 1996). I will argue, therefore, that there are links between the dynamics of Empire and the geopolitical techniques of security. In the final section I will conclude the argument by noting that a poststructuralist encounter with IPE demonstrates that an enquiry into the nature of global order in the early twenty-first century is, first and foremost, an enquiry into the manner in which the global (bio)political economy is secured.

The imperial as motif for global order and terrain of theoretical encounter

The motif of globalization has dominated attempts to understand the nature of world order and political economy at the end of the twentieth century (Scholte 2000; Shaw 2000; Rosenberg 2000). Globalization theory could be said to be constituted around the central proposition that contemporary world order is characterized by supra-territoriality caused by the decline or dissolution of the territorial interstate system in the face of a set of deterritorializing forces (cf. Scholte 2000: 46–61;

Held, McGrew, Goldblatt and Perraton 1999: 440–4). Commonly, such a proposition is interpreted as the triumph of the deterritorializing logics of capital over the territorial logics of statecraft. In the light of the September 11 attacks on the Pentagon and World Trade Centre and the subsequent reassertion of American military dominance, however, the claims of globalization theory have been taken to be problematized (cf. Gray 2001; see also Aitken this volume). As Roach notes, '[t]errorism puts sand in the gears of cross-border connectivity and [thus] threatens...globalization' (Roach 2001). Compounding the problematization of globalization by terrorism, American statecraft under the regime of George W. Bush comprised a revivification of seemingly unilateral political-military power (Cox 2003: 3; Rosenberg 2005: 2).

However, whilst representing a problematization of the supra-territorial claims of globalization theory, neither transnational terrorism nor seemingly unilateral practices of statecraft should be taken to signal a simple evaporation of globalization and a return of territorial sovereignty. Neither American statecraft under George W. Bush nor the borderless jihad envisioned (or actualized) by al-Qaeda cells has undermined the various de-territorializing forces of capital, or the transversal flows of people, goods, information and communication. Scholars of global politics are thus faced with reconciling the territorially-based sovereignty evinced by American statecraft or the borders hardened to fight terrorism with the deterritorializing transversal forces that have shaped the post-Cold War era. One could call this the problem of global order in the contemporary conjuncture.[2]

This question of global order is not soluble within the conceptual antinomies offered by territorial sovereignty and supra-territorial globality. Given the manner in which the present conjuncture is marked by elements of both, reducing this question to an either/or decision between one of two poles is particularly unsatisfactory. The principal problem of being intellectually shackled to such a binary opposition is the manner in which it rests on largely mythical or fictitious suppositions. As Justin Rosenberg (2000: 27–44) has made clear, the supposition of a modern, preglobalized interstate system based upon 'constitutional separateness' – the so-called 'Westphalian system' – is itself a fictional, or mythological, understanding of world order contradicted by the various deterritorializing and transversal forces that have characterized the development and propagation of the European nation-state form. Flows of people, goods, money and ideas have both contested boundaries and formed the backdrop against which the sovereignty of states is articulated (Rosenberg 2000: 31–5; Abu-Lughod 1989).

One particularly popular response to the question of global order which has attempted to think beyond the conceptual antinomies of sovereignty and supra-territoriality is that which has characterized the contemporary conjuncture as an instance of imperialism. Indeed, one could say that scholarly examinations of global order in the contemporary conjuncture have given rise to a body of scholarship that could be referred to as the 'literature of the new imperialism/empire.'[3] This literature proposes the figure of the imperial as the defining characteristic of the contemporary global order. Variously interpreted as American imperialism or a wider empire predicated on certain globalized values and norms, this figure of global order combines the notion of expansiveness central to globalization theory with that of the exercise of power on which notions of territorial sovereignty are predicated. As such, the literature of the new imperialism/empire escapes the simplistic antinomy of the territorial sovereignty/supra-territorial globality debate.

Furthermore, insofar as it seeks to demonstrate the manner in which economic, political, military and cultural flows are implicated in contemporary global order, the literature of the new imperialism/empire offers an important opportunity for an analysis of global politics 'thicker' than the 'thin' (Barkawi and Laffey 2002, 110–11) classical accounts of inter-state politics. As such the motif of the imperial has been a fertile conceptual trope for a range of scholars seeking to delineate the various flows and hierarchies occluded by traditional IR scholarship. The imperial is thus a terrain in which different approaches to such broadening of IR categories and concepts might both encounter, and profitably engage with, each other. It is this role as terrain of encounter that suggests that the imperial comprises an ideal terrain on which to stage an encounter between IPE and poststructuralism.

Michael Hardt and Antonio Negri's *Empire* (2000) comprises precisely such an encounter between poststructuralist conceptual tropes and the subject matter of IPE. In particular, *Empire* can be read as an encounter between the IPE demand that dynamics of production, trade, exchange and migration be taken seriously and a poststructuralist concern for the examination of the manner in which the political comprises the constitution of boundaries (of self and other). It is, therefore, productive for any analysis of the possible mutual interpenetration of IPE and poststructuralism to examine the manner in which *Empire* could be said to provide an account of the problem of global order in the contemporary conjuncture.

The imperial character of the contemporary conjuncture

Generally speaking, the literature of the new imperialism/empire notes four distinguishing features of the contemporary global order. Firstly, that global politics is characterized by an *expansiveness* (Hardt and Negri 2000: 10). That is, deterritorializing logics which contest borders are a particularly salient feature of global order: from capitalism to the contestation of territorial sovereignty effected by the American invasion of Iraq. Secondly, the contemporary global order, like all forms of imperialism, is characterized by a certain *hierarchization* (Barkawi and Laffey 2002: 111ff.). Indeed, insofar as imperialism has in the past denoted a particular logic of exploitative subordination, so its deployment in regard to contemporary circumstances is intended to indicate a certain hierarchization. Thirdly, the contemporary era is marked by a particular *relation between forms of government/governance and modes of production/regimes of accumulation*. Imperialism has, in the past, been understood to comprise an expansionary pressure upon statecraft deriving from certain tendencies in capitalism. The literature of the new imperialism/empire similarly regards transformations in forms of government/governance to be intimately related to capitalism (Harvey 2003). Finally, the literature of the new imperialism/empire takes the present era to be characterized by the *motif of crisis* (Mann 2003). Whether American statecraft under George W. Bush is a response to, or catalyst for, such crisis depends upon the individual writer, and yet the sense of crisis pervades all accounts of the present era as imperial. I will examine the manner in which Hardt and Negri's *Empire* addresses each of these characteristics in turn.

The expansiveness of power

In order to understand the manner in which global order in the contemporary era is defined by an expansiveness of power it is important to examine Hardt and Negri's assertion that Empire is to be distinguished both from traditional forms of imperialism and notions of a contemporary *Pax Americana* (Hardt and Negri 2000: xii). This assertion is predicated upon the proposition that Empire is defined as a borderless realm. Without borders there can be no imperialist expansion from a colonizing, metropolitan center to a colonized periphery. Expansiveness must, therefore, take on a different form. Of course, such an assertion sounds similar to hyperbolic statements found in globalization theorists, prediction of the end of territorial sovereignty (cf. Ohmae 1992). And yet, Hardt and Negri do not, similarly, predict the demise of the sovereign state. Rather they assert that the form of juridical rule from which the state would draw its legitimacy is transformed from the form of metropolitan government first outlined in Hobbes' *Leviathan* (1985), to a set of global norms in which the state plays a role not of transcendent territorial government, but rather of a machine that facilitates transversal flows (Hardt and Negri 2000: 309–12). The state is not a source of governmental power, but rather a transmission belt for global governance. In this respect Hardt and Negri's Empire echoes Stephen Gill's (1990) understanding of the emergence of hegemonic forms of power or Rosenau and Czempiel's (1992) understanding of global governance. In both accounts diffuse intersubjective norms rather than power understood as a commodity to be wielded from a governmental, metropolitan center (across borders) serve as the basis for regulative control of the global political economy.[4]

It is as a consequence of this understanding of power as expansive that Hardt and Negri argue that the United Nations provides a model for the emergent imperial capitalist sovereignty. Hardt and Negri's United Nations should not be understood as a gathering of states alone, but rather as a complex global institution whose individual agencies/organs are constituted and given legitimacy by an accepted set of norms. The United Nations then is not only a forum for diplomatic (interstate) negotiation, but rather the name of a global, delocalized hegemonic network of norms regarding human life, its rights and normal conduct: a network wider than its own agencies/organs encompassing nongovernmental organizations, intergovernmental organizations, multi- and transnational corporations, and even civil society (Koenig-Archibugi 2002). These norms, whilst implemented by discrete agencies in specific places, are ultimately deterritorialized and diffuse. These norms are, moreover, a 'biopolitics,' a determination of the nature of human life itself (Foucault 1998). The biopolitics of the United Nations determine the character of human life: starting with the principle of autonomous individuality enshrined in widely circulating and circumscribed to notions of human rights (Foucault 1998; Foucault 2000; Dillon and Reid 2001).

Hierarchy and subordination

The hierarchization of Empire is harder to discern. Indeed, insofar as imperial power is characterized as a deterritorialized and diffuse set of global norms constitutive of a borderless realm, it is difficult to identify core and periphery. The notions of core and periphery are central to a notion of hierarchization predicated on the differentiation of two or more entities, the delineation of flows of money, goods and ideas from one entity to another and the demonstration that such flows comprise exploitation or domination insofar as they either represent expropriation without recompense or imposition without tolerance of indigenous life forms. Central to such hierarchies is differentiation, the distinction between one entity and another without which exploitation and domination cannot take place.

According to Hardt and Negri the differentiation of core and periphery is replaced in the contemporary global order with the distinction between Empire and its barbarian others. Insofar as Empire is a biopolitical form of rule, its normative regime is predicated upon a specific understanding of what constitutes defensible human life. This normative regime thus differentiates between imperial, defensible life and barbaric indefensible life. It is on the basis of this distinction that the new hierarchies of Empire are established: hierarchies of life that rank Empire's barbarians according to their potential for integration into the imperial domain. Empire is thus characterized, as Ulrich Beck has noted, by complex algorithms of risk (Beck 2002: 41). Such calculations of risk pertain not simply to possible threats to the security of Empire, but to the risk attached to ventures beyond Empire's borders for purposes of intervention. These algorithms of risk can be found in the insurance of companies and individuals taking part in the reconstruction of Iraq as well as the measures applied to disaster triage to determine the likelihood of successful outcomes. Such calculation of risk leads to the constitution of a biopolitical hierarchy on which Empire's interventions in the risky barbarian margins of the imperial domain are predicated.

The constitutive performance of Empire's normative regime is found in the fieldwork of various NGOs and UN organs where distinctions between viable and nonviable forms of life are made. For example, in 1997 the Sphere project – an NGO consortium with some involvement from UN agencies – was set up in order to establish minimum standards for humanitarian responses (Sphere Project 2004; Walker and Purdin 2004). The Sphere project gave rise to the Sphere handbook and the aim to implement minimum standards in key areas of humanitarian response across the 'humanitarian community' (Griekspoor and Collins 2001: 740). The key indicators set out in the Sphere handbook establish thresholds for humanitarian response. For example, Griekspoor and Collins (2001: 741) note that the usual level for admission of children by Médecins Sans Frontières to therapeutic feeding stations during the 1998 Sudan famine was 70 percent of weight for height.

Such standards and indicators should be seen as integral to a biopolitical imperial regime. Through such biopolitical indicators Empire – in the form of NGOs and UN agencies – is continually performing the distinction between the human and those, who by virtue of their barbaric condition fall below the levels thought to be normal for the persistence of human life. Such biopolitics may result in either intervention or abandonment. Griekspoor and Collins (2001: 741), for example, note that, given the difficulty of maintaining a response in the face of overwhelming needs during the 1998 Sudan famine, Médecins Sans Frontières might have prioritized 'less intensive treatment for those having better survival chances.' Moreover, they argue that such a 'triage strategy could have achieved a lower overall mortality by accepting higher death rates among the severely malnourished' (Griekspoor and Collins 2001: 742). However, such a strategy comprises the abandonment of those deemed to have failed to fall into the category of defensible life. Whilst it is not my argument that humanitarian response should not occur, it is important to note that the actions of humanitarian agencies are not simply the neutral nonpolitical provision of care. Rather these agencies are at the forefront of establishing what it is to be fully human and what it is to fall below that threshold. It is this difference that forms one of the principal hierarchies of Empire: the less than human being either abandoned or finding themselves the subject of intervention. It is only through the constitution of this threshold, therefore, that the flows characteristic of hierarchization can be mobilized.

The relation between government/governance and production/accumulation

The third aspect of global order in the contemporary era, an inextricable relationship between government/governance and the mode of production/accumulation, is, of course, that which has drawn some to label the present conjuncture 'imperialist' (for example, Harvey 2003). Theses concerning imperialism from Lenin to Luxemburg via Kautsky, are predicated upon a proposition regarding the relationship between capitalism and the state that asserts that tendencies in the former drive expansionary policies by the latter (Brewer 1990). Thus arguments that regard the present conjuncture as an instance of American imperialism (for example, Harvey 2003) argue that global capitalism has reached a point at which a crisis in accumulation has driven the USA to military adventurism in order to open new markets and acquire cheaper raw materials (specifically oil). Whilst Hardt and Negri do not deny that

Empire is characterized by a relationship between governance and capitalism (the mode of production/accumulation), they contest the mechanistic, economic determinism of many accounts of imperialism.

For Hardt and Negri, Empire is not the mere facilitator of capitalism. Indeed, imperial rule has morphed capitalism in important ways – not least by extending its possible range of markets and sources of labor into realms hitherto thought of as private and outside the economy. The notion that a crisis of accumulation has given rise to the regime of norms that characterizes Empire, is taken to be a far too simplistic picture of the emergence of the contemporary global order. Rather it is possible to say that the diffuse and deterritorialized norms that define imperial rule comprise a society of control constitutive of a specific form of subjectivity which is the sufficient, rather than necessary, condition of a certain form of capitalism. The forms of individuality constituted by norms of human rights and the recomposition of this individual into a seller not only of labor but also affect, recomposes capitalism from the industrial form characteristic of imperialism in which fixed capital and raw materials are central to the dynamics of production and accumulation, into the flexible and diffuse form of capitalism that characterizes the present conjuncture in which immaterial resources (such as affect) and information networks are key drivers of production and accumulation.

The motif of crisis

The fourth and final characteristic of the present conjuncture is that of crisis. The imperial form encounters crisis in two specific forms. On the one hand, Empire is constituted in and through an agonistic dialectical encounter with the multitude – the mass that is both subject of biopolitical strategies and yet always in excess of the regimes of governance that characterize Empire (Hardt and Negri 2000: 43–62). The multitude confronts Empire in a whole host of minor crises – the most recent of which could be said to be the anti-globalization protests that have accompanied meetings of organizations such as the G8 and the World Economic Forum (cf. Notes From Nowhere 2003). Yet such sporadic crises cannot be taken to be a systemic crisis from which Empire cannot recover. Indeed, as Amoore and Langley (2004: 100–2) have noted, in many instances the various actions of the organizations that are taken to compose global civil society might be said to be integrated into, rather than a decisive contestation of, global governance regimes.

However, Empire finds a greater, more intractable crisis in its encounter with its others: in the zones where those who fall outside or below what can be considered human reside. As the complex emergencies leading to famine and concomitant starvation, or the genocidal massacres to which Empire has been a spectator, or the wars of pacification fought in Afghanistan and Iraq testify, in such confrontations with alterity Empire finds its central values – universality and civility (Hardt and Negri 2000: xiv; Coward 2005a) – questioned. Whether in its inability to provide development assistance in order to combat the systemic failures that lead to catastrophic famine, or in the so-called collateral damage of noncombatant death that has progressively marked imperial combat, Empire's others comprehensively question both the universality and civility of its rule. Such crises are central, then, to the nature of global order in the present conjuncture.

De- and reterritorialization: Empire and the performance of liminal boundaries

Despite having outlined four defining features, Empire can be reduced to a logic of expansive becoming, rather than static being (Hardt and Negri 2000: 28–9). The hierarchization, regimes of accumulation and modes of crisis that pertain to Empire are all, at root, functions of expansiveness. Without the expansion of the domain of imperial governance, empire would not encounter, nor dominate, intervene in, or subordinate its barbaric others. Similarly, expansiveness is the motor of the incorporation of ever increasing numbers of affective forms of labor into Empire's economy, or the integration of NGOs and other civil society actors into global governance.

This expansive becoming is best understood according to the (poststructuralist) motif of de- and reterritorialization (cf. Connolly 1995). Whilst the sovereign state is predicated upon a logic of territorialization, the transversal flows of Empire are deterritorializing. Deterritorialization and expansion only make sense against the backdrop of exceeded or dissolved borders. It is only looking back at such borders that it is possible to note their permeability or contestation. Thus it is possible to say that the drawing of boundaries is the ground upon which the logics of deterritorialization and reterritorialization rest. Moreover, this allows us to acknowledge that Empire is not merely a de- and reterritorializing expansive force in geographical terms, but also in biopolitical terms. That is to say, Empire does not merely expand across land borders, but also through the boundaries of what is taken to constitute the human. As I noted with regard to the Sphere project, the boundaries of what is taken to constitute defensible humanity have been decomposed and recomposed in various ways. If the drawing of boundaries is the principal moment of territorialization, then these biopolitical moments are in themselves also instances of de- and reterritorialization.

The drawing of the boundary might also be said to constitute the establishment of the limen: the threshold through which bodies might pass in order to become imperial. Such a notion conforms to the ideas of agonistic identity advanced by William E. Connolly (1995; 1991). Connolly (1991) characterizes existence as a complex network of identity and difference. All notions of selfhood are derived in and through a relation with otherness. Central to this characterization of existence is the notion of the boundary between self and otherness, identity and difference. The relation between either term traverses a border identifiable as a threshold – the limen – where self becomes otherness, and identity becomes difference. These relations are agonistic insofar as difference and alterity stand as provocations to identity and selfhood to assert or perform their presence (Foucault 1982: 222; Connolly 1991: x). Insofar as the self is continually challenged by an otherness that would contest its self-contained and naturally constituted nature, otherness is an agonistic provocation of the self to assert its presence. As such, then, the limen is a threshold that defines the place of an agonistic encounter central to the constitution, or territorialization, of identity. At the limen one always finds an agonistic provocation of identity by difference. In Empire, one finds the threshold not only in geographical locales, but in the constitution of what it is to be human. Human rights, minimum standards of care, rules of disaster triage, and so on, all constitute thresholds at which imperial identity agonistically encounters its others.

The contemporary, imperial global order, is therefore characterized by what R. B. J. Walker (1999: 173) calls an 'unstable dialectic of inclusion and exclusion.' Such dialectics of inclusion and exclusion are 'unstable' insofar as they are in a continual state of transformation. The liminal boundaries that mark the relation between one term and another in the dialectic are constantly shifting according to the success, or lack thereof, of performative invocations of such limits. The notion of the performative constitution of boundaries requires, as Campbell (citing Judith Butler) notes, that we regard global order as having 'no ontological status apart from the various acts that constitute its reality' (Butler cited in Campbell 1998: 9). If global order has no ontological status beyond the acts that constitute it, and global order is predicated upon the various boundaries that establish unstable dialectics indicating where imperial identity starts and stops, then global order is constituted 'through a stylized repetition of acts' (Butler cited in Campbell 1998: 10). That is to say, Empire is constituted in and through 'a regulated process of repetition' (Butler cited in Campbell 1998: 10) of boundaries. To say that Empire is performed, then, is to say that Empire is constituted in and through the stylized liminal boundaries drawn between its self and its others on a repetitive (day-to-day) basis.

On an everyday basis, the various thresholds of imperial power are thus being performatively reasserted. The normalization of certain notions of life, community, and safety is never fully secured, but must rather be performatively reiterated. The normalization of bodies and their needs is performed in and through the various technologies of medicine, therapy and so on (Rose 1999). The limits of the community are performed in discursive invocations of the proper function of the family, the neighbourhood, the nation (Billig 1995). The security of Empire is performed in the continual policing of zones of incivility to defer the alterity that would otherwise erupt, contesting imperial rule (Caygill 2001).

Securing the global (bio)political economy

The key, therefore, to understanding the contemporary global order, is the constitution of the threshold, or boundaries of Empire: the points at which the dialectic of inclusion and exclusion is performed and Empire's identity is secured. Such liminal limits establish the extent of, and secure, the pacific zone of civility in which biopolitical norms establish conditions for a specific regime of accumulation. The centrality of the border, the liminal limit, or the boundary, suggests, however, that underneath concerns with the political and the economic, is a need for examining a certain *logic of encounter*. That is to say, if the present political economic order can only be understood in reference to the limits that are constitutive of its identity, then it is only in and through tracing the various imperial encounters with alterity that we can establish any of the political or economic forms that we wish to delineate.

This logic of encounter – a relation across a threshold – might more properly be referred to as the *logic of security*. The logic of security comprises a moment of contestation and ambiguity that demands a certain performance of a threshold in order to clarify what would otherwise be an instance of confusion and indistinction. The logic of security is thus the performance of a certain separation of relational terms, self from other, identity from difference. Performances of separation are only successful insofar as they naturalize an imaginary and stable limit between self and other, identity and difference. Such separation is never a real gap, never the opposition of two positive terms (present in and for themselves), but rather the relational encounter of two identities constituted in and through a shared, relational threshold (cf. Caygill 1997: 21).

One possible encounter between the subject matter of IPE and certain poststructuralist conceptual tropes leads, therefore, to the conclusion that a logic of security underlies the study of the present conjuncture. That is to say, that one possible poststructuralist IPE would always already be an examination of the various logics of security that define Empire. Thus this 'poststructuralist IPE' would examine the various instances in which an attempted separation marked a threshold. First and foremost then this would require a concern with the imaginative geographies that drive both the war on terror and the evolving notions of productivity that mark the extent of the imperial regime of accumulation. The invasion of zones of incivility, the distinction of speculation from gambling (de Goede 2000; 2005), free markets from gangster oligopolies and despotic mercantilism, the separation of righteous ways of life from their fanatical others, the recomposition of the threshold defining life itself at the level of genetic code (Rose 2001), and the redefinition of productive labor to include forms of reproduction previously taken to be extra-economic, all mark moments in which a logic of security is at work in geo-graphing the limits of imperial rule.

It is thus to such encounters and the logics of security that attempt to render them as moments of separation that a poststructuralist IPE might turn. Such separations mask a liminal relationality – and all such relationality comprises an inseparability of self and other insofar as a relation cannot be constituted by one of these terms alone. Delineating the logics of security at the core of the global (bio)political economy is thus always already a delineation of the liminal relations constitutive of that global order. Moreover, insofar as a poststructuralist IPE comprises a delineation of the liminal relationality constitutive of contemporary global order, it is also a repoliticization of the various identities and entities within that order that are – insofar as they are taken to be separate and secure – traditionally taken to be simply natural and objective.

Notes

1 This essay is based on Coward (2005a). I am grateful to Shahid Qadir, Editor of *Third World Quarterly* for permission to reprint a substantial amount of that paper. I would also like to thank Marieke de Goede for the invitation to take part in this project, without which I would not have had time or cause to consider the intersection of poststructuralism and global political economy. The argument was presented to the British International Studies Association Annual Conference, December 2004 and Brighton Philosophy Society, May 2005. I have benefited from several comments made on those occasions. I also received helpful suggestions from Julian Reid. Beate Jahn and Justin Rosenberg commented on a previous argument concerning Empire as a motif for the postglobalization era and, whilst I was unable to alter that paper in the light of their suggestions, my argument here has benefited from their insights. Of course, the responsibility for the final argument is entirely my own.

2 On the concept of 'historical conjuncture' see Rosenberg (2005: 29–40). Whilst my argument here might be said in some ways to constitute what Rosenberg calls a 'conjunctural analysis,' it does not share his own Marxist orientation to such a task.

3 See Coward (2005b) for a discussion of this literature. An exhaustive list of contributors to this literature is beyond the scope of this paper. However, a representative sample would include: Ferguson (2004); Gregory (2004); Hardt and Negri (2000); Harvey (2003); Ignatieff (2003); Joxe (2002); Mann (2003); and Todd (2004).

4 On the notion of power as a commodity see Campbell (1996: 11).

References

Abu-Lughod, J. L. (1989) *Before European Hegemony: The World System A.D. 1250–1350*. Oxford: Oxford University Press.

Amoore, L. and Langley, P. (2004) 'Ambiguities of Global Civil Society,' *Review of International Studies* 30 (1): 89–110.

Barkawi, T. and Laffey, M. (2002) 'Retrieving the Imperial: Empire and International Relations,' *Millennium* 31 (1): 109–27.

Beck, U. (2002) 'The Terrorist Threat: World Risk Society Revisited,' *Theory, Culture & Society* 19 (4) 39–55.

Billig, M. (1995) *Banal Nationalism*. London: Sage.

Brewer, A. (1990) *Marxist Theories of Imperialism: A Critical Survey*, second edn. London: Routledge.

Campbell, D. (1996) 'Political Prosaics, Transversal Politics and the Anarchical World,' in Shapiro, M. J. and Alker, H. R. (eds) *Challenging Boundaries: Global Flows, Territorial Identities*. Minneapolis: University of Minnesota Press.

Campbell, D. (1998) *Writing Security: United States Foreign Policy and the Politics of Identity*, revised edn. Minneapolis: University of Minnesota Press.

Caygill, H. (1997) 'The Shared World: Philosophy, Violence, Freedom,' in Sheppard, D., Sparks, S. and Thomas, C. (eds) *On Jean-Luc Nancy: The Sense of Philosophy*. London: Routledge.

Caygill, H. (2001) 'Perpetual Police? Kosovo and The Elision of Police and Military Violence,' *European Journal of Social Theory* 4 (1): 73–80.

Connolly, W. E. (1991) *Identity/Difference: Democratic Negotiations of Political Paradox*. Ithaca: Cornell University Press.
Connolly, W. E. (1995) *The Ethos of Pluralization*. Minneapolis: University of Minnesota Press.
Coward, M. (2005a) 'The Globalization of Enclosure: Interrogating the Geopolitics of Empire,' *Third World Quarterly* 26 (6): 855–71.
Coward, M. (2005b) 'The Imperial Character Of The Contemporary World Order,' *Theory and Event* 8 (1), http://muse.jhu.edu/journals/tae/.
Cox, M. (2003) 'The Empire's Back in Town: Or America's Imperial Temptation – Again,' *Millennium* 32 (1): 1–27.
Daly, G. (1991) 'The Discursive Construction of Economic Space: Logics of Organization and Disorganization,' *Economy and Society* 20 (1): 79–102.
de Goede, M. (2000) 'Mastering Lady Credit: Discourses of Financial Crisis in Historical Perspective,' *International Feminist Journal of Politics* 2 (1): 58–81.
de Goede, M. (2003) 'Beyond Economism in International Political Economy,' *Review of International Studies* 29 (1): 79–97.
de Goede, M. (2005) *Virtue, Fortune, and Faith: A Genealogy of Finance*. Minneapolis: University of Minnesota Press.
Dillon, M. (1996) *Politics of Security: Towards a Political Philosophy of Continental Thought*. London: Routledge.
Dillon, M. and Reid, J. (2001) 'Global Liberal Governance: Biopolitics, Security and War,' *Millennium* 30 (1): 41–65.
Ferguson, N. (2004) *Colossus: The Rise and Fall of the American Empire*. London: Allen Lane.
Foucault, M. (1982) 'Afterword: The Subject and Power,' in Dreyfus, H. L. and Rabinow, P. (eds) *Michel Foucault: Beyond Structuralism and Hermeneutics*. Brighton: Harvester Press.
Foucault, M. (1998) *The History of Sexuality Volume 1: The Will to Knowledge*. London: Penguin.
Foucault, M. (2000) 'The Birth of Biopolitics,' in Rabinow, P. (ed.) *Essential Works of Foucault 1954–1984, Volume 1: Ethics, Subjectivity and Truth*. London: Penguin.
Gill, S. (1990) *American Hegemony And The Trilateral Commission*. Cambridge: Cambridge University Press.
Gray, J. (2001) 'The Era of Globalization Is Over,' *New Statesman*, September 24: 25–7.
Gregory, D. (2004) *The Colonial Present: Afghanistan, Palestine, Iraq*. Oxford: Blackwell.
Griekspoor, A. and Collins, S. (2001) 'Raising Standards in Emergency Relief: How Useful are Sphere Minimum Standards for Humanitarian Assistance?' *British Medical Journal* 323 (7315): 740–2.
Hardt, M. and Negri, A. (2000) *Empire*. London: Harvard University Press.
Harvey, D. (2003) *The New Imperialism*. Oxford: Oxford University Press.
Held, D., McGrew, A., Goldblatt, D. and Perraton, J. (1999) *Global Transformations: Politics, Economics and Culture*. Oxford: Polity.
Hobbes, T. (1985) *Leviathan*. London: Penguin.
Ignatieff, M. (2003) *Empire Lite: Nation Building in Bosnia, Kosovo and Afghanistan*. London: Vintage.
Joxe, A. (2002) *The Empire of Disorder*. New York: Semiotex(e).

Koenig-Archibugi, M. (2002) 'Mapping Global Governance,' in Held, D. and McGrew, A. (eds) *Governing Globalization: Power, Authority and Global Governance*. Cambridge: Polity.

Mann, M. (2003) *Incoherent Empire*. London: Verso.

Notes From Nowhere (ed.) (2003) *We Are Everywhere: The Irresistible Rise Of Global Anti-Capitalism*. London: Verso.

O'Brien, R. and Williams, M. (2004) *Global Political Economy: Evolution and Dynamics*. London: Palgrave.

Ohmae, K. (1992) *The Borderless World: Power and Strategy in the Interlinked Economy*. London: Fontana.

Roach, S. (2001) 'Back to Borders,' *Financial Times*, September 28, Available at http://www.globalpolicy.org/globaliz/econ/2001/1003glo.htm.

Rose, N. (1999) *Governing The Soul: The Shaping Of The Private Self*, second edn. London: Free Association.

Rose, N. (2001) 'The Politics Of Life Itself,' *Theory, Culture and Society* 18 (6): 1–30.

Rosenau, J. N. and Czempiel E.-O. (eds) (1992) *Governance without Government: Order and Change in World Politics*. Cambridge: Cambridge University Press.

Rosenberg, J. (2000), *The Follies of Globalization Theory: Polemical Essays*. London: Verso.

Rosenberg, J. (2005) 'Globalization Theory: A Post Mortem,' *International Politics* 42: 2–74.

Scholte, J. A. (2000) *Globalization: A Critical Introduction*. London: Macmillan.

Shaw, M. (2000) *Theory of the Global State: Globality as Unfinished Revolution*. Cambridge: Cambridge University Press.

Sphere Project (2004) *The Sphere Handbook 2004 Edition*, http://www.sphereproject.org/handbook/index.htm

Todd, E. (2004) *After The Empire: The Breakdown of the American Order*. London: Constable.

Walker, P. and Purdin, S. (2004) 'Birthing Sphere,' *Disasters* 28 (2): 100–11.

Walker, R. B. J. (1999) 'Citizenship after the Modern Subject' in Hutchings, K. and Dannreuther, R. (eds) *Cosmopolitan Citizenship*. Basingstoke: Macmillan.

4

Performativity, Popular Finance and Security in the Global Political Economy

Rob Aitken

> ...we should focus on security as a pervasive and complex system of political, social, and economic power, which reaches from the most private spaces of being to the vast flows and conflicts of geopolitics and global economic circulation.
>
> Anthony Burke, *Aporias of Security* (2002)

Throughout the fall of 1954 and into 1955 and 1956 the US Advertising Council managed a complicated public service campaign it called *People's Capitalism*. Buoyed by the earlier successes of its *Our American Heritage* campaigns of the early 1950s (which featured the Freedom Train, a portable public service advertisement that criss-crossed America), the Council trained its attention onto more explicitly geopolitical topics. 'It was felt,' the Council emphatically claimed, 'that a dramatic rebuttal was needed of the communist claim that the common man must turn to communism to be "saved"' (The Advertising Council 1956: 9). This confrontation with the communist threat did not, however, inspire a campaign directed explicitly against the Soviet Union. Rather, the Council sketched its dramatic response by targeting the practices and habits of America's own working and middle classes. Its campaign, consisting of radio, print and television advertisements, paid particular attention to the ownership of capital and attempted to dramatize the ways in which the American economy and its productive enterprises were owned and controlled by its great mass of workers. The campaign was conceived, the Council reports, 'as a way of dramatizing the fact that in the US of today the people both supply much of the capital and receive the benefits' (The Advertising Council 1956).

This dramatization provokes some intriguing questions. How could something as seemingly remote from concerns of national security as individual economic practice be connected to the domain of foreign policy? How and through what processes did it become possible to imagine individual and national security as part of a shared field? This chapter addresses these questions by paying attention to the ways in which 'popular finance' became deeply implicated in issues of national security and in forms of geopolitical reasoning over the interwar and postwar periods. Popular finance refers to a disparate range of attempts to incorporate working-class and 'everyday' populations into private financial spaces and to ask those populations to seek some conception of their own security within those spaces. This chapter explores a very particular ambition which many programs of popular finance pursue: the framing of popular finance as a special set of practices with which everyday individuals could make themselves active in the question of national security. Throughout the postwar period a connection was forged between geopolitical, national and individual security in which, I argue, the confrontation with geopolitical risk and danger became, in some important ways, inseparable from the risks individuals were asked to confront as they enter private financial spaces. At the same time, this chapter highlights the way in which 'capital' itself – or at least one particular form of capital connected to popular finance – had to be constituted, often in the everyday spaces where it did not already exist.

This chapter frames the ambition to connect geopolitical and individual economic security by drawing on several concepts which are broadly consistent with 'poststructuralist' forms of analysis but which are only beginning to creep into conversations within International Political Economy (IPE). Influenced by notions of genealogy and 'cultural economy,' this chapter argues for a fuller critical interrogation of the question of security in IPE.[1] Although the question of geopolitical reasoning has been usefully problematized by the 'critical geopolitics' literature in International Relations (IR), less critical attention has been focused on questions of everyday economic security. Neither has there been much attention to the connections between economic and geopolitical conceptions of security. This chapter argues that national and individual economic security were, at least for a cluster of programs of popular finance, deeply implicated in and constitutive of each other. Developing a genealogy – a cultural economy – of one line of connections between national/geopolitical reasoning and everyday financial security can, I argue, help open up the question of economic security by highlighting the ways in which 'economic' identities and practices are 'performatively constituted.' This kind of cultural economy, I conclude, can open space for more heterogeneous and diverse critical accounts of 'economic' categories and practices; a space in which we might usefully develop more concrete and situated analyses of global political-economic practice.

Performativity and (popular) finance

Among the most productive contributions of poststructuralist analysis has been an attempt to reframe identity and subjectivity as unstable, 'dislocated' or relational categories. As David Campbell notes, identity is not a given or unproblematic aspect of social life. Rather the identities of all bodies are constituted in particular processes and performances. 'Identity,' argues Campbell, 'is not fixed by nature, given by God, or planned by intentional behaviour...Whether we are talking of "the body" or "the state" or of particular bodies and states, the identity of each is performatively constituted' (Campbell 1998: 9).

A particularly resonant concept in Campbell's discussion is performativity. Performativity is a methodological stance which emphasizes the ways in which the identity of any body is 'performed' into being through the repeated iteration of its basic features. 'Overview, simplifications,' writes John Law (2002: 28), 'the mastery of time and space, are not given in the order of things. Rather, they are artfully performed into being.' Rooted in the work of Judith Butler, 'performativity' underscores the ways in which subjects come to constitute themselves, or become constituted, through the repetition of norms and discourses which mark them out from other processes, categories or subjects. 'Performativity,' argues Butler, 'is a matter of reiterating or repeating the norms by which one is constituted...It is a compulsory repetition of prior and subjectivating norms, ones which cannot be thrown off at will, but which work, animate, and constrain the...subject' (Roden 2001: 27, see also Butler 1997).

There has, however, been relatively little attention to the constitution and performativity of *economic* identity and practice (Mitchell 2002). Frequently, key concepts in IPE such as 'capital,' 'economy,' and 'finance' are assumed as given categories with stable or self-evident identities (de Goede 2004; see also Gammon and Palan this volume). This is particularly true of capital, a category that often serves as a key protagonist in both critical and more mainstream accounts in the field. Often depicted in macrostructural terms, capital is assumed to be a self-possessed and unified force central to the very contours of political-economic life. Despite its centrality, however, little attention is paid to the precise, and often mundane, ways in which capital itself is constituted. As Marieke de Goede (2003: 81) has argued, capital in IPE is often conceived as 'a transformative agent, capable of "self-expansion."'

By sketching capital as an implacable kind of force, both critics and proponents alike contribute to the mystification of finance and the financial world as an unknowable and, importantly, undoable center of power and domination. In contrast, I argue that a critical genealogy, what some writers have recently termed a cultural economy, can help make capital visible as something decentered and as something made, and potentially remade, in the diverse and sometimes incoherent space of everyday life. Genealogy, argues Foucault, 'disturbs what was previously considered immobile; it fragments what was thought unified; it shows the heterogeneity of what was imagined consistent with itself' (quoted in Rosow 1997: 44). This is not to suggest that capital is not central to the political and economic trajectories of the past two centuries. Rather, this is to suggest that capital can be diagrammed in less centered ways than it often is. To sketch capital in monolithic tones, is to provide it a status and unity it may not 'independently' have. As one nineteenth-century critic observes (1882), images of an omnipotent power offers a conception of capital in which its capacities to influence social, political and even natural rhythms are dramatically overstated:

> To be true, it would require that the half-dozen men recognized as great operators should hold in their hands all the elements...They should be able to give or withhold from us bountiful harvests; to blast the grain-fields of Europe when we have a large surplus to sell; to give us mild or severe winters, floods or drought; to call up the devouring swarms of grasshoppers in the West...to increase or diminish the stream of immigration into the country; to make commerce and manufacturing flourish or wither as they may will it (Anonymous 1882: 50).

Apart from and alongside centered stories of capital, then, there is an 'other' history of capital. For a diverse set of programs and campaigns throughout the past 100 years, capital is, precisely, something made particularly possible only when it occupies the space of everyday life or when it is created by and through everyday or working class populations. This 'other' side of capital is the space of 'popular finance' which entails all of the diverse, although mainly American, attempts – both historical and more contemporary – to incorporate popular and working class populations into private financial spaces.

These programs of 'popular finance' are deeply implicated in processes of performativity. At one level, and in direct reference to Butler's understanding, these spaces and practices of popular finance are one set of attempts to create and cultivate capital, often in places where it does not already exist.[2]

At another level, however, programs of popular finance imply a second and slightly broader notion of performance. These programs often conceive of capital as something that has to be performed in a quite literal sense, as something that can only be instrumentalized when actually embodied by everyday populations. In this regard 'performance' is an active verb signifying the ways in which 'capital' is literally performed by everyday populations in the name or pursuit of our own freedom, security, ethical choice or some other objective.[3] These are performances, however, that are also animated by the question of risk; a question key not only to individual security, but also to the broader contours of geopolitical reasoning.

Popular finance, national space, geopolitics

At a most immediate level, programs of popular finance are centrally concerned with forms of individual economic/financial security which often require individuals to navigate economic risk in a direct manner. Even historical cases of popular finance have often invoked something of an 'entrepreneurial' notion of citizenship. 'The language of the entrepreneurial individual,' Rose and Miller (1997: 200–1) argue, diagrams an agent 'endowed with freedom and autonomy [mobilized]...in the energetic pursuit of personal fulfilment and the incessant calculations that are to enable this to be achieved.' The individualized risks of everyday economic spaces, however, are not conceived as separate from or outside of the spaces of national security. 'Making up' individual financial security has often, at the same time, also been implicated in the making up of national security. 'Sovereignty-thinking,' notes Warren Magnusson (2000: 80), 'suggests that people must be distinct and self-governing, both individually and collectively.' As they experiment in the first part of the twentieth century, the experts and institutions keen to foster popular finance, begin also to diagram a connection between individual financial security and the integrity or security of national space in a number of ways.[4] The connection between individual and national security is perhaps most forcefully drawn, however, in relation to the question of risk and geopolitics.

The critical geopolitics of popular finance

State identity, reminds Campbell (1998: 9), 'is constituted in relation to difference...the constitution of identity is achieved through the inscription of boundaries that serve to demarcate an "inside" from an "outside," a "self" from an "other," a "domestic" from a "foreign." Borders and boundaries do not surround or 'hold together' categories that naturally exist, but rather help define the identities of those categories by marking them out in space and delineating the frontiers within which categories are contained (Weiskopf 2002; Weldes *et al.* 1999). The articulation of danger emanating from the external environment (in terms of a dangerous enemy, 'other', risk or general threat) is less a 'real' or objective entity as much as it is a discourse which functions precisely to stabilize the identity of the inside against or in relation to an identifiable outside or other. In contrast to realist images of global politics, insecurity and danger are not threats to the internal terrain of the nation, but are discursive materials from which the nation itself gains identity and definition. 'The constant articulation of danger through foreign policy,' attests Campbell (1998: 11–12), 'is thus not a threat to a state's identity or existence: it is its condition of possibility' (see also Shapiro 1997: O'Tuathail 1996).

One way to read images and practices of popular finance is as a site where a particular form of national identity is developed and made real in these terms. Many images in American popular finance campaigns operate, precisely, as places where American identity is formulated in a particular kind of way. Marketing material mobilized as part of the US Savings Bonds programs of the early 1950s, for example, were indicative of Cold War campaigns organized around images of an external threat. One striking image depicts a kind of simultaneity between personal and national security by featuring a lone figure using his savings to fight a menacing Soviet presence. The real danger represented by this external threat is not the force of violence, but rather the risk of losing a particular kind of American identity dedicated to freedom and individualism. Framing investment as a 'hitting out at the enemies of our way of life,' the whole question of international threat becomes one connected to the intimate contours of American culture and values. (The Advertising Council, ca. 1950–1955)

In this Cold War context, American identity became squarely focused on the exceptional obligations to maintain and secure the free world. American values, in this configuration, are both required to meet this international obligation and yet are also threatened by forces external to the nation. The advertising of popular financial vehicles (including of course those connected to US Savings and Defence Bonds) were often key diagrams of this exact kind of international obligation and exceptionalism. In *Trouble in Foreign Places,* the 'good American life' is clearly (and perhaps most fundamentally) connected to an almost unknowable amount of 'trouble in foreign places.' In this formulation, American culture (the 'kind of future we want') is most clearly defined in opposition to the instabilities and difficulties of 'foreign' space. The work of personal investment is clearly framed in terms of an equation between domestic culture/values and a particular requirement to respond to foreign 'trouble':

> Sometimes I can't understand all I see in the newspapers about trouble in foreign places. But nowadays we can't turn our backs on what's happening somewhere else. The world's too small. If my youngsters are going to grow up to enjoy the good American life, it's going to take some doing...if there's going to be the kind of future we want...Savings Bonds are a kind of 'insurance policy' for me and my country (The Advertising Council, ca. 1950).

Active citizenship and individual/national security

The advertising of popular finance gave particular prominence to diagrams of national identity which, in particular, defined the terrain of the nation in relation to images of geopolitical danger. What is perhaps most striking about this connection between national and geopolitical identity are the ways in which the risks central to individual economic security are often conceived as internal to (part of the same moment as) the dangers of geopolitical space. Many programs of popular finance both locate individuals directly within forms of economic risk and, at the same time, connect that individual risk to the processes with which the nation bears itself in the context of international risk/danger. The ability of the nation to bear itself within international space (and to confront its international obligations and dangers) is directly connected to individual citizens and their capacities to bear and govern themselves in the little risks they face in economic and financial spaces.

The attempt to connect individual practice with the broader confrontations of geopolitical space is first hinted in some of the modes of economic citizenship associated with nineteenth-century imperialism. In the British context, for example, nineteenth-century thrift and money management advice often clarified a relationship between individual conduct and the international (imperial) obligations of the nation. Explicitly targeted at working class audiences, advice writers defined sound financial practice as an act of denying the 'savage' self within. The capacity to govern the self autonomously is an act of overcoming the 'natural' tendencies of the 'lower' or 'animal' self (often conceived as a trace of savage life) by denying appeals to sensual gratification and impulse. Careful and regulated saving was one practice through which working class individuals could begin to develop capacities for autonomous self-government (Payot 1893).

A similar general theme is apparent in many examples from twentieth-century American advertising campaigns for popular financial vehicles. One of the most striking examples is *In His Hand*, a 1954 copy from the US Savings Bonds series, where male obligation to and sacrifice for the unspeaking members of his domestic space, is conceived not only as an act of family necessity, but also one of national security. This image foregrounds a little girl praying with the barely visible hand of her father covering her clasped-prayer hands (teaching her?) and emphasizes the necessity, and immense burden of manly saving. The requirement to save is expressed as both an act of prudential manliness as well as a godly act of national freedom and security. This is a formulation in which the 'strength of America' is most visibly connected to the security provided by its individual citizens in the pursuit of their own personal or gendered obligation:

> ...the guide is Dad, the goal is a security not even he can provide.
> But the pattern is security, and it is Dad's privilege to supply his part of it for the little hearts in his care...The security of our homes is our worthiest goal. And providing it is a privilege unique in a country like ours, where each of us is free to choose his way.
> And think: The security that begins in *your* home, joined to that of other homes, builds the strength of America.
> Saving for Security is easy!...For your sake, and your family's, too, how about signing up today? (U.S. Savings Bond Program 1954)

In these formulations an 'intimate association' is depicted between the risk that the nation faces in geopolitical space and the risks individuals directly confront by managing their own savings or investments in a prudential manner. In these terms, those who sought to provoke forms of individual economic/financial security, were also, and at the same time, pursuing a kind of geopolitical reasoning. These experts and advocates were trying to strengthen the nation and its security by 'making up' an individual form of citizenship capable of securing both individuals and the nations they populate. Practices of popular finance were depicted as a method with which individual citizens could become active in the government of themselves *and* the nation, a way of securing the nation within the geopolitical spaces it inhabits.

These lines of force, however, did not seek a singular or universal condition. Like many liberal modes of government, programs of popular finance seem as much preoccupied with the populations which are unable to develop capacities of self-government as they are with those which can realize such capacities (Dean 2002; Hindess 2002, 2005). The practices of popular finance help constitute the parameters and meaning of national space not only by specifying an account of geopolitical danger, but also by delineating, in concrete terms, who is capable of exercising citizenship and who remains outside of its privileged space (see also Coward this volume). In some campaigns, aboriginal populations, racial minorities, and others are depicted as special populations unable to practice the kind of financial autonomy and self-government available to normal populations. In many of the thrift and financial advice books from the late nineteenth century, this connection was made explicit by directly representing inappropriate financial conduct as a part of a 'savage economy.' 'The savage,' claims Smiles (1875: 44), 'is the greatest of spendthrifts, for he has no forethought, no tomorrow. The prehistoric man saved nothing…like savages…Saving for the future forms no part of the savage economy' (also Thornduke 1920, Gammon and Palan this volume)

Several twentieth-century campaigns also, in different ways, share this sense of populations unable to govern financial life in an appropriate manner. The American investment firm Dreyfus & Co, for example, launched a series of advertising campaigns throughout the 1950s that invoked this kind of theme. One image, *'Confidentially … I'm Bearish'*, features a stylized 'noble savage' image (featuring a dark-skinned figure with simple adornments and hunting tools). The caption underneath this orientalist image notes that 'this gentleman thinks that the market is going to go down'. This 'primitive' figure is invoked as an emblem of those populations that are incapable of assuming any of the roles associated with competent participation in markets (understanding the status of markets, exercising informed agency in market settings). 'It's amazing,' the text asserts, 'how many unqualified people have opinions on the market.' (Drefyus and Company, 1954)

Although it makes an appeal to seemingly universal conditions (reason, citizenship) the practices of popular finance are actually implicated in the making of particularities. Popular finance marks out a set of practices available only to the populations which exist within particular (often raced or gendered) parameters. In this sense, popular finance is implicated not in a single, but in multiple forms of identity which, although often made visible in terms of national security, are not contained, in any simple ways, to a single – national – conception of financial identity.

From national security to globalization?

The kinds of national political affiliation made visible in practices of popular finance through the early and middle years of the twentieth century are now often said to be eclipsed by global processes. Finance is often located at the very core of the processes of 'time-space compression' which are said to erode the very authority and status of national sovereignty. Figuring a new economy of flows and mobilities, many 'globalist' commentators, an increasingly common position within the IPE literature, have understood globalization, precisely, as the erosion of the sovereign state and its capacities to pursue national macro-economic economic security (Ohmae 1990; see also Hirst and Thompson 1996; Robinson 2002; Glassman 1999). Globalization, argues Urry (2000: 33), 'presupposes the metaphors of network and flow' rather than the logic of sovereignty (see also Helleiner 1999; Scholte 2000). Although finance was 'contained' within the postwar moment of 'embedded liberalism' through the use of capital controls and a fixed system of exchange rates, the dismantling of the Bretton Woods framework in the early 1970s and the emergence of the Eurodollar markets resulted in the dramatic development of global financial markets much less responsive to public authority and control (Germain 1997; Langley 2002). This has triggered a rapid growth in complex financial markets which undermine the capacity of states to pursue macroeconomic policy development and which, accordingly, challenge the overall sovereignty of the state. In this view, finance exists as a macrostructural force well beyond the scope of sovereign states, or in Castells' terms, as a 'collective capitalist' which is capable of 'unifying' and 'commanding' accumulation above any national or sovereign authority:

> There is not, sociologically and economically, such a thing as a global capitalist class. But there is an integrated, global capital network, whose movements and variable logic ultimately determine economies and influence society. Thus above a diversity of human-

> flesh capitalists and capitalist groups there is a faceless collective capitalist, made up of financial flows operated by electronic networks...this network of networks of capital both unifies and commands specific centers of capitalist accumulation, structuring the behavior of capitalists around their submission to the global network (Castells 2000: 78).

When conceived at a less macrostructural level, however, the connections of 'finance capital' to forms of spatial affiliation are more complex and multiple than often presented in the global finance/postsovereignty debate. At one level, the ways in which different financial institutions have made popular finance visible in recent years have indeed tended, in certain respects, to foreground a kind of global form of identification seemingly outside of the logic of individual/national security. Some of the recent images of personal finance, for example, have focused around the possibilities of a kind of investing-cosmopolitanism. One example of an attempt to make visible this kind of rationality is *It's Your World. Invest in It.* This image, produced in the mutual-fund boom of the 1990s, draws an expansive image of unbounded nature and frames individuals within the limitless space of the earth itself. 'Each of us,' the advertisement asserts, 'is part of a larger picture today. A global economy. Which is why we believe it makes sense to look beyond our national boundaries for investment opportunities.' (G.T. Global Mutual Funds 1995)

Alongside this cosmopolitan vein, however, the world of personal and popular finance is increasingly imagined in terms of a different confrontation between everyday individuals and risk. This confrontation exists not as part of the broader risk shouldered by the nation in the context of geopolitical danger, but as a more fully individualized experience generated though direct and unmediated participation in global spaces (Starchild 2000). For Ted Cadsby, for example, one of the irrationalities which prevent individuals from asserting the kind of rational authority over financial life is a misplaced affiliation with national markets and national financial instruments. 'Investors around the world,' writes Cadsby (2000: 157), 'are psychologically inclined to favour their home markets. This is...distorted thinking that results from attachment to one's own country.'

Global markets have also been made visible in terms of a language of difference and cultural otherness. A tension exists in these discourses between openness to the investing life beyond national borders and a deep concern for the risk inherent in the difference and strangeness of 'foreign' places. These images make visible a good kind of risk (confronting the competitive forces in a global setting) and a bad form of risk (exposure to cultural difference). Borders, reminds R. B. J. Walker (1994: 162), 'still provide our most powerful sense of what it means to look over the horizon.' Cadsby, for example, understands reluctance to enter global markets as a 'natural' reaction to the unfamiliarity and mystery of global spaces. 'We make our investment decisions,' writes Cadsby (2000: 150), 'within the frame of our experiences...Foreign markets can seem mysterious to us.' A striking diagram of this discourse of global markets as different and dangerous is a Bankers Trust campaign from the early 1990s. 'It's hard enough to recognize risk at home,' the advertisement asserts, but 'venture abroad and risk is even more disguised.' The image of the advertisement features a jovial mask hiding the sinister presence of a ghostly figure underneath. In this image foreign markets are never knowable in certain and pure terms but exist as sources of difference and danger. In the context of this indecipherable fear and danger, many investment firms have developed strategies to make themselves visible as bodies of expertise capable of negotiating and overcoming cultural or geographical difference. (Bankers Trust 1994)

Do these various lines emphasizing popular finance as a kind of cosmopolitan or global practice entail, as globalists might predict, a turning away from the individual-national-geopolitical nexus first made visible in the earlier parts of the twentieth century? To answer this question, I want to use the remainder of this chapter to suggest that the lines occupied by popular finance are more complicated than any singular or epochal account might suggest. Although there has been an increasing attempt in recent years to situate popular finance within global fields, this process does not correspond easily to any simple epochal story in which national political-economic identities have been supplanted by global forms of affiliation.

On the one hand, attempts to make visible a connection between everyday investors and global space predate the 'globalizations' of the past decades. Throughout the 1920s, for example, financial identity is often situated in global fields (see also Conant 1899). One campaign of the 1920s by S. W. Strauss & Co., consistently stressed the centrality of investment in a process that might loosely be called 'time-space compression' on a global scale. The series entitled *'Are You Keeping Pace with this Changing World?'* features images of technological progress which enable human action across space and time in ways previously unimaginable. Figure 4.1 highlights the ways in which increased travel shatters differences across space. This increased spatial accessibility reformulates conventional forms of identity and human connection and allows individuals to forge personal and geographical connections across a wider field. 'When land-walking humans, seated in a great three-motored air plane,' the text reads, 'make jaunty stops at Honolulu and the Fiji Islands...who shall say that a weekend rendezvous in Hongkong, for any two of us, is far remote?' Making references to a

Figure 4.1 'See You Next Saturday – in Hongkong' (S. W. Straus & Co., 1928)

shrinking world, the copy proclaims a new, boundless era in which technological and spatial barriers are systematically eliminated. 'And who,' the copy questions rhetorically, 'shall dare to place a limit on the expansion of industry and commerce destined to be born of such adventurings across the skies?'

On the other hand, the rationality outlined earlier which connects popular financial practice with national security remains resonant. Merrill Lynch, for example, has recently developed campaigns focusing precisely on 'national security'. An image from this campaign, *Merrill Lynch on National Security,* foregrounds the figure of a man, cradling a child. The corner of the advertisement features a small map of the United States. In this image, the basis of national security remains rooted in the financial security of its individuals. 'When its people are financially secure,' the copy attests, 'a nation's security is enhanced.' (Merrill Lynch and Co. Inc. 1997)

Perhaps, however, it is in the wake of the 'terror' of 11 September 2001 that the themes of national/individual security in everyday financial practice have been reframed most vigorously. Almost immediately after the attacks, 'war' or 'freedom' bond proposals were developed. Both houses of Congress passed legislation including the *Freedom Bonds Act of 2001* in response to which a hesitant Treasury eventually relaunched a regular EE Series of Savings Bonds as Patriot Bonds.[1]

These bonds are depicted as a mechanism through which individuals can connect their own security to the security of the nation and can help the nation sustain itself in the context of extraordinary geopolitical danger. Representative Levin, speaking in the Congressional Freedom Bonds debate, restates a line of force which figures the war against terrorism as a fight rooted, in some regard, in the conduct and unity of individual citizens:

> If we are to win the long war against global terrorism, it is clear that the fight must be waged not only by the Federal Government, but by the united American people. The war bond is both a symbol and an expression of this unity...This bill is one way to tap the resources of individuals, of countless citizens of this country, to help fight, keeping within American traditions, the fight against terrorism (United States Congress 2001: H7138).

This formulation is perhaps given a certain currency because the attacks targeted key symbols of American economy and finance, including the financial district of New York. Healing the damage inflicted on New York's financial institutions requires the mobilization of individual self-governance and enterprise. It is, in this view, a kind of everyday citizenship, made real in investment practices, that can reverse the damage inflicted to the very heart of American finance. Speaking on 20 September 2001 in an address to a joint session of Congress, President Bush clearly links the work of rebuilding the financial district (a task itself critical to confrontations with geopolitical danger) to the conduct and enterprise of American citizens. 'Terrorists attacked a symbol of American prosperity,' Bush affirms, however 'they did not touch its source. America is successful because of the hard work and creativity and enterprise of our people. These were the true strengths of our economy before September 11, and they are our strengths today' (Bush 2001).

In these terms, the relationship between national and global financial imaginaries occupies cross-cutting – and not single – trajectories. In contrast to epochal narratives which sketch a decisive shift between worlds organized around national and global logics, the worlds of popular finance have been more complicated. Appeals to global forms of affiliation predate the more recent round of globalization often dated to the crises of the early 1970s. In addition, the lines which link prudent investing/financial practice with national security remain a key way in which financial identity can be organized.

The shifting forms of everyday financial identity occupy a kind of history of assertions and slippages in which, at different moments (World War II, the Cold War, 9/11) a rationality connecting individual practice/citizenship with national is mobilized. At other moments, other kinds of diverse spatialities (global, local, fluid) are asserted in particular kinds of way. Different rationalities of popular finance become available at specific moments in a series of rhythms and discontinuities not easily read in terms of a straight or progressive line. This straight-line narrative can be replaced by a story of discontinuities in which different rationalities assert themselves in or become available to specific contexts only to be displaced by or refracted through other, shifting, ideas of identity or affiliation. Although, as this chapter has tried to emphasize, a key link between individual financial practice and national security was forged throughout the twentieth century, this link has neither been singular throughout the past century, nor has it been displaced in any categorical manner. Rather it has existed in uneasy relationship with other forms of popular financial affiliation which at times occupy their own – often fleeting – visibility. 'There is no simple evolution or succession,' writes Nikolas Rose (1999: 153), 'in knowledges and practices of subjectification. Many specifications of subjectivity coexist. They are deployed in diverse practices at similar times, sometimes without being troubled by their discrepancies. At other times they are set off against one another.'

Conclusion

This chapter has retold one story of a line which has often been transcribed between individual and national security. This connection centered individual financial security as a practice central to the nation as it bears itself in the dangers of geopolitical space. It is also a practice with which individuals could make themselves active in the space and geopolitical security of the nation. The risk that individuals bear in the spaces of popular finance are connected, in this relation, to the risk the state assumes in the anarchy of global space.

I have highlighted this individual/national security line not as a historical curiosity but to provide one example of the kinds of concrete analyses that can be generated by a particular form of poststructuralism in IPE. One way that a cultural economy perspective can contribute to broader conversations in the field is by disturbing key concepts like 'capital' as unproblematic categories, and by facilitating what we might term 'purposely heterogeneous' accounts of how those categories came into being in the first place. The story retold in this chapter has contributed to such a task in two broad ways. First, and in contrast to macrostructural conceptions of capital, this chapter highlights the way in which 'capital' itself had to be constituted. In more particular terms, it emphasizes the ways in which capital is performed and constituted, often in nonobvious and surprising ways. The claim in this chapter is that one site at which capital is constituted is the space of national security. By situating it directly within the logic of geopolitical reasoning, I have tried to make capital's emergence 'strange' to us; to confront capital, in other words, by placing it in a context that is alien to our conventional accounts in political economy and which might interrupt our understanding of it as a coherent and self-consistent category.

A second way in which this chapter has tried to introduce a more heterogeneous analysis is by highlighting the complexity of the economic changes associated with globalization. In contrast to lines which might sketch out epochal accounts of global political-economic change, I have tried to foreground a story of discontinuity and slippage in which national forms of identification exist, sometimes uneasily, with more globalized conceptions of self and citizenship.

In doing to, this chapter has situated 'capital' in a multiple and diverse set of contexts; not as a macrostructural and already-existing reality but as a force that itself needs to be constituted in complex ways. This kind of heterogeneous analysis, I want to suggest, is key to the ways in which we might develop critical analyses of 'finance' and 'capital' not as unimpeachable and mystified categories of global political-economic life, but as multiple categories deeply implicated in a diverse range of mundane contexts. 'Investigations,' writes Rose (1999: 58), 'are...used not for knowing but for cutting...to disturb that which forms the very groundwork of our present, to make the given once more strange and to cause us to wonder at how it came to appear so natural.' What is required are analyses which can contribute to a 'making strange' and a demystifying of the financial world; a task of some importance for a category so urgently a part of our neoliberal and globalized present.

Notes

1 As defined by Paul du Gay and Michael Pryke, cultural economy offers an 'understanding of economics as "culture" [which] focuses attention on the practical ways in which "economically relevant activity" is performed and enacted. It serves to show, in other words, the ways in which the "making up" or "construction" of economic realities is undertaken and achieved; how those activities, objects and persons we categorize as "economic" are built up or assembled from a number of parts, many of them supplied by the discipline of economics but many drawn from other sources, including, of course, forms of ostensibly non-economic cultural practice.' (du Gay and Pryke 2002: 5; also Aitken 2005)

2 A number of recent interventions in IPE have begun to emphasize the question of 'performance,' see Cameron and Palan (2004); Clark, Thrift and Tickell (2004).

3 This sense of individual performance, and its connection to government 'of the self by the self,' is influenced by key work on governmentality, see Dean and Hindess (1998); Dean (1999) and Rose (1993).

4 Many images in early popular finance campaigns, for example, imagine participation in everyday financial spaces in relation to broader narratives of national integration or a kind of 'normative whiteness' in which populations outside of (or ambiguous in relation to) the space of the nation can come to occupy a form of responsible citizenship through the habitual practices of saving/investing entailed in programs of popular finance.

5 United States Congress, *Freedom Bonds Act of 2001,* October 2001, Washington, DC: HR 2899. Almost simultaneously, another act was introduced in the House, *The Terrorism Elimination Act of 2001* which provided for 'the creation of a Counter-Terrorism Trust Fund, to provide for the issuance of Freedom Bonds, to allow tax-payers to contribute income tax funds and other amounts to support counter-terrorism efforts, and for other purposes.' See also the Avalon Project at Yale Law School for further details regarding this initiative.

References

Advertising Council (ca 1950–1955) *America Depends on Americans*. John W. Hartman Centre for Advertising and Marketing History, Rare Book, Manuscript and Special Collections Library, Duke University, Durham, NC. J. Walter Thompson Archives, Domestic Advertisements Collection, Advertising and Public Service Collection, 'U.S. Savings Bonds', Box #5.

Advertising Council (ca 1950–1955) *Hit Him Hard! and do Yourself a Big Favor*. John W. Hartman Centre for Advertising and Marketing History, Rare Book, Manuscript and Special Collections Library, Duke University, Durham, NC. J. Walter Thompson Archives, Domestic Advertisements Collection, Advertising and Public Service Collection, 'U.S. Savings Bonds', Box #5.

Advertising Council (1956) *People's Capitalism: A Contribution to U.S. Overseas Information. Advertising Council: Annual Report 1955–56*, New York: The Advertising Council.

Aitken, R. (2005) '"A Direct Personal Stake": Mass Investment, Cultural Economy and the New York Stock Exchange,' *Review of International Political Economy* 12 (2): 334–63.

Anonymous (1882) 'Hydraulic Pressure in Wall Street,' *The North American Review*, 135: 308.

Bankers Trust (1994) *Risk Doesn't Always Wear a Familiar Face*, New York: Bankers Trust, originally published in *The Economist*, October 1994.

Burke, A. (2002) 'Aporias of Security,' *Alternatives* 27 (1): 1–27.

Bush, G. W. (2001) *Address to a Joint Session of Congress*. Washington, DC: 20 September.

Butler, J. (1997) *Excitable Speech: A Politics of the Performative*. New York: Routledge.

Cadsby, T. (2000) *The 10 Biggest Investment Mistakes Canadians Make and How to Avoid Them*. Toronto: Stoddart Publishing Co.

Cameron, A. and Palan, R. (2004) *The Imagined Economies of Globalization*. London: Sage Publications.

Campbell, D. (1998) *Writing Security: United States Foreign Policy and the Politics of Identity*. Minneapolis: University of Minnesota Press.

Castells, M. (2000) 'The Network Society,' in Held, D. and McGrew, A. (eds) *The Global Transformations Reader*. Cambridge: Polity Press.

Clark, G., Thrift, N. and Tickell, A. (2004) 'Performing Finance: The Industry, the Media and its Image,' *Review of International Political Economy* 11 (2): 289–310.

Conant, C. A. (1899) 'The Economic Basis of Imperialism,' *The North American Review* 167 (502).

Dean, M. (1999) *Governmentality: Power and Rule in Modern Society*. London: Sage Publications.

Dean, M. (2002) 'Liberal Government and Authoritarianism,' *Economy and Society* 31 (1): 37–61.

Dean, M. and Hindess, B. (1998) 'Introduction: Government, Liberalism, Society,' in Dean, M. and Hindess, B. (eds) *Governing Australia: Studies in Contemporary Rationalities of Government*. Cambridge: Cambridge University Press.

de Goede, M. (2003) 'Beyond Economism in International Political Economy,' *Review of International Studies* 29 (1): 79–97.

de Goede, M. (2004) 'Repoliticizing Financial Risk,' *Economy and Society* 33 (2): 197–217.
Dreyfus & Co. (1954) *Confidentially...I'm Bearish.* D'Arcy Agency Collection, Champaign Illinois: University of Illinois Urbana-Champaign, Communications Library, Reel #86, originally published in *Life* 1 November 1954: 82.
du Gay, P. and Pryke, M. (2002) 'Cultural Economy: An Introduction,' in du Gay, P. and Pryke, M. (eds) *Cultural Economy: Cultural Analysis and Commercial Life*. London: Sage Publications, 1–19.
G. T. Global Mutual Funds (1995) *It's Your World. Invest In It.* San Francisco: G. T. Global Financial Services Inc., originally published in *The Economist* 7 October 1995: 78.
Germain, R. D. (1997) *The International Organization of Credit: States and Global Finance*. Cambridge: Cambridge University Press.
Glassman, J. (1999) 'State Power Beyond the "Territorial Trap": The Internationalization of the State,' *Political Geography* 18 (6): 669–96.
Helleiner, E. (1999) 'Sovereignty, Territoriality and the Globalization of Finance,' in Smith, D. A., Solinger, D. J. and Topik, S. C. (eds) *States and Sovereignty in the Global Economy*. New York: Routledge.
Hindess, B. (2002) 'The Liberal Government of Unfreedom,' *Alternatives* 26 (2): 93–111.
Hindess, B. (2005) 'Liberalism – What's in a Name?' in Larner, W. and Walters, W. (eds) *Global Governmentality: Governing International Spaces*. London: Routledge.
Hirst, P. and Thompson, G. (1996) *Globalization in Question*. Cambridge: Polity Press.
Langley, P. (2002) *World Financial Orders*. London: Routledge.
Law, J. (2002) 'Economics as Interference,' in du Gay, P. and Pryke, M. (eds) *Cultural Economy: Cultural Analysis and Commercial Life*. London: Sage.
Magnusson, W. (2000) 'Hyperspace: A Political Ontology of the Global City,' in Ericson, R. V. and Stehr, N. (eds) *Governing Modern Societies*. Toronto: University of Toronto Press.
Merrill Lynch and Co. Inc. (1997) *Merrill Lynch on National Security*. New York: Merrill Lynch and Co. Inc., originally published in the *Economist* 10 May 1997: 37.
Mitchell, T. (2002) *Rule of Experts: Egypt, Techno-Politics, Modernity*. Berkeley: University of California Press.
Ohmae, K. (1990) *The Borderless World: Power and Strategy in the Interlinked Economy*. London: HarperCollins.
O'Tuathail, G. (1996) *Critical Geopolitics: The Politics of Writing Global Space*. Minneapolis: University of Minnesota Press.
Payot, J. (1893) *The Education of the Will: The Theory and Practice of Self-Culture*. Reprinted in 1910 by New York: Funk and Wagnalls Company.
Robinson, W. I. (2002) 'Capitalist Globalization and the Transnationalization of the State,' in Rupert, M. and Smith, H. (eds) *Historical Materialism and Globalization*. London: Routledge.
Roden, F. (2001) 'Becoming Butlerian: On the Discursive Limits (and Potentials) of Gender Trouble at Ten Years of Age,' *International Journal of Sexuality and Gender Studies* 6 (1/2): 25–33.

Rose, N. (1993) 'Government, Authority and Expertise in Advanced Liberalism,' *Economy and Society* 22 (3): 283–99.

Rose, N. (1999) *Powers of Freedom: Reframing Political Thought.* Cambridge: Cambridge University Press.

Rose, N. and Miller, P. (1997) 'Political Power Beyond the State: Problematics of Government,' *British Journal of Sociology* 43 (2): 173–205.

Rosow, S. J. (1997) 'Echoes of Commercial Society: Liberal Political Theory in Mainstream IPE,' in Burch, K. and Denemark, R. A. (eds) *Constituting International Political Economy: International Political Economy Yearbook, Vol. 10.* Boulder CO: Lynne Rienner.

S. W. Strauss & Co. (1928) *See You Next Saturday in Hongkong,* originally published in *New York Times* 10 September 1928. J. Walter Thompson Archives, J. Walter Thompson Microfilm Collection, John W. Hartman Centre for Sales, Advertising and Marketing History, Durham NC: Duke University. Reel #35.

Scholte, J. A. (2000) *Globalization: A Critical Introduction.* Basingstoke: Palgrave.

Shapiro, M. J. (1997) *Violent Cartographies: Mapping Cultures of War.* Minneapolis: University of Michigan Press.

Smiles, S. (1875) *Thrift: A Domestic Counsel.* New York: Harper and Brothers.

Starchild, A. (2000) *The Offshore Entrepreneur: Profit and Opportunity Have No Borders.* San Francisco: First Street Press.

Thornduke, E. L. (1920) 'Psychological Notes on the Motives for Thrift,' *The Annals of the American Academy of Political and Social Sciences.* LXXXVII.

Urry, J. (2000) *Sociology Beyond Societies: Mobilities for the Twenty-First Century.* New York: Routledge.

United States Congress (2001) *Freedom Bonds Act of 2001,* October, Washington, DC: HR 2899.

U.S. Savings Bond Program (1954) *In His Hand,* John W. Hartman Centre for Sales, Advertising and Marketing History, Rare Book, Manuscript and Special Collections Library, Duke University, Durham, NC. J. Walter Thompson Archives, Domestic Advertisements Collection, Advertising and Public Service Collection, 'U.S. Savings Bonds', Box #5. Folder 1.

Walker, R. B. J. (1994) *Inside/Outside: International Relations as Political Theory.* Cambridge: Cambridge University Press.

Weiskopf, R. (2002) 'Deconstructing The Iron Cage: Towards an Aesthetic of Folding,' *Consumption, Markets and Culture* 5 (1): 79–97.

Weldes, J., Laffey, M., Gusterson, H. and Duvall, R. (1999) 'Introduction: Constructing Insecurity,' in Weldes, J., Laffey, M., Gusterson, H. and Duvall, R. (eds) *Cultures of Insecurity: States, Communities and the Production of Danger.* Minneapolis: University of Minnesota Press.

Yale Law School. The Avalon Project at Yale Law School. New Haven: Yale Law School, http://www.yale.edu/lawweb/avalon/avalon.htm.

5

Libidinal International Political Economy[1]

Earl Gammon and Ronen Palan

> ...the fundamental problem of political philosophy is still precisely the one that Spinoza saw so clearly, and that Wilhelm Reich rediscovered: 'Why do men fight for their servitude as stubbornly as though it were their salvation?'
>
> Deleuze and Guattari, *Anti-Oedipus* (1984)

Introduction

In 'Libidinal Economy,' a reflection that was conceived in response to Deleuze and Guattari's seminal studies on 'Capitalism and Schizophrenia' (1984; 1987), Jean-François Lyotard (1993) observes that capital is the only remaining totalizing force in modern society. He adds, 'everyone knows' that 'state officials' primary duty nowadays is to ensure the health and long term stability of capital. The idea that capital is the principal structuring force in the modern world, a force that determines in a complex and multifaceted manner the set of options available to states and governments is, of course, a shared theme among the disparate range of theories of political economy, and by extension International Political Economy (IPE). But if capital is considered the only remaining totalizing force in modern society, the nature of capital itself remains curiously a mystery (Bichler and Nitzan 1996).

In fact, there are as many different theories of capital as there are different approaches to political economy. Best known in IPE are the traditions of neoclassical economics, which treats capital as tangible assets or 'capital goods,' and the Marxist tradition of political economy, which considers capital a particular form of disciplinary power (van der Pijl 1998). An equally important tradition, although less well known in IPE, is evolutionary institutionalism, which treats capital from a collective perspective, as the collective knowledge of society (Veblen 1919). The approach that we are discussing in this chapter is distinct, although has close, if largely unexplored, affinities with the institutionalist perspective (Palan 2000). It draws upon what is described sometimes as *pulsional*[2] (Lyotard 1993), or *biunivocal* (Deleuze and Guattari 1984) theories of capital. Habitually referred to as 'post-structuralism,' it is better understood, we argue, as a distinct tradition of political economy known sometimes as 'libidinal economy.' And since 'every political economy is libidinal' (Lyotard 1993: 111), so IPE must be libidinal as well, in the sense that like any other theory of political economy it is simultaneously founded upon, as well as constructs a theory of, a desiring subject (desiring 'objects,' 'status,' 'power' or desire itself).

Libidinal economy is different from other traditions of political economy not in its emphasis on desire – neo-classical economy advances a theory of a 'rational' advantage-maximizing desiring subject as well, and so does Marxism – but because it constructs a theory of capital as the contemporary totalizing force operating within the Freudian-derived schema of pulsional forces, Eros and the death drive. While the notion of libidinal economy is explicit in the work of Deleuze and Guattari along with Lyotard, this chapter also takes its cue from the early metapsychology of Freud at the beginning of the twentieth century, returning to his analyses of parapraxes,[3] dreams and jokes, which would be determinant of his later topographies of the functioning of the psychical processes and the functioning of the psychical economy of groups. Much as Lacan found tremendous inspiration for his own theories regarding the articulation of desire in these earlier works of Freud, the approach that we aim towards will find in them instruction in the variegated means through which the unconscious speaks through socially constituted forms of representation. It is in these earlier works that Freud dealt most readily with the *economy* of desire (indeed, Freud talks of libidinal economy) that comes into play when the unconscious speaks through the Symbolic.

Due to the complexity of libidinal economy, this chapter can do no more than present some basic ideas about the possibilities for post-structuralist – or more appropriately, libidinal economy – inspired theories of capital and IPE. We would like to stress from the outset, that our understanding of poststructuralism is very different from the school of thought conventionally associated with poststructuralism in International Relations (IR) (Hoadley 2001; 2003 Hoadley and Palan 2004). In saying so, we would agree that it is not at all easy to define poststructuralism (and indeed, most of the authors associated with poststructuralism, like Foucault, strongly denied any adherence to such a school of thought! See also the comments in the introduction).

What is libidinal economy?

Broadly speaking, libidinal economic theories assume that the typical items of political economy should be seen as surface phenomena driven by psychical energies, or more properly, what Freud referred to as the *investment*[4] of the psychical drives. Libidinal economy suggests, in other words, that there is more to political economy than meets the eye. Such an approach is associated with a political program as advanced among others by Lyotard, Bataille, and Deleuze and Guattari, and possibly Foucault. It is a self-avowed 'militant' program founded on a Lacanian (or post-Lacanian, depending on one's interpretation of Lacan's work) theory of the subject as a constructed Self.

With his use of *investment*, Freud was attempting to give a quantitative (or economic) dimension to the means through which psychical energy, which he called, the libido, was discharged by the mental apparatus in its efforts to maintain ego-syntonic relations with the outer world [*Umwelt*].[5] The notion of investment corresponds with what Freud referred to as the secondary psychical processes, which, are contrary to the highly mobile discharges that typify the primary processes and which are governed entirely by the pleasure principle, are defined by the binding of libido to objects through a process of disjunction and idealization that aims at maintaining the integrity of the ego construct and reducing unpleasure. In Freud's work this notion takes on a largely defensive connotation, relating to the more literal translation of *besetzung* as 'occupation' or 'squatting,' whereby libidinal energy is directed towards stabilizing the relationship between the *innerwelt* and *umwelt* of the subject, of creating a stable relationship between the subject and the objects that constitute its world.

Bearing this in mind, libidinal economy may be conceived, therefore, as an approach that seeks to come to terms with the patterns of these psychical investments, the flows of libidinal energy that bring forth what is taken by the more conventional approaches of political economy as rationality and intelligence. Indeed, libidinal economists seek to identify that which creates the very conditions of causality (and hence rationality) that underwrite production (understood very broadly) within the social field. The libidinal economist attempts to tap into the unconscious dynamic of the social and 'proposes to demonstrate the existence of an unconscious libidinal investment of sociohistorical production, distinct from the conscious investments coexisting with it' (Deleuze and Guattari 1984: 98).

The libido is conceived by Freud as one of the primary drives that fuels the subject's desire to combine, to create, to unite, what at a later stage he would denominate as Eros.[6] The realm of primordial desires is referred to by Freud as the unconscious. The unconscious according to Freud is a theoretical space that is timeless and without contradictions between the drives originating there. In the unconscious the drives are not yet fully invested in representative forms, of which the two most basic are those of temporal and spatial reference. As the drives in the unconscious seek articulation, limited only by a quantitative dimension of libido that supports the notion of an economy of the psychical apparatus, they are guided entirely by the pursuit of pleasure, or the pleasure principle. Operating on the basis of the primary processes, the unconscious is not yet restricted in the way in which representations are conjoined and the paths of libidinal flows are not yet inhibited – for in this theoretical space, the ego does not yet directly intervene, nor does it come up against the repression of the super-ego, of society. Libidinal energies or flows extend, therefore, beyond sexuality understood in the limited terms of genitality. It is only as drives lead to representative articulation in the conscious, leading to motility, that contradictions are met.[7] Consequently, for Freud the divide between the unconscious and conscious only comes into existence with accession to language – as the child is 'socialized,' or as Foucault would have it, 'normalized' into society.

According to Freud, therefore, the energy that is spent in unifying object relations is a central concept in understanding the constitution of the ego and the relation of the subject (or what other approaches refer to as individuality or subjectivity) to the social other. Political economy that fails to connect to these energies fails to comprehend an important dimension of its own economy.

The notion of flows of energy that are vital to Freud's conception of the psychical economy is not a unitary conception, but one which is marked by a tension and ambivalence that calls into question the motivation of the subject. Unlike positivistic conceptions of the subject, which premise a unified subject whose actions can be discerned on the basis of ascribed rationalities, Freud's subject does not enjoy complete sovereignty, but is fragmented by an internal conflictual dynamic as it seeks to stabilize its object relations. In its quest for stasis, the subject must integrate the objects of others into its psyche, a process Freud referred to as identification, whereby the subject invests in the schema of another's object relations as if they were its own. This series of identifications, constituting what Freud referred to as the super-ego, loosely associated with what we normally call 'society,' transforms the subject's desire, sanctioning its pursuit of pleasure and its capture of additional objects.[8]

But this complex and conflictual process of taking and assuming mastery of objects, of eradicating the persecutory threat of these objects turning against the subject, ultimately led Freud to theorize the existence a second drive, the death drive. The death drive works towards conditions of stasis, of aggressively investing in objects and working towards the annihilation of their independent subjectivity, in order that they reaffirm the unity of the subject. Ultimately, all psychical investments are deployed to shore up the ego construct of, in effect, seeking a psychical dividend of subjective reaffirmation. While Eros is present in the social field in the act of binding and uniting, the death drive is always working, if silently, at exclusion and control, of preventing an excess of stimulation. As Freud emphasized, the two drives are coterminus and indissociable, and cannot be functionally separated. Despite the attempts of some, we cannot denominate one act as being of Eros, and another of the death drive.

This coterminus nature of the psychical drives is a key aspect within the work of libidinal economists. In his *Libidinal Economy*, Lyotard (1993) redeems the sense of ambivalence that is patent in Freud's theory of drives, or *pulsions* as Lyotard refers to them, whence the reference to his approach as *pulsional*. Lyotard inveighs against the functionalism that arises from the mechanical and thermodynamic interpretations of Freud's conception of the psychical economy. Lyotard goes on to reiterate the lesson that we derive from Freud, which is that there is always pleasure, or *jouissance*, in repetition in symbolic deployment, as well as the expression of annihilatory tendencies that seek to eradicate any dissipation in the symbolic economy. Consequently, Lyotard emphasizes the theatricality that maintains coherence in the social field, that is, the impression of a unified social body. At the same time, this theatricality is simultaneously a process of dissimulation, that is, negation that silently works to eradicate those forces which threaten the objects that define our subjectivity.

Libidinal economy and political economy

Libidinal economy refuses to take capital in its own words; to accept, for example, concepts employed in marginalist economics such as 'saving,' 'investment,' 'accumulation,' 'profit,' 'growth,' 'money supply' and 'credit' or, alternatively, Marxist concepts such as 'surplus value' or 'primitive accumulation,' and so on, at face value – as if they refer to self-explanatory, real phenomena. Like a structural anthropologist who refuses to accept the myth of so-called primitive societies (but believes that all human beliefs systems are myth-based) and interprets myths in the general economy of that society, effectively, as a systematic relationship, or an 'economy' of communication and desire, so the libidinal theorist treats capitalism and its attendant concepts not as a mere system of exploitation – a theory that assumes that accumulated wealth is the possession of things and that potential consumption power is the ultimate driving force of individual advancement. This, according to libidinal economists, is a naive understanding of human motives and the psyche, as much of this apparent wealth is symbolic and has not much value outside a historically specific societal condition. To confuse symbolic wealth with wealth is precisely to confuse psychical processes of identification, constituting the superego, for the 'real,' and to avoid the crucial question of how a particular society, or rationality, is an organization of flows of desire. After all, the possession of fast cars, beautiful houses or expensive clothes is meaningless outside the social conditioning of the subject (see also Shapiro this volume).

In contrast to such naive materialism, which confuses symbolic investment with 'real' wealth, libidinal economy advances a theory of the economy as a surface expression of an economy of desire, and the central concepts of capitalism as an expression of libidinal energies – or a specific organization of flows of desire.[9] As such, libidinal economy interrogates the power of capitalist concepts, in particular their hold, we could say, stronghold, on the human imagination. It suspects that these energies do not emanate directly from some transhistorically given 'human nature,' as the general propensity to truck and barter, nor as a futile power game, but as a particular and powerful articulation of libidinal energies. The study of libidinal energies should help therefore in our understanding of the power and force of capital.

In its understanding of capital, libidinal economy attempts to come to terms with the notion of production, understood in a significantly broader dimension than that which would normally arise from analyses classed under the rubric of political economy. Libidinal economy approaches production not in terms of wealth generation or marginal product, but rather as the deployment and exchange of symbols for the purpose of reconstituting the hierarchy values in the social field. The notion of production in libidinal economy transcends, in other words, the narrowly circumscribed definition that prevails in modern political economy, one which defines it in terms of the transformation of social and natural inputs into exchangeable outputs, or, more explicitly, into outputs that become coextensive with the quantitative dimension of money. In the sense conveyed by the biunivocalism of Freud's Eros and the death drive, 'consumption' and 'production' are no longer treated as simple expressions of needs and desires of the sovereign subject, as if it is self-evidently true that the subject wishes to maximise their 'scarce resources.' On the contrary, the rationality of such historically constituted subjectivity is brought back, by libidinal economists, into an ambiguous and inextricable relationship aimed at giving expression to the flows of desire that charge the theatricality that defines the movements within modern capitalism.

Here, libidinal economy approximates an ethnographic analysis of production, moving away from signification defined in terms of intermediary equivalences, examining the inscription of the representatives of desire on the social body. By this we mean production understood as the investment in representatives of time and space that allow for the circulation of symbols and the conjunction of our most basic rituals, namely those dealing with how we eat, copulate and defecate. In examining production, political economic notions such as circulation, exchange, and surplus value are to be viewed as libidinal constructs, or more properly perversions, whose incessant reinvestment in the social field is indicative of unconscious group desires. In essence, it is coming to terms with the dramaturgical dimension that resonates in even the most modern and 'scientific' techniques of production, techniques that conceal the primitivism that abounds in all production.

Libidinal economists' concern is, therefore, to capture the dynamic of the libidinal investments and flows that eventuate the incandescence of forms within the material world – forms whose 'reproduction' allows the conceptualization of time and space at any given moment, a conceptualization that ultimately gives coherence to what Castoriadis calls the social-historical dimension.[10] The social-historical dimension, which is often taken as an empirical given, is the dimension of the collective, and is understood here as that which initiates, through those whom it is reproduced, a 'simultaneous relation of interiority and of exteriority, of participation and of exclusion' (1987: 113).

Libidinal economy attempts to understand the inscription of rationalities through ritual, theatricality in social discourse, and engagement with the material world. The interest of the libidinal economist lies, therefore, not in effacing the analytical categories that are the mainstay of political economic analyses, amongst them being the state, capital, the commodity, labor, and so on, but rather in descending below the level of their assumed causal relations and phenomenal expression to the level of desire and its relation to the constitution of subjectivity. As Deleuze and Guattari (1984: 345) argued, political economy and libidinal economy represent two different modes of libidinal investment in the same social reality. This also means that libidinal economy is not to be confused for an alternative approach to a more conventional political economy, but rather as a complementary element, adding in a rigorous manner certain 'cultural' and 'psychological' dimensions to our understanding of the ways a political economy operates.

Consequently, through their program of schizoanalysis, Deleuze and Guattari (1984) attempted to reveal the libidinal economic underpinnings of modern capitalist political economy and the historically unique manifestation of oedipal neuroses or perversions that arise as consequences of capitalist libidinal economy. Michel Foucault (1991: 184) investigates the forms of 'normalization' of the subject in the power-structures of capitalism held primarily through self-discipline and self-repression. In a similar vein, Lyotard (1993) attempted to draw attention to the repressive investments that maintained the dissimulation of exchange relations, to retranscribe political economy in a libidinal discourse in order to reveal the incessant contradictions that arise within political economy and which remain inexplicable without an understanding of the economy of desire. In doing so, they called for a breaking down of the barriers between psychology and psychoanalysis and traditional political economy – calling effectively for a libidinal political economy. One of the distinctive features of the libidinal economic approach is its emphasis on daily practices within the social field. In many regards, those aspects of IPE that would strike us in the here and now as mundane are exactly those which are of special interest; those forms that are most readily interpreted within a social-historical formation by its constituents are those that experience the highest levels of libidinal investment.

Libidinal economy – or what is often confused for 'poststructuralism' – consists therefore, of a range of heterodox and multidisciplinary approaches that aim ultimately to get a grip on the mysterious powers of capital on human imagination: its seductive and beguiling nature, the 'cunning' of capital as Marx would have it (1990: 285). But at the same time, capital fiercely represses all that which would deny its claim as the *omnitudo realitatis*, with the capitalist subject's anxiety leading, as libidinal economists protest with their program of liberation, to annihilatory libidinal investments that seek to elide the subject's illegitimate descent from nature and the polymorphous nature of sexuality.

Conceptualizing an economy of desire

The economy of desire arises from the complex inter-subjectivity that defines the group, an inter-subjectivity that is based on mutual identification, as well as identification with symbolic figures, be they ancestors, deities, or such. The quest of subjective-reaffirmation, of overcoming the subject's fragmented nature, provokes the subject to invest its psychical drives in representatives that will bring it some sort of foreclosure on reality. Desire in libidinal economy is seen in the series of identifications, many of them extremely costly in psychical terms, that the subject undertakes in order to bring stability in its object relations.

The problem for the subject is that desire is never satiated. While Freud placed emphasis on the quantitative dimension of the psychical economy, this was not an economy of a zero sum and absolute rationality, but an economy of dissipation, a psychical economy operating within entropy.[11] Given this universal condition of increasing entropy, notions of profit and dividend, which rely on deferral to a static and objectified future, only make sense within a libidinally invested rationality. Following in the same vein, for the libidinal economist, returns on the future are only possible with investments in what Deleuze and Guattari (1984) referred to as the socius, with an inscription of libidinal energies of the present to sanctify the investments of the past. Deferral – which is a fundamental factor in capitalist mentality: thinking about the future, anticipating the future, factoring time-delay on 'investment' in order to satisfy some desire in the 'future,' may appear a fairly straightforward proposition for the businessmen, but it is an extremely difficult and complex mental process for the subject. The psychology of deferral, of anticipation, of 'savings' and delayed satisfaction relies on repression, the accession to language, a signifier endlessly chasing the signified. How does an entire capitalist system evolve on such a difficult mental process? How have subjects learned to repress their desires in such a way? What sort of psychical processes are at work in a society that evolved, as John Commons (1961: 7) notes, into a structure in which the future shapes the present! For Deleuze and Guattari, the Oedipus complex, which, contrary to Freud, they believe is a distinctive effect of the capitalist mentality, 'presupposes a fantastic repression of desiring-machines.' And why, they ask in the name of libidinal economists, 'are they repressed? To what end? Is it really necessary or desirable to submit to such repression? And what means are to be used to accomplish this?' (1984: 3) These are no doubt difficult questions. But they are certainly worth posing. They might bring us face to face with the powerful myths and the disciplinary power of capital. And this must be considered one of the key questions facing IPE.

To the libidinal economist, the 'capitalist mentality' of deferral relies, therefore, on a primordial social contract that lays down the law of sociality, primarily in the form of taboos. This in turn leads us to Freud's understanding of the unconscious, the language that is always spoken and heard below the rhetorical deployment of representation in the social field.

Following in that vein, Deleuze and Guattari proposed the concept of the socius to capture the essence of the shared psychical body that holds together a libidinal economy, the series of the foundational investments by the members of a society that delimit the bounds of acceptable/worthwhile social production. The socius 'appears as the natural or divine presupposition' of production, which in contemporary IPE is the body of capital (1984: 10). But the investments in the socius, particularly those that find explicit articulation in the language of daily production, through means of figural displacement, often speak for that which is always present, but never spoken of. What we speak of here is the realm of the repressed, the primordial desires that the socius, which in modern times is the capitalist socius, seeks to contain.

The problems of general economics

Libidinal economy challenges the concept of the economy as we saw, by seeking to develop a holistic approach to the economy, or to open up the question of 'general economics' (Bataille 1988). As Bataille points out, a central aspect of all economies is the expenditure of the excess energy that they produce. Be it through ritual, religious or military organization, or sumptuary tendencies, all economies must find a means of channeling this surplus energy. While Bataille's notion of general economy does not invoke the terminology of psychoanalysis, in many ways it dovetails with Freud's (1995) understanding of the investment of the psychical drives in the composition of civilization;

whereas Freud points to the necessity of civilization in dissipating or channeling the aggressivity that works against the program of civilization, Bataille points to the necessity of all societies to deal with the excess of 'life force.' As he writes, 'Ancient societies found relief in festivals; some erected admirable monuments that had no useful purpose; we use the excess to multiply "services" that make life smoother, and we are led to reabsorb part of it by increasing leisure time' (1988: 24).

While Adam Smith talks about 'a certain propensity in human nature ... to truck, barter, and exchange one thing for another' (1999: 117), he loses sight of the fact that the problem of general economy is not merely one of acquisition, but also of expending the excess of energy through controlled rituals of exchange. The libidinal economist understands that there is no corner of human nature from whence such a 'propensity' arises, nor are truck, barter and exchange to be treated in the same breadth. While anthropologists see universalizing tendencies of exchange, they do not accord the same universalizing tendencies to truck and barter. When we theoretically shift from the concept of human 'needs' to the concept of desire, the entire issue of economic 'surplus' (surplus that is then traded) takes on a new meaning. What is the meaning, after all, of surplus in the economy of desire? This is a problematic that was explored already by early twentieth-century anthropologists such as Malinowski and Mauss.

An important point in the development of libidinal interpretation of the economy was Malinowski's famous studies of the Trobriand islands. Malinowski observes with regard to the native Melanesians who inhabit the Trobriand Archipelago that:

> With the most rudimentary implements, a pointed digging stick and a small axe, they are able to raise crops sufficient to maintain a dense population and even yielding a surplus, *which in olden days was allowed to rot unconsumed* (1948: 27, emphasis ours).

It is this odd treatment of societal *surplus* – particularly surplus that is expanded and destroyed in a way that appears to us, moderns, as irrational and wasteful – that is of particular interest to the libidinal economist. Surplus is something that we intuitively understand – or so we think. When Malinowski speaks of a surplus of crops, we can almost see, feel, sense and smell the food rotting, as a material expression of something that is treated as superfluous. The corollary of this evidence of the treatment of surplus is that the societies Malinowski speaks of are 'savage' or 'primitive,' and never learned the secrets of 'accumulation' of surplus for their benefit. Hence, the common conclusion that these are nothing but static, non-class societies; they are still at an 'infantile' stage of humanity (an interesting libidinal allusion widely used by nineteenth-century thinkers to describe the 'noble' savage). We, 'moderns,' in contrast, know better, we have marshaled savings and investment to create a system founded on growth and are amazed, therefore, at the spectacle of such apparent waste (see also Aitken's reading, in this volume, of discourses of saving that distinguish the responsible citizen from the savage). But such 'waste,' from a 'surface' understanding of political economy, is hugely significant if we delve deeper, for it represents the energy that binds the 'primitive' socius. Such waste is actually part of the compact of that society, one that prohibits claims upon the future by individuals, of claiming power over others, much as Bataille pointed out that scholastic invocations against usury acted to prevent transgressions in a realm reserved for God the Father himself.

Our amazement, combined with our sense of superiority when confronted with the wastefulness of our irrational forefathers, may turn sour, therefore, when we take on board what Bataille has demonstrated, namely, that our, modern 'rational' economists seem to be perfectly happy with only half of the story of economy. Economists are just too content to investigate the process of accumulation (whatever accumulation may be), 'forgetting' the problem of general economics, the problem of general equivalence as libidinal economy teaches us. In many ways, the 'secret' of the economy – and by implication, the 'secret' of the modern IPE – is how societies discharge of the 'accumulated surplus' – for the surplus has no objective 'meaning' outside a social context.

All societies are waste machines

All societies are waste machines, and the problem they face is not simply of accumulation, but equally important, or more central to the understanding of their primary codes of organization of the flows of desire, is the problem of the dissipation of accumulation. The ancient Egyptians produced a superbly organized 'accumulation machine' in order to construct huge pyramids of stone to bury their kings. An entire economy and society, complex and multifaceted as it was, evolved to mobilize resources during the lifetime of the king to construct his tomb! No doubt, the priests of rationality of that era saw nothing strange or bizarre about such an undertaking, much as their modern-day equivalents see nothing irrational in the allocation of resources by financial markets. Similarly, the period that Marxists describe as 'primitive accumulation' in capitalism has generated, or was accompanied by, the moral code of frugality, abstinence, temperance and sobriety compared with the 'excesses' of the Baroque, which was the 'ancien regime.' In fact each society develops its own language, its own codes, within which it is perfectly rational (in the eyes of its members) to accumulate in order to leave things to rot, whether food, buildings, machines, or excess symbolic exchange. Ultimately, accumulation is not always seen as beneficial, but is often recognized for the potential of reigniting internecine conflicts, by unbalancing equivalences, unraveling the socius and unleashing destructive drives.

As modern capitalism has learned to expand by 'borrowing on the future,' it has developed theoretically limitless possibilities of accumulation – for in such a system the only check on accumulation is the social convention on the number of years we can borrow on the future. Such a system had to learn new techniques of allowing excess 'capital' (often symbolic capital) to rot. Seven trillion dollars were wiped off the US stock market between the years 2000 and 2002, a huge 'waste' of symbolic exchange – and the implication of the cycle and accumulation and waste that is played out in the stock market is something that requires a libidinal understanding. Every society must let things go to waste, only that, within its internal code and discourse, this waste is not recognized as such, just as the people of the Trobriand archipelago did not recognize their behavior as wasteful.

Informed by institutionalist approaches, Bichler and Nitzan (2000) raise the problem of 'general economics' in an interesting way – although they do not use Bataille's ideas. The hedonist economists, who understand the discharge of accumulation in individual and hedonistic terms as the pleasure of consumption, must be puzzled by the behavior of the multinational owned by absentee owners. Why, Bichler and Nitzan ask, does General Motors (GM) seek increased profit? Surely, GM cannot spend the excess surplus on consumption? What is the ultimate goal of the process? The mechanism they argue is 'differential accumulation,' but the goal is power – and capital measures power differentials. Of course, one hedonistic response to the puzzle is that GM represents an alliance of hedonists, joined together temporarily as shareholders because they believe they can 'milk' GM for their hedonistic pleasures. These are the mass of 'absentee owners,' company-hopping in search of higher return, to be discharged ultimately in consumption.

But this response by the hedonist economist is a meek one, as it does not wish to dwell more profoundly on the causes of these absurd but powerful processes, and the role the capitalist plays in them. In his masterful study of the development of late nineteenth-century US capitalism, *The Robber Barons*, Josephson begins to contemplate how the barons were taught to discharge their 'accumulated' profits – and here the pulsional drives of Eros and the death drive, pleasure and death are so clearly at play. He depicts a bunch of moody, brooding old men deeply unhappy and disappointed, desperately seeking hedonistic discharges for their accumulated surplus to no avail. These men draw upon a future of which they can never possibly partake. First, many of the barons turned to religion. 'The booty of so many providentially profitable engagements was then, "God's God"...' (1934: 318). Then they moved to conspicuous consumption. 'Mansions and châteaux of French, Gothic, Italian, barocco and Oriental style lined both sides of upper Fifth Avenue... railroad barons and mine-owners and oil magnates vied with each other in making town houses and country villas which were imitations of everything under the sun, and were filled with what-nots, old drapery, old armor, old Tudor chests and chairs...' (1934: 332). Here, we are told, old Vanderbilt buys an old French master's painting of dubious quality for a million dollars, because 'the breasts look just as they should.'

But as much as the robber barons wanted to spend, with the enthusiastic support of their spouses and children, none was of much help – they ended up more desperate. Here we see Eros dissimulating the death drive, and the death drive dissimulating Eros. 'The truth is that once arrived in the metropolis of fastidious luxury, installed at last in the palaces of Dives, the nobility of American business seemed bored, bewildered, lost... the masters of money and industry such as Morgan, Vanderbilt, Harriman, Stillman, William Rockefeller, were all of them typically "great silence men" with little enough to say in polite conversation' (335–6). 'James Stillman, the narrow-eyed "sphinx" of the banking world... confessed in his last years... that he knew not how to enjoy himself. "I have never in all my life done anything I wanted," he said, "and cannot now".'(336). As one society commentator of the time noted with regard to the lives of the 'colossally rich,' they were generally 'no more worth living than those of their cooks' (337). Indeed, 'Limited in their capacity of enjoyment and bored, yet prompted to outdo each other in prodigality, the New Rich experimented with ever new patterns and devices of consumption... One season, it is a ball on horseback which is the chief sensation... finally, a costume ball given by Bradley

Martin, in 1897 reached the very climax of lavish expenditure and "dazed the entire Western world". The interior of the Waldorf-Astoria Hotel was transformed into a replica of Versailles... [etc.]' (338–9). But eventually these balls reached their logical conclusion, 'the real':

> Thus in later years the 'Poverty Social' came strongly into vogue. At one such reunion held at the home of a Western millionaire, the thirty guests came attired in rags and tatters. At a cost of $14,000 per head, ... 'scraps of food were served on wooden plates. The diners sat about on broken soap boxes, buckets and coalhods. Newspapers, dust cloths and old skirts used as napkins, and beer served in a rusty tin can...!' (339–40)

In their attempt to foreclose on the future, to close the next deal, the pathology is revealed, as their attempts to accumulate ever more, their drive to combine and amass, leaves their drive to obliterate unabated. It is an unchecked narcissism that ultimately works against the subject. Think of a Michael Jackson or a Howard Hughes.

Conclusion

Like any approach, libidinal economy is a contradictory one. On the one hand, it firmly rejects, or so it appears, the 'grand narrative' themes of the twentieth century, the ideologies that pitted the masses of humanity one against the other in battles that made the last century the most cruel and bloodthirsty in human history. But its rejection is advanced, paradoxically, in the name of the grandest of all narratives, a totalizing political economy spanning from psychoanalysis and anthropology. It is paradoxically a Hegelian enterprise in vision and grandeur (and intuition), and it seeks to found political economy on a robust and coherent totalizing theory that leads all the way from the subject to the global political economy and back. Here lies a second dimension of its contradictory tendencies, while largely rooted in a tradition of the critique of capitalism, Marxism in fact, the focus on the subject has rendered it, in many ways, closer to 'methodological individualism,' though libidinal economy's subject is fragmented and knows not how to distinguish its pain from its pleasure. In fact, with its notion of liberation and emancipation, viewed as a personal journey of freedom, libidinal economy has clearly shifted its focus from class to the subject. There are, therefore, strong libertarian and liberal themes in this so-called post-Marxist theory.

The unifying force of capital bears the same primitivism in its conduction of libidinal intensities as all other social-historical formations, a point that is missed by those who, with their scathing attacks on capital's edifice, remain some of its most reliable/least resistant conduits. As Lyotard puts it: 'There is one thing, then, which makes us say: there is no primitive society, that is to say: there is no external reference, even if immanent, from which the separation of what belongs to capital (or political economy) and what belongs to subversion (or libidinal economy), can always be made, and cleanly; where desire would be clearly legible, where its *proper economy* would not be scrambled' (1993: 108). Even Marx, who 'discovered' in the supports of his house and the springs of his mattress the pangs of human labor, did not give full recognition to the cries of *jouissance* with which they resonated, of the ambivalence immanent in the libidinal investment that maintained his notion of equivalence within political economy.

For the libidinal economist, our aim is to reinvigorate the analysis of capital, which for too long has been the sole preserve of Marxism, and which has all too often been willing to understand capital in its own words. Given the renewed interest in the institutionalists Veblen and Commons, who also looked at the social constitution of capital, libidinal economy is not isolated in this desire to open new avenues for investigating what makes capital such a potent force in our day-to-day lives. Our hope is that by giving recognition to the ambivalence of the psychical investments that maintain the representatives of capitalism, and of the coextensive expression of the Eros and the death drive that marks capitalism's expansion and renewal, we come one step closer to being able to effectively inscribe the primary narcissism in forms of production that are less injurious to our continued survival.

Notes

1 We would like to thank Marieke de Goede, Lilly Ling and Yoshihiro Nakano for their comments on earlier versions of this paper.
2 Pulsion-al plays on Lacan's French translation of Freud's 'Trieb,' which best translates in English as 'drive.' Here we follow the lead of the translator of Lyotard's *Libidinal Economy* (1993) in using pulsional instead of the contested use of 'instinctual' by Freud's English translators.
3 Parapraxes refer to mistakes such as slips of the tongue and slips in writing, which Freud used to elucidate the workings of the unconscious.
4 Translated as the neologism 'cathexis' throughout the *Standard Edition*.
5 Regarding the qualitative aspect of investment, though, Freud remained ambiguous in his usage of the term, even in his later writings when he elaborated on his notions of Eros and the death drive, between which he

avoided any sort of functional separation, an intentional ambiguity that echoes in Deleuze and Guattari's notion of biunivocalism.

6 In attempting to fulfill the primary narcissism, what Freud termed the pleasure principle – and the idea of libido.

7 See 'The Unconscious,' (Freud 1995, vol. 14: 187).

8 The purpose of all psychical investments, as both Freud and Lacan conclude, including those repressive investments that go into maintaining the socius, resides entirely in narcissism. Quoting Lacan, 'When speaking of the problem of repression, Freud asks himself where the ego obtains the energy it puts at the service of the "reality principle" – we need look no further. ... There can be no doubt that it derives from the "narcissistic passion" ...'(2001: 24). It is the investment in the socius and the containment of the unconscious desires in language, in ritual, and in production in general, that the libidinal economist is most interested.

9 'The prime function incumbent upon the socius has always been to codify the flows of desire, to inscribe them, to record them, to see to it that no flow exists that is not properly dammed up, channeled, regulated' (Deleuze and Guattari 1984: 33).

10 Libidinal economy incorporates hermeutics into its broader conception of social forms. Forms are never reproduced *per se*. The constitution of forms is multi-determinant and the nature of the libidinal investment is never identical with the 'reappearance' of a form. The social-historical is delimited by what Lacan (2001) calls the 'Real,' which is loosely defined as that which is always beyond the symbolic, that which escapes the presence and absence defined in the process signfication. It is the limitation of the possible at a given moment in time.

11 Entropy refers to the observed universal tendency of dissipation, of the movement from structure and heterogeneity, as in the case of forms of knowledge, towards randomness and homogeneity (noise).

References

Bataille, G. (1988) *The Accursed Share: An Essay on General Economy, Volume I: Consumption* (Hurley, R., Trans.). New York: Zone Books. (Original French published 1967).

Bichler, S. and Nitzan, J. (1996) 'Putting the State in its Place: US Foreign Policy and Differential Capital Accumulation in Middle East "Energy Conflicts,"' *Review of International Political Economy* 3 (4): 608–61.

Bichler, S. and Nitzan, J. (2000) 'Capital Accumulation: Breaking the Dualism of "Economics" and "Politics,"' in Palan, R. (ed.), *Global Political Economy: Contemporary Theories*. London: Routledge.

Castoriadis, C. (1987) *The Imaginary Institution of Society* (Blamey, K., Trans.) Cambridge: Polity Press.

Commons, J. R. [1934] (1961) *Institutional Economics: its Place in Political Economy*, University of Wisconsin Press.

Deleuze, G. and Guattari, F. (1984) *Anti-Oedipus: Capitalism and Schizophrenia* (Hurley, R. *et al.*, Trans.). London: The Athlone Press. (Original French published 1972).

Deleuze, G. and Guattari, F. (1987) *A Thousand Plateaus: Capitalism and Schizophrenia* (Hurley, R. *et al.*, Trans.). Minneapolis: University of Minnesota Press. (Original French published 1980).

Foucault, M. (1991) *Discipline and Punish* (Sheridan, A., Trans.). London: Penguin. (Original French published 1975).

Freud, S. (1995) *The Standard Edition of the Complete Psychological Works of Sigmund Freud* (Strachey, J., Trans.). London: The Hogarth Press, Vol 1–24.

Hoadley, C. (2001) 'Machiavelli, a Man of "His" Time: R. B. J. Walker and The Prince,' *Millennium*, 30 (1): 1–18.

Hoadley, C. (2003) *An Archaeology of Poststructural Intent in International Relations*, unpublished PhD. University of Sussex.

Hoadley, C. and Palan, R. (2004) *Structuralism Or Poststructuralism: An Evaluation Of The 'Poststructural' Critique In International Relations*. Unpublished.

Josephson, M. [1934](1995) *The Robber Barons: The Great American Capitalists*. London: Harcourt Brace.

Lacan, J. (2001) *Ecrits: A Selection* (Sheridan, A., Trans.). Routledge Classics.

Lyotard, J.-F. (1993) *Libidinal Economy* (Grant, I. H., Trans.). London: Anthlone Press. (Original French published 1974).

Malinowski, B. (1948) *Magic, Science and Religion and Other Essays*. New York: The Free Press.

Marx, K. (1990) *Capital Volume 1* (Ben Fowkes, Trans.). London: Penguin Books.

Palan, R. (2000) 'The Constructivist Underpinning of the New International Political Economy,' in Palan, R. (ed.) *Global Political Economy: Contemporary Theories*. London: Routledge.

Smith, A. [1776] (1999) *An Inquiry into the Nature and Causes of the Wealth of Nations*. London: Penguin Books.

van der Pijl, K. (1998) *Transnational Classes and International Relations*. London: Routledge.

Veblen, T. (1919) *The Vested Interests and the Common Man*. London: George Allen & Unwin.

Part II

Discourse, Materiality and Economy

This section confronts the question of materiality and representation which governs much of the debate around international political economy (IPE) and poststructuralism, as briefly outlined in the introduction. If, as Shapiro, Aitken and others argue in the previous chapters, economics is to be understood foremost as a culturally contingent and discursively performed practice, what becomes of the study of material resources and inequality? Does a focus on discourse and representation still have eye for the very material questions of poverty and wealth, power and repression that are traditionally at the heart of critical IPE? In general, poststructuralism collapses the epistemological distinction between the realms of the 'ideal' and the 'material' on the grounds that reality outside language is not *knowable*. As Laclau and Mouffe (2000: 207) put it, 'Our analysis rejects the distinction between discursive and non-discursive practices. It affirms...that every object is constituted as an object of discourse.' In order to make sense of material reality, in order to answer the question 'what happened,' a (discursive) process of interpretation and meaning-making is necessary, that is in itself political. According to Campbell (2001: 444),

> the body lying on the ground, the bullet in the head, and the shell casing lying not far away – tells us nothing itself about the meaning and significance of those elements...For example, did the body and the bullet get to be as they are because of suicide, manslaughter, murder, ethnic cleansing, tribal war, genocide, a war of inter-state rivalry, or...? Each of those terms signifies a larger discursive formation through which a whole set of identities, social relations, political possibilities and ethical outcomes are made more or less possible.

It is precisely this insistence on the discursive constitution of the material, and on the political processes of meaning-making required for knowing reality, that worries some of poststructuralism's critics – and that this volume needs to engage with.

This section does not pretend to resolve the tension between these positions on discourse and materiality, nor will it settle the debates. But it does collect a diversity of opinions on the issue of discourse, materiality and economy, and offers the reader a variety of positions to identify with. First, Spike Peterson delivers a passionate plea for approaching the global political economy through a poststructural lens, without losing sight of material inequalities. One of the most important aspects of poststructural readings, for Peterson, is that they make possible a critical analysis of the politics of stabilizations. All stabilizations of meaning, Peterson points out, are 'historically contingent,...precarious and partial,' and 'continually at odds with reality.' At the same time, discursive stabilizations exercise power as they work to 'reproduce hierarchical orderings' and silence alternatives. From this starting-point, Peterson works to destabilize neoliberalism as a discursive category by showing that, firstly, it is not what it claims to be, and secondly, it depends upon marginalizations that may breed anger, violence and resistance. In analyzing, respectively, the productive, reproductive, and virtual economies, Peterson challenges the boundaries of what traditionally constitutes the global political economy and maps 'identities and culture as co-constituting what are conventionally described as material...phenomena.'

Secondly, Magnus Ryner offers a sympathetic but critical reading of poststructural political economy, that concurs with some of the most important critiques in the discourse-materiality debate. Ryner begins his contribution by establishing the need for IPE to engage with poststructuralist and post-Marxist philosophies, and he offers a critical appraisal of a number of authors who have already taken on this task. He then raises two questions that are crucial to the debate in this section. First, Ryner asks whether it is still possible to talk about a meaningful material world outside discourse, that can be analyzed with rational conceptual frameworks. Secondly, Ryner addresses the question whether critical political economy can still be geared towards a hermeneutic of emancipation, which seeks to transform the material world to enable a sustainable satisfaction of humanity's needs. Ryner develops a critical historical materialism that incorporates poststructural insights while seeking to answer both these questions in the affirmative. Ryner's chapter, then, can be seen as perhaps the most critical assessment of the poststructuralist promise in IPE in the present volume.

Thirdly, Jessop and Sum offer the concept of Cultural Political Economy as a way to move beyond the perceived impasse between poststructural and Gramscian IPE. Cultural Political Economy emphasizes, first, the need to view political economy's technical objects as socially constructed and historically specific; second, the contextuality and historicity of all claims to knowledge; and third, the methodological importance of critical discourse analysis in the study of the global political economy. In the context of Cultural Political Economy, Jessop and Sum stage an encounter between Gramsci and Foucault, and draw out these thinkers' similarities and differences in order to offer the reader a choice of positions. At the end of their paper, Jessop and Sum turn to the question of hegemony and counter-hegemony, in order to explore everyday life as a site of resistance. If hegemony needs to be (re)produced in the space of everyday life, then everyday practices of resistance become theoretically important for a critical political economy. Jessop and Sum thus foreshadow the theoretical explorations of the politics of dissent that follow in Part III.

In the final contribution to this section, Daly offers what is perhaps the most poststructural position within the discourse-materiality debate. For Daly, the economy is fully a discursive construction. Daly sees no need, as Ryner does, to defend an extra-discursive element to economy – in fact, for Daly it is precisely the discursivity of economy that makes it *political*, and essentially prone to political subversion and recomposition. Daly develops this position through a rereading of Niklas Luhmann's systems theory, that enables the economy to be understood as a system without ontological grounding. Understood in this manner, it becomes clear that the economy is both foundationless and endeavors to discursively construct foundations through political processes of inclusion and exclusion. Daly concludes with a critical reading of the processes of inclusion and exclusion that are the foundations of contemporary political economy, and that regulate the limits of the thinkable and the possible in contemporary economic practice.

References

Campbell, D. (2001) 'International Engagements: the Politics of North American International Relations Theory,' *Political Theory* 29 (3): 432–48.

Laclau, E. and Mouffe, C. (2000) *Hegemony and Socialist Strategy*. London: Verso.

6

Getting Real: The Necessity of Critical Poststructuralism in Global Political Economy

V. Spike Peterson

> The complicity between cultural and economic value systems is acted out in almost every decision we make.
>
> Gayatri Chakravorty Spivak, *In Other Worlds* (1987)

As others have noted (see introduction and Zalewski this volume), IPE scholars continue to resist poststructuralist approaches and interventions. I attempt to overcome some of that resistance by demonstrating not only the relevance but the *necessity* of critical poststructuralist approaches for making sense of, and responding critically to, neoliberal globalization. Moving beyond theoretical debates, this chapter focuses on a central issue for the theory/practice of global political economy (GPE) today: the purported hegemony, hence presumed stability, of neoliberalism (see also Larner this volume). Through a critical poststructuralist lens I analyze actually existing – 'real' – conditions of GPE to reveal that neoliberal hegemony is not what it claims in theory or practice, and simultaneously generates exclusions and marginalizations that belie its purported stability, in theory and practice.

To develop the argument I draw on theoretical framing and empirical data from my recent book, *A Critical Rewriting of Global Political Economy: Integrating Reproductive, Productive and Virtual Economies* (2003). The chapter first addresses theoretical issues regarding poststructuralism, the discursive construction of 'stability' as it relates to hegemony, and instabilities as they relate to neoliberal globalization. I then briefly introduce the book and its analytical innovations, and schematically describe the three (reproductive, productive, and virtual) economies, major trends ('real' conditions) within them, and linkages among them. A final section summarizes how neoliberalism is neither hegemonic nor stable and how critical poststructuralism is necessary for *seeing* this reality and revising our theory/practice accordingly.

Theory as practice and neoliberalism as politics

> One thing is essential methodologically and even more important politically: not to take anything for granted.
>
> Anne Showstack Sassoon, *Globalization, Hegemony and Passive Revolution* (2001)

The elements of poststructuralist approaches to IPE have been elaborated in the introduction. I here draw attention to those features especially relevant to the argumentation of this chapter. As a starting point, poststructuralists reject foundational dichotomies in favor of recognizing the inescapable uncertainty, ambiguity, and inconstancy of meanings ascribed to words/concepts/terms. Similarly, the presumption of stable, singular identities (fully coherent, self-transparent, rational) is rejected in favor of recognizing identities – or subjectivities – as complex, multiple, and hybrid (not necessarily coherent), and continuously (re)negotiated/created as an effect of contingency and context. As a corollary, poststructuralists emphasize the historical, contingent conditions (representations, discourses, practices, institutions) that *produce* and regulate particular forms of subjectivity (and speech), and how this effectively 'authorizes' and differentially validates some, with the effect of devalorizing, marginalizing or excluding others. Agency, self-representation, and 'real power' are not denied by poststructuralists. Rather, they are reformulated as 'enactments of variation within regulated, normative and habitual processes of signification' (Sawicki 1998: 99) that are historical, contingent, and *necessarily* embedded in relations of power.

In this sense, signifying systems and their differentiations are *inseparable* from the material conditions of their production and the material effects of their differential authorization/valorization. Poststructuralism then denies a separation of symbols/discourse/culture from material/structure/economics, or ideology/culture/theory from politics/economics/practice. A central question becomes: how does power operate (through representations, discourses, practices) within specific contexts to stabilize – with a tendency to normalize and depoliticize – particular discourses and their effects? Poststructuralism is also then political: it pursues critical genealogies to expose how differential 'authority' and power are produced; focuses on 'difference' to reveal what is marginalized/excluded/

devalorized; and directs our attention to the consequences, especially the 'costs,' of normalizing/stabilizing/depoliticizing *particular* discourses and institutionalized practices *at the expense of others*. To address this chapter's focus I further clarify the relationship between language/discourse and the politics of 'stabilizations.'

Poststructuralists understand language not as referential (words/signs name pre-existing, 'real' categories or 'things') but as *producing* the meaning of categories and 'things' through processes of signification (involving stabilizations) that are embedded in power relations. As a condition of their actualization, language and social relations require some 'ordering' – some stabilization of the infinite possibility of differences, meanings, and practices – that will afford mutual intelligibility and sustainable patterns of social activity. While necessary, this 'fixing' of particular meanings and actions is nonetheless deeply problematic.

On the one hand, because change is constant and stabilizations are historically contingent, all stabilizations are precarious and partial. They are not absolutely congruent with but continuously at odds with 'reality' and therefore subject to disruption and contestation by the surplus meanings ('excess') and contradictory practices that are suppressed or excluded. In this sense, uncritical adherence to particular stabilizations frustrates attempts to adequately understand 'reality.' On the other hand, stabilizations marginalize other possible meanings, interpretations, and 'orderings.' This has obvious cultural *and* political implications, especially as the power to 'name' and impose particular stabilizations is unevenly distributed. Critical genealogies expose how this power has historically been dominated by religious, political, military and economic elites who for the most part, intentionally and otherwise, favor stabilizations that reproduce hierarchical ordering and the silencing of alternatives.[1]

In our pursuit of meaning and sociality, we necessarily seek 'ordering' and stabilizations are inescapable. The 'reality' then is an unavoidable and irresolvable tension between the stabilization/fixing/bounding process and the inexorably disruptive (destabilizing) effects and political consequences of the surplus/incongruities/marginalizations of meanings and differences that are not and cannot be 'contained.' *The objective of political analysis is then not to abolish power but to expose how it operates to produce and privilege particular stabilizations at the expense of others*; to render visible and critically evaluate – to *politicize* – the specific effects and trade-offs of stabilizations, dominant orderings, and especially, what becomes normalized (depoliticized) as 'common sense.' Insofar as we deem the trade-offs less desirable than those imposed by other possible orderings, we are not without agency in shaping change; neither the symbolic nor the social is a closed system.

The hegemony of neoliberalism is ostensibly evidenced in the discursive/cultural/ideological acceptance of its premises as 'common sense.' The latter includes first, believing that 'there is no alternative' to capitalism (see also Daly this volume). Adherents argue that this claim is supported by the historical, cumulative success of capitalist development and the displacement or collapse of all alternatives. The second and related belief is that neoliberalism is (ultimately) good for everyone: providing efficiency, creativity, growth, and even security (for example, by ensuring the greatest growth to fulfill increasing material 'needs,' and promoting democratization to engender justice and equality that reduce conflict).

I argue that this hegemony is both analytically/ideologically and materially unstable. On the one hand, neoliberalism is not what it claims: the realities of contemporary globalization do not conform to the conditions, stabilization or coherence it projects. These realities are not simply the inevitable excess confounding all stabilizations but much more extensive and systemic 'differences' that *contradict* what neoliberalism claims. On the other hand, the exclusions and marginalizing effects of neoliberalism are themselves destabilizing. For example, suppressing alternative viewpoints (environmentalism, postcolonialism, poststructuralist IPE) may preclude 'disruptive' but valuable knowledge, and excluding social groups (discarded workers, disenfranchised migrants, demonized countermovements) may breed anger, resistance, or violence. Whether the outcome is deemed 'desirable' or not, my point here is that marginalization must be taken seriously as a destabilizing force. When marginalizations are extensive – as I argue they are under neoliberal globalization – they threaten the apparent coherence, legitimacy and even viability of the stabilization we understand as hegemony.

Most poststructuralist scholarship focuses on how power operates through discursive practices to *produce* particular stabilizations.[2] My title's claim to 'getting real' suggests a different strategy. I take as given that familiar (linguistic) representations – of work, family, skill, value, money, production, and so on – are not separate from (non-linguistic) 'reality'; how these representations are produced and are currently shifting is a thread throughout the analysis. But the primary focus here is specifying, through a critical poststructuralist lens, actually existing conditions of today's GPE, that is, phenomena conventionally regarded as 'real.' Insofar as this exposes the excesses and contradictions of neoliberalism, it undermines the latter's claims to accurately represent reality. At the same time, it reveals the 'costs' of favoring this stabilization at the expense of others. The objective is to expose how thoroughly inadequate conventional accounts are, and how necessary critical poststructuralism is *not only* but *especially* at this juncture and for analyzing GPE.

'Real' global political economy

> Economics is only a system of values.
>
> Gloria Steinem, *Revving Up for the Next 25 Years* (1997)

A Critical Rewriting of Global Political Economy moves beyond a narrow definition of economics to develop an alternative analytical framing of reproductive, productive, and virtual (RPV) economies. Economies are here understood poststructurally: as mutually constituted (therefore coexisting and interactive) systemic sites through and across which power operates. These sites include socio-cultural processes of self-formation and cultural socialization that underpin identities/subjectivities and their political effects. The subjective, conceptual, and cultural dimensions of these sites are understood as inextricable from (mutually constituted by) material effects, social practices, and institutional structures.

At its simplest, the framing of three (RPV) intersecting economies is a heuristic device that builds on conventional economics but is more inclusive. In essence, the RPV framing brings the conceptual and material dimensions of 'social **reproduction**,' non-wage labor, and informalization into relation with the familiar but increasingly global, flexibilized, information-based and service-oriented '**productive** economy,' as well as with the less familiar but increasingly consequential '**virtual** economy' of financial markets, commodified knowledge, and the exchange less of goods than of signs. The goal is to move beyond the limitations of prevailing accounts, while building on their insights and addressing important but neglected features of today's global political economy.

Retaining the productive economy permits continuity with conventional economic analyses, illuminates current global developments in relation to production, and links this economy to the others. Including the reproductive economy invites attention to otherwise marginalized agents and activities, and acknowledges especially the importance of feminist research and analysis. Including the virtual economy addresses developments in 'symbolic money,' informationalism, and the commodification of intangibles and aesthetics. It confirms the necessity of poststructuralist approaches for analyzing how symbols and cultural phenomena underpin today's GPE.

One objective of the RPV framing is to move beyond disciplinary boundaries and map identities and culture as *coconstituting* what are conventionally understood as material and 'structural' phenomena. Another objective is to advance critical theory by illuminating the intersection of race, gender, and economic inequalities (within and among states) as structural features of globalization. In support of these objectives the book introduces a second analytical innovation – 'triad analytics' – that is applicable to social relations more generally.

The positivist/modernist dichotomies of conventional social science tend to obscure relations of interdependence and embeddedness and to marginalize issues of identity and subjectivity. To facilitate a shift from the binary tendencies of conventional framing, my triad analytics posits identities (subjectivity, self-formation, sexualities), meaning systems (symbols, discourse, ideologies), and social practices/institutions (actions, social structures) as coconstituting dimensions of social reality. Stated simply, the triad insists on fully integrating 'who we are,' 'how we think,' and 'what we do.'

This framing invokes familiar categories (conceptual 'thinking' and concrete 'doing') but also insists on complicating these in crucial, even transformative, ways. First, it rejects dichotomized constructions (for example, symbolic-material, discursive-structural, analytical-empirical) that encumber conventional theorizing and divide academic disciplines; rather, its poststructuralist orientation understands the symbolic and material relationally, as interactive and codetermining. Second, triad analytics insists that conceptual habits and social practices are equally inextricable from identification processes and the emotional investments they elicit. This draws our attention to issues of subjectivity, sexuality, and self-formation as well as the social hierarchies and 'micro-power' that structure identity formation and ideological preferences. These are issues that have been too long neglected, even excluded, from mainstream analyses, due largely to positivist commitments in the social 'sciences.'

Dominant accounts of GPE originate from the disciplines of economics and international relations, where economistic, modernist/positivist, and masculinist commitments prevail.[3] In particular, these preclude adequate analyses of two central features of global restructuring. First, today's globalization is distinguished by its dependence on information and communication technologies (ICTs) specific to the late twentieth century.[4] These technologies not only enable the 'global' in globalization but – due to the inherently conceptual/cultural nature of information – transform the world as we 'know' it. The issue then is not only empirically observable changes in speed, scale and scope, but also analytical challenges posed by the unprecedented fusion of culture and economy – of virtual and material dimensions – afforded by ICTs. In this sense, the symbolic/virtual aspects of today's GPE are so extensive as to *decisively* expose the (positivist) fallacy of separating culture from economy. Hence, the *necessity* of poststructuralist lenses appropriate for interpreting the symbolic, cultural, and virtual.[5]

Second, even as these technologies enhance some forms of integration and homogenization, globalization and its effects are extremely uneven – manifested starkly in global, intersecting stratifications of ethnicity/race, class, gender, and nation. These hierarchies of difference have long histories of stabilization and corollary exclusions. Hence, the *necessity* of critical lenses appropriate for analyzing structural hierarchies exacerbated (and complicated) by neoliberalism.

Critics tend to focus on one or another of these hierarchies, or at best 'add' one to another. The *interconnections* among them remain underdeveloped. As a contribution to theorizing the intersection of global hierarchies I deploy gender analytically. Extensive feminist research documents the deeply sedimented coding of gender as a hierarchical opposition between masculinity and femininity. The historical result is gender as a governing code that valorizes practices and people (not only men) that are characterized as masculine, at the expense of those stigmatized as feminine (lacking agency, 'skills,' control, reason, or power). The claim here is that gender – and its denigration of the feminine – pervades language and culture, with systemic effects on how we 'take for granted' (normalize and effectively naturalize) the devaluation of feminized bodies, identities, *and* activities. In short, I argue that *feminization of identities and practices effectively devalues them* – in cultural as well as economic terms. Applying this insight to globalization permits us to see and theorize interconnections among previously 'disconnected' categories; in particular, feminization devalorizes not only women but also racially, culturally, and economically marginalized men *and* work that is deemed unskilled, menial, and 'merely' reproductive.

The Productive Economy, or PE

I start with the most familiar economy, conventionally understood as the sphere of formal (contractual, regulated) exchanges. Here I note only major trends to provide context for discerning the contradictions and instabilities they generate. Each has implications for the practices, identities, and valorization of workers.

First, the dramatic decline in world prices of and demand for (non-oil) primary products has been devastating to 'third world' economies where primary production dominates: unemployment problems are exacerbated, ability to attract foreign investment is reduced, and debt dependency may be increased. One effect is viewing (unregulated) labor as a competitive resource and/or encouraging outward migration in search of work.

Second, 'deindustrialization' especially affects advanced economies and major cities, manifested variously through downsizing, 'jobless growth,' loss of skilled and often unionized positions, growth in low-wage, semi- and unskilled jobs, and relocation of production to lower wage areas. Job security is additionally eroded for all but elite workers through 'flexibilization': more temporary, part-time, non-unionized jobs with fewer benefits, and more just-in-time, decentralized, and sub-contracted production processes. These shifts tend to increase un- and underemployment (especially of men) and coupled with erosion of union power translate into a decline in real incomes and household resources.

Third, employment shifts from manufacturing to information-based services as technologies transform the nature of work worldwide. Income polarization is exacerbated insofar as service jobs tend to be either skilled and high-waged (professional-managerial jobs) or semi-, unskilled and poorly paid (personal, cleaning, retail, and clerical services). Differential access to education, training, and career opportunities, structures who does what work and tends to reinforce historical stabilizations of gender, race, class, and national location.

The fourth trend is *feminized* flexibilization: simultaneously a material, embodied transformation of labor markets, a conceptual characterization of devalorized labor conditions, and a reconfiguration of worker identities. As an increasing proportion of jobs require few skills, the most desirable workers are those who are perceived to be undemanding (unorganized), docile but reliable, available for part-time and temporary work, and willing to accept low-wages. Gender stereotypes depict women as more attractive candidates for these jobs and especially since the 1980s, women's proportion of the formal workplace has been increasing worldwide, while male participation has been falling.[6] In short, as more jobs are casual, irregular, flexible and precarious (read: feminized), more women – and feminized men – are doing them.

Fifth, globalization increases flows of people: to urban areas, export processing zones, seasonal agricultural sites, and tourism locales. Migrations are shaped by colonial histories, geopolitics, immigration policies, capital flows, labor markets, cultural stereotypes, skill attributions, kinship networks, and identity markers. Given the nature of 'unskilled' jobs most frequently available (cleaning, harvesting, domestic service, sex work), migrant worker populations are especially marked by gender and race/ethnicity.[7] Being on the move – for work, recreation, or escape – affects personal and collective identities and cultural reproduction. Not least, traditional family forms and divisions of labor are disrupted, destabilizing men's and women's identities and gender relations more generally. Shifting identities have complex effects at numerous 'levels,' whether expressed in anti-immigrant racism, nationalist state-building, ethno-cultural diasporas, ethnic cleansing, or patriarchal religious fundamentalisms.

Flexibilization tends to increase the power and autonomy of management and be attractive to those with highly valued skills. Some find flexible arrangements better suit their life conditions. Specific trade-offs depend on specific contexts, but a general point remains: in the absence of regulatory frameworks that protect workers' rights and generate *living* wages, flexibilization translates into greater *insecurity* of employment and income for the majority of workers, with destabilizing effects.

The Reproductive Economy, or RE

Unlike the PE, the RE is rarely analyzed in accounts of GPE. This neglect is due largely to stabilized binaries that locate men/masculinity in the (valorized) public sphere of power and formal (paid) work, and women/femininity in the (marginalized) family/private sphere of emotional maintenance, leisure, and caring (unpaid) labor. Here I focus on three reasons for taking the RE seriously: the significance of subject formation and socialization, the devalorization of 'women's work,' and increasing informalization.

Socialization is about learning how to be human according to the codes of a particular cultural environment and is essential for stable reproduction of social relations. Family life is where subject formation begins (within/through signifying systems) and the 'ordering' (language, cultural rules, ideologies) we acritically imbibe in childhood is especially influential. This is where we first observe and internalize gender differences, their respective identities, and divisions of labor. Moreover, gender acculturation is inextricable from beliefs about race/ethnicity, age, class, religion, and other axes of 'difference' (see also Zalewski this volume).

Subject formation matters *structurally* for neoliberalism. It produces individuals who are then able to 'work' and this unpaid reproductive labor saves capital the costs of producing labor inputs. And it instills attitudes, identities and meaning systems that enable societies to function. Capitalism, for instance, requires not only that 'workers' accept and perform their role in 'production,' but that individuals more generally accept hierarchical divisions of labor and their corollary: differential valorization of who does what kind of work.

Socialization and the caring labor required to sustain family relations are stereotyped as '**women's work**' worldwide. Yet in spite of romanticized motherhood and a glut of pro-family *rhetoric*, neoliberal globalization reduces the emotional, cultural and material resources necessary for the well-being of most women and families. While the traditional ideology of patriarchal states, religions, and families locates women in the home as loyal dependents and loving service providers, economic realities (and consumerist ideologies) are at odds with this and increasingly *compel* women to seek formal employment and/or undertake additional 'home-work.' As families worldwide confront shrinking economic resources, women are disproportionately expected to compensate – to absorb the costs of 'adjustment.' Women have fewer legal protections than men, fewer property rights, and less access to education, training, and work opportunities that are associated with highly valued skills. As a survival strategy, women especially rely on informal work to ensure family well-being.

Informal activities are not unique to but have greatly expanded in the context of neoliberal restructuring[8] as conditions of formal employment deteriorate, privatization undercuts welfare provisioning, deregulation expands entrepreneurial and 'irregular' activities, and flexibilization entails declining real incomes and decreased job security worldwide. People are thus 'pushed' to engage in informal activities as a strategy for securing income however they can. Yet these activities are 'outside' of and contravene theoretical expectations regarding capitalist development, which presumed an increasingly *formalized* workforce.

Moreover, informalization has a variety of direct and indirect effects on labor relations. In general, it decreases the structural power of workers, reaps higher profits for capital, depresses formal wages, disciplines all workers, and through the isolation of informalized labor, impedes collective resistance. Women, the poor, migrants, and recent immigrants are the prototypical (feminized) workers of the informal economy; in the context of increasing flexibilization, the devalued (and unstable?) conditions of informalization are arguably the future for all but elite workers worldwide.

Informalization is heterogeneous and controversial. Some individuals prosper: in microenterprises (favored by neoliberals) where innovation may breed success and multiplying effects; in tax evasion and international pricing schemes that favor larger operations; in developing countries where informal activities are crucial for income generation; and in criminal activities that are 'big business' worldwide.[9] Informalization is then crucial to GPE because it defies theoretical expectations, erodes safe and secure labor conditions, is growing explosively, and its often semi- or illegal activities are problematic. It thus poses fundamental questions for 'realistically' analyzing GPE (what 'counts' – and what *gets* counted/recorded – as economic activity) and exposes multiple sites of instability.

The virtual economy, or VE

Globalization is especially visible in flows of symbols, information, and communication through electronic and wireless transmissions that defy territorial constraints. It is not only the new scale and velocity of these transmissions but the different (symbolic, non-material, virtual) *nature* of these processes that we must address. Intangible symbols contravene familiar notions of time and space as well as conventional analyses of material goods. Because symbols are inherently cultural their circulation fuses culture and economy in novel ways. In short, manifestations of the VE effectively 'force' analysts to adopt a post-structuralist lens that accommodates interpretation. To be clear: I am not arguing that poststructuralism has only recently become relevant, but that current developments undercut any claims to the adequacy of non-interpretive accounts. I focus on three (interactive) modes of the VE involving respectively the exchange of symbolic/virtual money, information/knowledge, and cultural/aesthetic symbols.

Since the 1970s, floating exchange rates, reduced capital controls, offshore transactions, desegmentation, new financial instruments, securitization, and the rise of institutional investors, have interacted to amplify the speed, scale and complexity of **global financial transactions**. Powerful states have been complicit in, and technologies have been decisive for, enabling the mobility of capital and its enhanced power. The result is an 'enormous mass of "world money"...[that] is not being created by economic activity like investment, production, consumption, or trade...It is virtual [symbolic] rather than real [commodity] money' (Drucker 1997: 162). The point is not that this 'delinking' (of symbolic from commodity money) insulates the real economy from global finance because prices 'set' in the VE (for example, through interest and exchange rates) have decisive effects throughout the socio-economic order: they shape investments (in financial instruments or human resources?), the production of goods and services (labor intensive or capital and technology intensive?) and the structure of labor markets (what types of labor, where located, with what compensation and under what conditions?). But symbolic money is differently constituted than commodity money: its symbolic/informational content is continually open to interpretation, and that interpretation depends less on objective indicators than on subjective ideas, identities, and expectations.

Effects of global finance are multiple. The allure of financial trading encourages short term speculation over long term investments in industry and infrastructure. The expansion, complexity, and non-transparency of global financial transactions makes money laundering easier, which enhances opportunities for illicit financial trading as well as organized crime. Increasing urgency in regard to 'managing money' and investment strategies shifts status and decision-making power within households, businesses, governments, and global institutions. These changes disrupt conventional identities, functions, and sites of authority. Most visible are the risks of financial crises, technical breakdowns, and hacker disruptions that are clearly destabilizing. Critics argue that prevailing economic theories fail both to adequately acknowledge the risk-prone tendencies of financial liberalization or take seriously the 'disturbing effects' when crises ensue.

The **informational** mode of the VE features the exchange of knowledge, information or 'intellectual capital.' While all processes involve information/knowledge, in this mode information *is* the commodity: ideas, codes, concepts, knowledge are what is being exchanged. Conventional analyses fail to address questions posed by the unique characteristics of the informational economy: its self-transforming feedback loop, the imperative of accelerating innovation, defiance of exclusive possession, capacity to increase in value through use, and intrinsic dissolution of cultural-economic distinctions. Hence, the informational economy *necessarily* involves a transformation not only of goods but also of thinking, knowledge, and cultural codes.

Computer-based digitization enables the conversion of information, arts, and even human experience into a binary code available, virtually without the constraints of time and space, to anyone with the relevant 'reading' capacity (conceptual and technological). Digitization also effectively 'objectifies' these diverse phenomena, rendering them objects/commodities that are tradable. The selection of what is deemed worthy of digitization and circulation is inherently political, shaped by the cultural preferences and interests of those with greater ownership and control of relevant media. Many voices and viewpoints are marginalized. Similarly, access to and control over 'valued' informational goods, training and technologies are structured by familiar exclusions. Whatever celebrations and resentments accrue, the processes themselves transform conventional boundaries, cultural representations, and knowledge claims on an unprecedented scale.

The third mode of the VE features the exchange of aesthetic or cultural signs/symbols, treated here as heightened **consumerism**. This involves the creation of a social imaginary of particular tastes and desires, and the extensive commodification and marketization of tastes, pleasure, and leisure. Aesthetics and *cultural symbols* figure prominently here, emphasizing not the material aspects of commodities but the signs, symbols, and codes that invest these commodities with (cultural) meaning and value. In an important sense, capital focuses less on producing consumer goods than on producing consumer *subjectivities* and a totalizing 'market *culture*' that sustain consumption (see also Shapiro, and Gammon and Palan this volume, on the political economy of taste and desire).

The significance of cultural coding is amplified as commodification penetrates all aspects of culture, and the production of desire and rapidly changing tastes are key to surplus accumulation. The 'aestheticization of commodities' fuses economic and cultural activity by 'enlivening everyday life at the same time as legitimating consumerism and social acceptance of the imperatives of capitalism,' while the 'commodification of aesthetics' transforms culture and cultural activity 'into cultural industries, that is, commodities sold in the market,' thereby encouraging consumers to 'increasingly identify cultural gratification with consumption,' rather than other perhaps more meaningful and less profit-oriented activities (Amin 1994: 31).

Affluent consumption is the privilege of only a small percentage of the world's population, but it shapes the desires, choices, and valorization of those without affluence. The political economy of consumption involves the effects of consumerism as an ideology (fueled by pervasive advertising and global media that propel even the poorest to desire consumer goods as an expression of self-worth), and the power-laden issue of practicing consumption. Whose needs, desires, and interests are served? Whose bodies and environments are devalorized in pursuit of consumerism and the neoliberal commitment to growth (rather than redistribution) that fuels it? Finally, consumerism requires purchasing power, increasingly sought through access to credit. Patterns regarding who has it, how much they have, and how they use it correspond tellingly to class, race/ethnicity, gender, and geopolitical stratifications.

In summary, the VE is so-named not because it escapes materiality but because it forces us to 'get real' about the *power of symbols* to determine (by assigning differential 'value' to goods and workers) who wins and loses in neoliberal capitalism. In all of the economies, neoclassical precepts and positivist models tell us too little about how values and entitlements are determined; they omit too much of the symbolic, discursive, cultural and social. These omissions are simply untenable when analyzing the VE, where 'symbolic money,' digitized information, and commodified aesthetics constitute the 'goods' that are circulated and exchanged. Hence, in addition to and also more than any other, the VE proves the *necessity* of poststructuralism.

Conclusion

> It is exactly the business of tracing and retracing contexts that puts things in a different light.
>
> Teresa Brennan, *Between Feminism and Psychoanalysis* (1989).

Neoliberalism represents itself as a coherent and structurally homogenizing set of policies; based on neoclassical economics, it claims to be the optimal – and historically triumphant – system of economic ordering and one that is good for *all* of us, at least in the long run. This chapter reviewed actually existing – 'real' – conditions of GPE to argue otherwise: that reality 'exceeds' and contradicts what neoliberalism claims, and critical poststructuralism is required both to see 'real' conditions and produce more 'accurate' and politically adequate theory/practice.

Analytical claims of neoliberalism are at odds with the following realities. Capitalist markets have always required state supports. 'Real' shifts today reflect less a diminution of state power than an expansion of private/corporate power to affect state agencies, such that pursuit of minority (elite) economic interests increasingly displaces delivery of public goods to the majority (nonelites). Neither is capitalism's homogenizing claim persuasive: it has never been monolithic but always a mix of economic modes: barter, social, informal, formal. Linear and totalizing narratives of capitalist development are similarly at odds with its always contested, always changing character. And the 'real' history of capitalism is deeply marked by unevenness; some argue for its fundamentally cyclical nature, others for its inherent *unsustainability*: environmentally, socially, ethically. Historical development is always the result of struggle between social forces, and opposition to capitalism continues today in spite of neoliberalism failing to account for it.

Worsening conditions of employment, increased inequalities, growth of informal activities, crises of welfare provision, and feminization of the labor force contradict neoliberal expectations. Structural changes in the three economies are transforming identities of workers and nonworkers and upsetting 'expected' divisions of labor, sites of decision-making power, and sources of income. Work outside of the formal economy is neither coincidental to nor diminishing with capitalist development. The latter (historically and today) *relies on* 'noneconomic' social relations (for example, families, communities) and cultural codes (for example, validation of competition, acquisitiveness) for its successful – and effectively subsidized – 'reproduction.' Similarly, the *majority* of work (historically and increasingly today) is informal, and in this sense, outside of formal capitalist structures. This would be visible if analysts examined the everyday lives of women, peasants, migrants, artisans, microentrepreneurs and those operating in the 'underworld' of illicit activities. At the same time, neoliberal globalization is disrupting conventional families, communities, and cultural codes, and this disruption has destabilizing, though not predictable, effects.

ICTs not only enable unprecedented speed, scale and complexity of transactions, but their commodification of 'money' itself, knowledge, and cultural phenomena entails unique features that confound orthodox theories. ICTs transform processes of production, exchange, marketing, and consumption as well as modalities of thinking, knowing, and reflexivity. This occurs at an accelerating pace, affecting and linking local and global cultural codes, without necessarily homogenizing them. Relative to conventional commodities, virtual goods and processes of exchanging them are less predictable, controllable, or stable.

Neither does global capital conform to neoliberal, economistic analyses. While ostensibly mobile, its flows are highly patterned, selective, and often inconsistent with theoretical expectations. The delinking of symbolic/world money from commodity money continues to be underanalyzed even as its effects are recognized as problematic. The speculative, volatile and risk-prone tendencies of financial markets are exacerbated by deregulation and, as recent crises confirm, the consequences are systemically threatening. The subjective, interpretive dimensions of financial markets are by definition 'outside' of theoretical models that code them as 'exogenous' variables. Yet financial markets in particular rely on intersubjective relations (of trust and confidence) for their successful operation (see Thrift 1996; de Goede 2001). Lack of transparency and money laundering permits 'shady' trading and organized crime to proliferate. The latter economy is enormous, increasing, and unregulated; it has multiple effects on GPE that are neither accounted for analytically nor addressed politically.

The biases, blind spots, and failures of neoliberal 'theory' are inseparable from its suppression of alternative analytics. The latter offer extensive resources for making 'better' sense of global processes and conditions but are marginalized by the dominance of positivist/economistic/rationalist paradigms in economics and IR. This involves academic and epistemic communities, the political economy of universities, and the training of practitioners in business administration, management and marketing programs.

Neoliberalism's limited 'grasp' of actually existing conditions is due in part to theoretical blinders and in part to its top down vantage point. In spite of the manifestly global processes they cultivate, neoliberal advocates pay little heed to voices and viewpoints outside of rich, powerful states, indeed outside of elite sites of power and authority within those states. Through their selective lenses the 'reality' in developing countries, the 'discarded fourth world,' urban ghettos, and overburdened families is rendered invisible and hence unaccounted for. Yet each of these is a site of knowledge-production as well as alienation and resentment that are potentially destabilizing.

Beyond the failures and omissions of neoliberal analytics (but inextricable from them) are *embodied marginalizations*. I refer here to processes of social exclusion, marked in particular by hierarchies of class, ethnicity/race, sexuality, gender, and nation. In spite of rhetoric, or promises 'in the long run,' neoliberalism has exacerbated global inequalities and effectively marginalized the majority of the world's population from its purported benefits. Inequalities do not originate with neoliberalism, nor do its proponents claim to intentionally exacerbate them. Rather, long and entwined stabilizations of classism, racism, heterosexism, and colonialism enable the deployment of already internalized and institutionalized 'difference' in support of neoliberal objectives. Capitalism is not after all homogenizing; it seeks not to eliminate differences and inequalities but to take advantage of them for naturalizing (depoliticizing) exploitative practices.

What distinguishes contemporary, specifically neoliberal, capitalism is its unprecedented global reach and apparent 'hegemony.' ICTs enable this reach and (under the direction of rich and powerful elites) the global promotion of capitalism as the only alternative – ostensibly, as 'common sense.' People everywhere are more aware of – and are encouraged to emulate – lifestyles of the rich/north. But due to global media, they are also acutely aware of inequalities, and for the majority, the impossibility of 'making real' the promise of rich, secure lives.

This is not to suggest a homogeneity of consciousness among those excluded, nor a global repudiation of what capitalism purports to offer. It is to insist that (in various and shifting forms) these exclusions are increasing, are increasingly debilitating, and responses to them threaten the stability of neoliberal marketization. Responses vary and depend on multiple factors. In psychological terms they include denial, indifference, frustration, despair, anger, resentment and hostility. In 'social action' terms they include individual, informal and collective resistance; seeking and developing alternatives; participation in countermovements; as well as fatalistic disengagement; scapegoating 'others'; enhancing self- and group-power through fundamentalist ideologies; and in- and out-group violence. Whatever their form and however we evaluate the outcomes, all of these responses are 'at odds with' the self-representations of neoliberal hegemony, even as they are central to understanding GPE. In a simplifying sense, I am arguing that neoliberalism deepens conditions of structural violence, and that these conditions cultivate acute (direct) violence that is structurally destabilizing.

Through a critical poststructuralist lens, I have attempted to politicize (denaturalize) the symbolic and structural stabilizations of neoliberal capitalism – its ideological coding and material effects. Because stabilizations are only that, they require constant reproduction. To disrupt and redirect the particular orderings 'at work' we must first be able to see them clearly. Documenting the failures, omissions, and excesses of neoliberalism undermines its claims to 'accuracy,' coherence, and legitimacy. Illuminating the social exclusions of neoliberalism shifts attention to the *costs* of perpetuating it as 'common sense.' Neoliberalism is not what it claims analytically, and in practice has not alleviated but exacerbated global inequalities and social exclusions. In short, the 'real' conditions of identifying, thinking, knowing, being, and having agency conform neither to the premises of neoliberal ideology nor its promise of the good life for all. These conditions render neoliberalism unstable.

The reality of being precarious and unstable does not guarantee neoliberalism's demise, much less its replacement by a more 'progressive' project. My point is rather the *necessity* of a critical poststructuralist lens for more 'accurately' analyzing the *realities* of GPE and for 'politically' assessing it in relation to alternative understandings and stabilizations. Prevailing accounts 'miss' and marginalize entirely too much; they cannot help but fail in their pursuit of the understanding and explanation so desperately needed today. By unmasking neoliberalism's pretensions, exposing its costs, and affording more adequate analysis, critical poststructuralism offers not only 'better' but more politically relevant understanding of GPE.

Notes

1 An important example is early 'western' state-making where the invention of writing afforded unprecedented 'sedimentation' of a particular symbolic order. For example, codifications in early Greek texts (especially the hierarchical dichotomies of mind-body, public-private, and civilized-barbarian) endure as the foundations of 'western philosophy' and have deeply affected subsequent politics and social ordering. Hierarchical divisions of labor and authority were also stabilized in this process (Lerner 1986; Peterson 1997) and have deeply affected subsequent political economy.

2 Exemplary elaborations regarding finance include de Goede (2001) and Thrift (2001).

3 These claims are elaborated in Peterson (1992) and regarding IPE specifically in 2003; see the latter for argumentation, empirical evidence, and citations supporting claims made subsequently in this chapter. On theory see also Amin and Palan (2001); Barker and Kuiper (2003); de Goede (2003); Gibson-Graham (1996); Hewitson (1999). I especially recommend the latter for an accessible and persuasive rebuttal of the most frequently repeated criticisms of poststructuralism.

4 I understand technologies as not deterministically but as historically contingent and socially embedded.

5 To clarify: I am arguing that the separation of culture from economy (due to positivist commitments) has been a persistent error that continuously impoverishes analysis, and *also* that 'real' conditions (due to ICTs) of today's

GPE expose – to an unprecedented extent and in new developments – how that separation is totally indefensible. In effect, to deny poststructuralist insights in the face of these real conditions is to preclude 'accurate' analyses of GPE.

6 Women continue to earn 30–40 percent less than men worldwide and in spite of heading almost one-third of the world's households, their lower wages are ideologically/culturally 'justified' by casting them as secondary earners. A corollary stereotype and sometimes reality, is that flexibilized work arrangements are therefore attractive to – and 'good for' – some women.

7 Migrant labor is particularly subject to informalization (treated under the RE) and often involves semi-clandestine and clandestine activities that link all three economies.

8 Debates regarding how to theorize, define, measure and evaluate informalization are addressed in Chapter 4 of my book (2003) where I reference an extensive and rapidly growing literature. The shadow or underground economy was in 1998 estimated to be US$9 trillion – the equivalent of approximately one-fourth of the world's gross domestic product for that year (*The Economist* 28 Aug 1999: 59). Sivard (1995: 11) estimates that including 'women's work' would add as much as one-third to the world's gross national product.

9 A variety of sources (see Peterson 2003: 196, 201) provide the following estimates (in US dollars, per year): of 'white collar crime' in the US: $200 billion; of profits from trafficking migrants: $3.5 billion; of money laundering: as much as $2.8 trillion; of tax revenue lost to the US by hiding assets offshore: $70 billion; of tax evasion costs to the US government: $195 billion.

References

Amin, A. (1994) 'Post-Fordism: Models, Fantasies and Phantoms of Transition,' in Amin, A. (ed.) *Post-Fordism: A Reader*. Oxford: Blackwell.

Amin, A. and Palan, R. (2001) Towards a Non-Rationalist International Political Economy,' *Review of International Political Economy* 8 (4): 559–77.

Barker, D. K. and Kuiper, E. (eds) (2003) *Toward a Feminist Philosophy of Economics*. London and New York: Routledge.

Brennan, T. (1989) *Between Feminism and Psychoanalysis*. London and New York: Routledge.

de Goede, M. (2001) 'Discourses of Scientific Finance and the Failure of Long-Term Capital Management,' *New Political Economy* 6 (2): 149–70.

de Goede, M. (2003) 'Beyond Economism in International Political Economy,' *Review of International Studies* 29 (1): 79–97.

Drucker, P. F. (1997) 'The Global Economy and the Nation-State,' *Foreign Affairs* 76 (5): 159–71.

Gibson-Graham, J. K. (1996) *The End of Capitalism (as we knew it): A Feminist Critique of Political Economy*. Cambridge, MA: Blackwell.

Hewitson, G. J. (1999) *Feminist Economics: Interrogating the Masculinity of Rational Economic Man*. Cheltenham: Edward Elgar.

Lerner, G. (1986) *The Creation of Patriarchy*. New York: Oxford University Press.

Peterson, V. S. (1992) 'Transgressing Boundaries: Theories of Knowledge, Gender, and International Relations,' *Millennium* 21 (2): 183–206.

Peterson, V. S. (1997) 'Whose Crisis? Early and Postmodern Masculinism,' in Gill, S. and Mittelman, J. H. (eds) *Innovation and Transformation in International Studies*. Cambridge: Cambridge University Press.

Peterson, V. S. (2003) *A Critical Rewriting of Global Political Economy: Integrating Reproductive, Productive and Virtual Economies*. London: Routledge.

Sassoon, A. S. (2001) 'Globalization, Hegemony and Passive Revolution,' *New Political Economy* 6 (1): 5–17.

Sawicki, J. (1998) 'Feminism, Foucault and "Subjects" of Power and Freedom,' in Moss, J. (ed.) *The Later Foucault*. London: Sage.

Sivard, R. L. (1995) *Women...A World Survey*, second edn. Washington, DC: World Priorities.

Spivak, G. C. (1987) *In Other Worlds: Essays in Cultural Politics*. London and New York: Methuen.

Steinem, G. (1997) 'Revving Up for the Next 25 Years,' *Ms.* VIII (2), Sept/Oct: 82–4.

Thrift, N. (1996) *Spatial Formations*. London: Sage Publications.

Thrift, N. (2001) '"It's the Romance, not the Finance, that Makes the Business Worth Pursuing": Disclosing a New Market Culture,' *Economy and Society* 30 (4): 412–32.

7
International Political Economy: Beyond the Poststructuralist/ Historical Materialist Dichotomy[1]

J. Magnus Ryner

Unless International Political Economy (IPE) is to merely produce instrumentalist 'problem solving' knowledge but is also to produce critical knowledge, an intellectually honest response to poststructuralism (compatible with enlightenment ideals) would require IPE to take seriously the question of discourse and discursive representation. Hence, any claim that this question amounts to no more than a distraction has to be rejected. However, dramatic claims by poststructuralism, that there are no significant economic 'facts' prior to discourse, are too strong and they can be refuted by the distinction that critical realists make between the intransitive and the transitive. On the basis of the ontological position that this argument implies, this chapter makes the case for a neo-Gramscian critical-theoretical approach to IPE, but one that is methodologically enriched by the profound contribution to semiotic awareness that poststructuralism makes.

The poststructural critique of historical materialism

In the introduction to *The Postmodern Condition* (1984: p. xxiii), Lyotard makes the point that, measured by their own yardsticks, the majority of modern sciences would prove to be fables. To be sure, their methods of observation can be deployed to shed light on empirically grounded and localized regularities. Lyotard does not deny that awareness of such regularities amount to instrumental and (from certain perspectives) useful knowledge. The problem arises when universal truth-claims are made from such observed regularities. Modern science is then '... obliged to legitimate the rules of its own game. It then produces a discourse of legitimation with respect to its own status, a discourse called philosophy.' Lyotard's characterization poses a fundamental challenge to the economism of neoliberalism and neorealism. Lyotard's characterization of science and philosophy as 'fables' is not dissimilar to Marx's (1973) characterization of neoclassical economics as 'Robinsonade.' However, Marxism and critical theory more generally have not been exempt from poststructuralist critiques.

Laclau and Mouffe

The most sustained critical work that has been written against historical materialism from a poststructuralist perspective is arguably *Hegemony and Socialist Strategy* (1985) by the erstwhile Althusserians, Ernesto Laclau and Chantal Mouffe. The first two chapters of this book apply the Derridean method of deconstruction to Marxist theory, to make the case that the social is fundamentally associated with a 'symbolic logic' of 'hegemony.' This, in turn, implies that social analysis must necessarily focus on questions of identity, representation and discourse rather than engage in class reductionism.

In this endeavor they first begin by 'overturning' what they see as the theoretical binary logic of Marxism and as such they trace (invoking Foucault) the 'genealogy' of the concept of hegemony. They show that Marxism, as it confronted the problems of revolutionary practice in the twentieth century, was unable to stick to its model of the 'base' determining 'the superstructure' and as a result it progressively had to assign the politico-ideological – the 'logic of hegemony' – a 'relative autonomy.' Focusing on this 'subordinate' element in the Marxian binary, Laclau and Mouffe show how this led to internal inconsistencies, which progressively led Marxists to yield more and more to the 'void' of the politico-ideological. This process is traced from the 'dilemma of Rosa Luxemburg' through to the 'last redoubt of essentialism – the economy' and the 'Gramscian watershed.' This, according to Laclau and Mouffe, leads us to a poststructuralist and a post-Marxist sensibility of 'radical democracy.' Progressively, then, the second Derridean tactic of 'displacement' is deployed until the theoretical framework is undermined: this progressive undermining through displacement proceeds because there is an 'undecidability' in the binary logic that cannot be pinned down.

The 'Dilemma of Rosa Luxemburg' (in *The Mass Strike, the Political Party and the Trade Unions*) concerns her attempt to understand why a revolution was possible in Russia in 1905 but not in Germany. She found that an essential difference in the two cases were the fact that in Russia any grievance (such as the shortage of bread) became associated with the Czarist regime, whereas in Germany it remained merely a shortage of bread. Hence, the revolutionary logic is that any antagonism 'overflows its own literality' and *metaphorically represents* a moment in a broader, general revolutionary movement. This stands in fundamental contrast to the base-superstructure model, where classes are defined in terms of fixed 'literal' positions in a mode of production (Laclau and Mouffe 1985: 8–19). This contradiction between the literal 'economic logic' and the symbolic 'political logic of hegemony' constitutes a split, in theory and practice, that, according to Laclau and Mouffe, Marxism – through Kautsky, Bernstein, the syndicalists, Lenin, and Gramsci – never resolves. The last 'redoubt of essentialism' in neo-Marxism is the economy itself, now conceived as a relatively autonomous 'region' among others in the social formation (cf. Poulantzas 1978). But the dual split is not 'mended' in these theories either and it cannot be resolved until the logic of the literal completely yields to the logic of the symbolic.

To be sure, with Gramsci, a fundamental transition takes place in Marxist theory (Gramsci 1971). Gramsci argued that social order required 'moral and intellectual leadership,' which in turn required that an ensemble of 'ideas' and 'values' was shared beyond the boundaries of class sectors. (And, for Gramsci, intellectual practice is an integral part also of production since the transformation of nature which in turn 'creates' humans, fundamentally requires intellectual inputs). With Gramsci, then, even class formation had an inescapable ideational dimension, a 'logic of hegemony' ('whose elements..., considered in themselves, do not have any necessary class belonging') (Laclau and Mouffe 1985: 66–71). But, according to Laclau and Mouffe (1985: 69), Gramsci also fails to overcome the dualism as the 'entire construction rests upon an ultimately incoherent conception,' because 'even though the diverse social elements have a merely relational identity – achieved through articulatory practices – there must always be a *single* unifying principle in every hegemonic formation, and this can only be a fundamental class.' Also Gramsci's conception is based then on that last redoubt of essentialism – the economy.

Laclau and Mouffe proceed to displace this last site of the 'literal logic.' They argue that the claim of existence of this literal realm of the economic, conceived as the rational substratum of history, can only be maintained if three specific conditions obtain. Firstly, if its 'laws of motion' are strictly endogenous; secondly, if the unity and homogeneity of the economic social agents result from these very laws of motion; and, thirdly, that these relations of production endow the agents with 'historical interests' so that the presence of such agents at other social levels must ultimately be explained on the basis of these economic interests (Laclau and Mouffe 1985: 76). They then proceed by juxtaposing Harry Braverman's classical study of Taylorist labor processes (*Labour and Monopoly Capital*) with the works of Marglin and Stone, Bowles and Gintis, Burawoy and Edwards to show that these conditions do not obtain. Thus, they conclude that also 'the space of the economy is structured as a political space' where the logic of the symbolic operates (Laclau and Mouffe 1985: 77–85).

Implications for IPE

It is broadly from such a theoretical position that a number of poststructuralist-inspired analyses are starting to emerge in IPE that emphasize the importance of discursive representation and identity. In my view, these are contributing with considerable original insight. They are also works of political importance because they seriously disturb claims that 'there are no alternatives' to the present configuration of the political economy of world order.

One such work is Marieke de Goede's (2001) study of Long-Term Capital Management (LTCM) and deconstruction of financial market modeling. De Goede shows convincingly how the mathematical modeling that current hedge fund investment decisions and arbitrage are based upon originate as a response to moral societal concerns of whether these practices do not amount to more than gambling as they are based on highly uncertain future outcomes. These mathematical models, though they cannot ontologically be seen as anything more than contestable constructions of a 'fair price' of financial instruments, have served a heraldic function for global finance as they are received as the scientific discovery of an absolute truth, underpinned by the authority to the economics profession. As such these models become constitutive ordering devices of financial practices. They also serve as a discourse of legitimization of these practices, even in lieu of the spectacular collapse and Federal Reserve bailout of the LTCM. Also de Goede hints at Derrida's 'overturning' and 'displacement' technique: Greenspan's insistence of the necessity of human maintenance of the financial system through 'scientific finance' is here juxtaposed with the 'fact' that the *episteme* of scientific finance is defined in terms of the discovery of underlying objective truths, which Greenspan's comments seriously put in doubt.

Questions can be raised, however, about whether de Goede's work is best understood as deconstruction, or as negative-dialectical *Ideologi-*

kritik in the Frankfurt School sense. There is, after all, an underlying rhetorical tone in de Goede's piece implying that there is something irrational and morally problematic in finance-as-gambling, and the LTCM practices were unsustainable. This, in turn, seems to imply a conception of rationality/morality and even systems-sustainability against which LTCM practices can be analyzed, which a mere invocation of discursive 'play of difference' cannot and will not provide. I will return to this below.

Other examples of how productive this type of political economy can be are Andrew Barry's (1993) and William Walters' (2000) Foucauldian analyses of the political economy of European integration. Their basic thesis is that the possibility of European (economic) government is not to be taken for granted. Rather, before this, discursive practices are necessary in order to construct that to be governed. Walters shows, for example, how the very construction of statistical categories, accounting procedures and the like was a *necessary precondition* for the formation of the European Coal and Steel Community (ECSC) as without them one could not conceptualize a 'European economy' that was governable. He also points to the importance of contingencies such as the strategy of Jean Monnet in the process of the formation of these categories. Monnet seized the moment to create an *esprit de corps* in the nascent High Authority (therein, Walters argues, lies the real 'Monnet Method'). This is a clear instance where particular *representations* of economic categories become essential to render economic practices effective and possible. In her recent review, de Goede (2003: especially 90–1) argues that this applies to IPE in general and she critiques any conception of an 'economy' existing outside discursive practices of representation, including Gramsci's 'structural moment' of relations of force.

Finally, works on the 'fault-lines' between IPE and development studies have demonstrated that analyses of the representational and discursive can be productive. An example of this is the work of L. H. M. Ling (1997). Drawing on a methodology of deconstruction of pictorial and audible signification in advertisement (pioneered by Barthes) she advances a feminist poststructuralist analysis of the political economy of East Asia. She uses this as a vehicle to problematize the inside/outside dichotomy of much of the work on globalization, which sees globalization as an inherent Western force which subsumes the periphery. Related to this, she challenges the notion of identities being closed, eternal and immutable. Through the advertisement media she demonstrates how East Asian socio-cultural power relations and construction play an active part in its own interpellation into the global political economy, through a gradual transformation of the representation of the male and female ideals. Clearly, however, this is a discourse that maintains female subjectivities in a subordinate position in the form of housewives, support staff workers and sex objects. From this position, Ling points to 'hypermasculism' as an articulating principle of a power bloc that transverses the 'east' and the 'west' in the global political economy.

More broadly, Ling has made a strong case elsewhere that replacing a subsumptionist conception of globalization, and its inside/outside distinction, with a more 'hybridic' conception is necessary if critical theory is to avoid the trap of orientalism, in Said's sense. In other words, a conception of 'the oppressed in the Third World' as victims, and empty exotic 'others,' whose possible standpoints are not reflected upon and represented in their own terms in critical-theoretical practice (Ling 1996).

These are considerable contributions. From a neo-Gramscian perspective, these conceptions of discourse provide us with more powerful and subtle methodological tools through which to understand the conditions for neoliberal hegemony (for a similar position, see Jessop and Sum 2001; also Jessop and Sum this volume). In my own work, I have argued that Foucault's conception of *episteme* is crucial for understanding the manner in which Swedish social democracy was interpellated into a transnational neoliberal hegemonic bloc. I have also argued that the conception of societal representation is crucial for understanding the external/internal dynamics and contradictions of Sweden's interpellation both into this hegemony and that of *Pax Americana* (Ryner 2002). Similarly, following the lead of Haeusler and Hirsch (1989), I have relied on a relational conception of hegemonic discourses to make sense of the contradictory nature of Germany's interpellation into neoliberalism. I would argue that it is only through this relational, contradictory and indeed hybridic conception of hegemony, that we can make sense of the fact that this erstwhile regional hegemonic power rejected its own creation, the Growth and Stability Pact of the EMU (Ryner 2003).

Furthermore, poststructuralist sensitivity to difference and otherness raise issues that critical theorists should simply not ignore if they are to ground the hermeneutics of critique ethically and responsibly (Hay 2002). This being said, I would nevertheless contend that the poststructuralist ontological and epistemological scepticism to critical theory is overstated.

In defence of historical materialism and critical theory

It is clear enough that poststructuralism renders a crude base-superstructure model less than compelling (Hall 1988: 41–4). I will nevertheless argue in this section that this critique is not as devastating for historical materialist critical theory as what might at first glance seem to be the case. I will defend the position that

a) it is still possible and desirable to engage in intellectual endeavor whereby we seek to develop increasingly *rational* conceptual frameworks and analytical models,
b) these frameworks and models can be conceived as rational because they serve a *hermeneutic of emancipation*. That is, the quest to transform the material world (nature in a broad sense) in such a way that it is consistent *inter alia* with a sustainable satisfaction of material needs of humanity as a whole (external socialization) and the self- and mutual recognition of human subjectivities and their aspirations (internal socialization). Such a hermeneutic of emancipation can be seen as served, when through a procedure of 'negative dialectics,' existing conceptual frameworks and analytical models are exposed in terms of *how they are not* serving these purposes.

Such a position faces two fundamental burdens of proof in relation to poststructuralism. It has to be demonstrated that it makes sense to talk about a meaningful 'material world' outside discourse. One also has to make the case that it is possible to envisage a hermeneutic standpoint of emancipation. As we have seen, poststructuralism has raised doubts over the possibility of this procedure on two grounds. First, it is argued that it maintains an untenable dualism between the material and the ideational. Second, the very possibility of emancipatory knowledge on behalf of a privileged 'oppressed subject,' devoid of power, is challenged as a dangerous intellectualist utopia.

My defence will proceed in three stages. First, I will return to Laclau and Mouffe's postulated 'split' between the logic of the literal and the symbolic in Marxism, and demonstrate that this critique, though perhaps valid for orthodox Marxism, ultimately is less than convincing for critical theory more broadly conceived. I will then spell out somewhat more concretely some of the implications of this for IPE by revisiting de Goede's recent critique of neo-Gramscian analysis. Finally, I will address the thorniest question of them all: how do we ground social criticism in a hermeneutic of emancipation? It is here that I think poststructuralism poses the most potent challenge to critical theory.

Laclau and Mouffe (and de Goede) revisited

Laclau and Mouffe's critique implies that an overly *concretist* conception of essential classes as privileged political subjects is untenable. That is, in concrete reality we should not reduce concrete subjects, positively to some fundamental class position as determined by a mode of production.

However, this does not mean that Marxism has not grasped some essential objective realities of capitalist society that *qua* critical theory generates 'coercive illusions,' or one might with Habermas (1984) suggest 'systematically distorted communication.' Whilst these realities hardly are extra discursive, they are not open to a free play of representation, interpretation and social construction either. Rather, they are necessitarian tendencies within the capitalist mode of production, which point to intransitive generative mechanisms that transcend a discursive logic of the symbolic. Central here is Marx's conception of 'commodity fetishism,' which is absolutely fundamental to the account of capital as a social force, with determinant generative mechanisms and emergent causal powers, that he gives in the 3 volumes of *Capital*.

It should be noted that Marx is not at all oblivious to the need to ground his account in relation to semiotics. Indeed, he talks about the exchange value of the commodity form as a *social hieroglyph*. This is a social hieroglyph which renders equivalent, in terms of exchange value, things that blatantly are of different physical quality and use (that is what makes a piece of cloth equal an ounce of precious metal) (Marx 1977: 167). With reference to his own assessment of Hegel, he suggests that commodity fetishism and the suppression of use value in favor of exchange value in the production and distribution of objects, creates an 'enchanted world' turned upside down. This system generates a form of intersubjectivity with a necessitarian logic. This logic is defined in terms of the relation of value-equivalences between commodities, mediated by the universal equivalence of money. The logic in question is experienced as an external constraint by the actors, because they have no choice but to engage in this 'language game.' As such, they become carriers of this necessity. The necessity is imposed on capitalists as they seek to survive by making average profit rates, or on workers as they seek to survive by offering their labor power on the 'free' labor market as 'abstract labour.'

Fundamentally, this necessitarian hieroglyphic form of communicative action applies, then, to the relationship between those who own the means of production through the institution of private property and those who are separated from them. It should be noted that, in this account, the language game becomes a *literal* one in a sutured discourse. In other words, whilst this can be expressed in discursive terms, one has to ask oneself is this the best way to understand matters? There is very little room for Derridean ambiguity and games of identity construction and interpretation in this language game. One problem in this context, pointed to by Anthony Giddens (1979: 45–6), is that when Derrida speaks about semiotics and societal communication being inherently ambiguous due to the logic of the 'trace' or the '*pharmakon*,' he is really referring to *writing* in opposition to *speaking*. It is far from certain that other forms of social *practices* (such as '*doing*'), whilst they can be understood semiotically as discourses, are characterized by the ambiguities and free-floating significations associated with the particular opposite of discursive practices defined by the *writing-speaking* duality.

Now, is Marx's abstract conception *Capital* relevant to contemporary analyses of the IPE? I think, yes. Whilst it is clear that in the concrete any capitalist economy is much more complex and shot through with contingencies than what is captured in *Capital*, capital in general is still one of the constituent determinants, arguably the most central constituent determinant, of the modern (international) political economy. Whilst markets are not characterized by the perfect competition and perfect information that Volume 1 of *Capital* (*via* Smith and Ricardo) seems to assume, this still to a significant degree captures central determinants of value and price formation of commodities in a capitalist market system. In this context capitalists have to acquire adequate profit rates and workers have to offer abstract labor on the labor market, and here *Capital* captures a central necessity pertaining to the relationship between expanded reproduction and the reproduction of labor power (for example, Albritton 1986). Insofar as concrete capitalism departs from this, it is understood in more illuminating ways in terms of *counter-tendencies* to the value form.

De Goede makes much of the fact that accounting techniques decisively constitute economic objects, such as commodities in the concrete and as such they can up to a point discursively construct value. Baudrillard (1981) has already quite a while ago made similar points about consumer demand, with reference to the fashion industry. There are no doubt elements of truth to this, but this inscription and encoding is not done on completely malleable material. In the end, there are limits to the extent to which discursive practices can construct commodities and their relations. This is not the least indicated by the LTCM case itself. After all, the hedge fund collapsed in the wake of Russia's default on loans, and, as pointed out above, de Goede even refers to its discursive practices as a 'failure.'[2]

An alternative account of the concrete situation in question would not deny de Goede's insights about the constructivist dimensions of scientific finance and accounting techniques, but would see them as part and parcel of what David Harvey (1982; 1990: 141–97) has called a *regime of flexible capital accumulation*. This is a regime of advanced capitalism where productive forces in the core are sufficiently highly developed to provide in abundance the materials required to reproduce essential human needs, and to provide humans with protection from natural contingencies. Here, the financial realm has developed tremendous capacities to displace tensions and contradictions as implied in maintaining the formula M-C-M on a social level. Tendencies towards overproduction/underconsumption are here temporally and spatially displaced through credit and investment functions and turnover-time is increased. Ultimately, however, such a system also has its limits of operation. The range of spatio-temporal displacement is not infinitive, and in the end also this form of accumulation is based on a material substratum of use values. Here surplus extraction still depends on the application of after-Fordist production technologies in absolute surplus value augmentation (in production processes employing flexible low wage workers) and relative surplus value augmentation (employing high value-added professional labor).

One could of course retort that production technology also can be configured in different ways, and as such they also are constituted by discursive practices. This is to some extent true. However, technologies are far from completely malleable to discursive practices. Rather, they do entail a fair degree of inertia and 'resistance' which in turn shapes the range of (possible) discursive practices. This is something that, for example, research into the deployment of cybernetics and communication technology has demonstrated (for example, Leborgne and Lipietz 1988).

Similarly, there seems to be an extradiscursive ecological subsystem at work, which is significant, for example, to an explanation of the unintended consequences and effects of imperialist strategies aimed at integrating sub-Saharan Sahel into the capitalist world market in the nineteenth century. Here the previous balance of a fragile ecosystem with agricultural production based on a sophisticated system of crop rotation and long-distance trade between farmers and nomads was replaced with monocultural peanut growing by the French colonial power. The implications were devastating in terms of desertification and attendant famines and destitution affecting the peasants and subsistence farmers of the area (Moore-Lappe and Collins 1982). The point is not to deny that human practices helped shape the ecology – they clearly did and that is what makes the case so striking – however, the ecological feedback effects – with profound politico-economic implication – in the form of desertification clearly indicate that something more than Lacanian semiosis was at work.

No doubt also such events *are only assigned social meaning* through discursive practices of socio-cultural representation, but this standard poststructuralist response misses the point. One needs to be careful not to conflate the real with the *empirical* here. Whilst it may be that any empirical politico-economic phenomenon has a discursive representational dimension, it does not mean that it captures the totality of the *real*. It rather seems to point to the importance of the distinction of the transitive and the intransitive as coconstitutive of the social (Archer *et al.* 1998).

I am not suggesting here that the account that Marx gives in *Capital* can be straightforwardly used in concrete analysis. The abstract capital relation is only one constituent determinant of many in concrete political economies. A more subtle and sophisticated historical materialism would hold that socio-economic order is shaped by the *longue duree* of a complex dialectic of commodification and societalization (*Vergesellschaftung*) imperatives, which draws on historically specific phases, defined by paradigmatic production and social technologies. Transitive, and contingent social practices and strategies, where the discursive and representational is central, play an important role here. But also intransitive aspects, which include the tendential impacts of the law of value, the abstract formal separation of the market and state in capitalism as well as intransitive dimensions of technology, play a crucial autonomous role (for example, Lipietz 1985; Albritton 1986; Jessop 1990a; 1990b; van der Pijl 1998). Such a conception of capitalism as an ontologically multilayered and 'deep' phenomenon implies that poststructuralist insights need to be subsumed within a *method of abstraction*. Abstraction in this context implies that a lot of things are going on at the same time in social situations. Abstraction is the practice of separating out these phenomena in order to identify the character of each constituent process and effect (accepting that they cannot be isolated experimentally) and to ascertain how they connect up to produce the societal situation in question (Sayer 1992). In Marx's famous formulation in the introduction to the *Grundrisse*, this is the movement from a 'chaotic conception' to an 'in thought concrete' conception. Subsuming de Goede's analysis into that of Harvey would be exactly for the purpose of giving it such ontological depth.

The thorny question of the hermeneutic of emancipation

What has been said so far cannot be sufficient, however, any more for critical theory than for poststructuralism. This is because contemporary critical theory also, like poststructuralism, accepts that there is no straightforward, and one-to-one, correspondence between patterns of determination and the social meaning that these patterns express. The meaning of patterns always has to be interpreted. Hence, there is an inevitable hermeneutic dimension to the social sciences (Taylor 1985). Whatever might be said about the reality of the intransitive by way of criticism of poststructuralism, then, critical theory still is liable to defend that it is possible to fix a point of reference of interpretation that can be plausibly related to emancipation. It is in relation to this question that poststructuralism poses the most difficult and important challenge to critical theory.

The reason for this should be clear. If identity formation is understood through the Lacan/Saussure/Derrida formula, it is so decentered that it questions the possibility of a fixed point of reference required to make the criticism meaningful for any particular subject (see Zalewski this volume, for an engagement with this critique). Whatever has been said above about commodity fetishism, the transitive, and attendant structuration effects, in the concrete, so many contingencies intervene that it may very well be, as Laclau and Mouffe (1985: 84–5) suggest, 'that there is no logical relationship whatsoever between position in the social relations of production and the mentality of the producers,' let alone the political stances that political subjects should take.

We can start to confront this question of a lack of vantage point of critique with a sarcastic, and characteristically quotable, remark by Terry Eagleton (1991: 215): 'This means presumably, that it is wholly coincidental that all capitalists are not also revolutionary socialists.' Approaching matters from the intuitive sense that there is something resonant in Eagleton's sarcasm and something suspect in Laclau and Mouffe's claim, Pierre Bourdieu's (1977) conception of *habitus* has a certain appeal. It allows us to scrutinize critically and in more detail the central ontological claims of poststructuralism, based as they are on their reading of the unconscious *via* Lacan. The upshot of Bourdieu's theory is that whilst the conscious cannot be reduced to material position, neither is it purely coincidental. Rather, there are transposable and durable *dispositions* of *habitus*.

The term *habitus* suggests that intransitive necessities operate as distinct determinants, which significantly shape the structured conditions in which cultural and overtly political processes take place. Contrary to a Derridean reading of Lacan, Bourdieu suggests that the former structure the 'unconscious principle of the ethos,' 'the commonplace' and the 'conventional and conditional stimulations' which are the very things that make communication between individual agents *possible*. He speaks of a 'homogeneity of habitus,' which is the very thing that makes one agent's practices and discourse 'sensible,' 'reasonable,' 'intelligible,' 'foreseeable' and 'taken for granted' by another agent. This homogeneity results from 'common conditions of material existence...which enables practices to be objectively harmonized without any intentional calculation or conscious reference to a norm' (Bourdieu 1977: 79–80; for a similar argument, but which rather draws on Luhmann's systems theory, see Jessop 2004).

The notable disagreement here is not so much with Lacan. Indeed, there is nothing that says that Bourdieu's commonplace habitus cannot be understood in semiotic terms. But contrary to Derrida, he maintains that the very possibility of social practices require some sense of a prestructured shared homogeneity which 'spontaneously' generates resonance and understanding. Whilst no doubt contingency and change has to be acknowledged both as a possibility and reality, at least in longer time-scales, the scope of contingency is limited by the dispositions defined by historically and materially produced homogeneities of habitus. Whereas it may be that semiotics can be understood as a sort of master-logic of social ontology, the *specific* practices of writing and speaking cannot, and broad practices associated with *habitus*, including *doing* are far less free floating than what the practice of writing/speaking implies.

The 'homogenizing conditions' should not be understood exclusively as 'economic corporate.' Indeed, Bourdieu operated with a much broader and 'cultural' conception of the 'commonplace' and praxis including Hegel's struggle for recognition. Hence, it is possible to talk about the *habitus* of a nation (for example, Elias 1996). Nevertheless, Bourdieu (1977: 80) assigns particular importance to *class/group habitus* because of the role social relations of (re-)production play as a determinant of 'homongeneities of existence.'

> [T]he objective homogenising of group or class habitus, which results from the homogeneity of conditions of existence, is what enables practices to be objectively harmonised without any intentional calculation…

Similarly, he talks about the 'social distance' between different classes separated by these social relations (Bourdieu 1977: 82). This does not mean that *habitus* cannot transcend social divisions. They clearly do in a national *habitus*. But different social groups need to be interpellated to this 'national unconsciousness' *in different ways*. Hence, whilst the 'economic corporate' does not exhaust the dynamics associated with *habitus*, following the method of abstraction, it is crucial to isolate and identify the homogenizing effects of the economic corporate as one of the constituent forces relevant, for example, to a critical understanding of the IPE.

According to Bourdieu one of the 'fundamental effects' of this 'orchestration of habitus' is the production of a 'common sense world.' 'Common sense,' of course, is crucial to Gramsci and in my view Bourdieu vindicates Gramsci from the critique poststructuralists have launched in his direction, as it asserts the importance of the 'economic corporate moment' without implying that society and history should be reduced to it. In this conception, there is dialectic of common sense, where the habitual/unconscious always tendentially threaten to undermine hegemonic articulations of common sense. It is in the field of these tensions that critical theory must operate in a struggle of representation, with the aim to become 'organic' (Simon 1982: 58–66).

Matt Davies and I have recently edited a volume that seeks to spell out some of the implications of the term *habitus* for a critical political economy of world order (Davies and Ryner 2006). Rather than pointing towards a move *away* from Gramsci's 'economic corporate moment' as poststructuralists suggest, it points towards the importance of retaining the concept. Most notably (and in disagreement with Jessop and Sum 2001), it points towards the importance of reconsidering much more seriously the concept of modes of social relations of production and their distinct rationalities as outlined in the neglected Part I of Robert Cox's *Production, Power and World Order* (1987) and the twin volumes of Jeffrey Harrod (1987). Insofar as the economic corporate moment and dispositions matter as *a* determinant, I would argue that it is dangerous and outright irresponsible to merely postulate a pure contingency between socio-economic position and the consciousness of political subjects as it distracts attention away from what should be done to change the socio-economic order.

Conclusion

What does this imply for social criticism beyond the fact that there might some kind of foundation of the real to ground it? Clearly, it is dangerous to go down the route of identifying a transcendent 'revolutionary subject' of world history, *qua* Hegelian-Marxism, and if nothing else, poststructuralism sensitizes us to the dangers.

An alternative would be to attempt to ground social criticism in a 'discourse ethics' as Habermas argues. This could provide a vantage point from which one could analyze the systematically distorted forms of communication in the global political economy (of which the LTCM would be a case in point). This is based on the idea that the very usage of language presupposes at least the possibility of rational persuasion, which Habermas seeks to grasp with his 'ideal speech situation.' Dynamics in IPE is thus to be understood with reference to this counter-factual in terms of 'systematically distorted communication' (hence in a negative-dialectical way in terms of what it is not).

It is of course possible to raise the Foucauldian objection to this, that there is no pattern of such Enlightenment thought, that has not at the same time been part of a disciplinary power technology. Hence, any claim of universality in this context constitutes an abstraction of violence (Foucault 1994a; 1994b). One possible way out of this would be to follow feminist explorations of Hannah Arendt's reading of Aristotle and ask if it is possible to separate out violence from power, and ascertain the potentials in a definition of power as 'action in concert,' 'actualisation' and 'action in public life' (Hartsock 1996: 32–3). We may then be in a position to understand social criticism in the global political economy as the identification of the 'systematic distortions' that are preventing subordinate subjects, in different cultures and civilizations, from realizing this actualization in mutual recognition and coexistence. (Hence, this also implies the identification of some sort of sense of mutual self-limitation). Here, Habermas' ideal speech community may still play a role, not as a universal truth but as the progressive Sorelian myth of an 'integral world order' in a Gramscian sense. As Hartsock (1996: 43) points out, this implies the extremely difficult task of intellectual representation working with Gramsci's dialectic between habituated common sense and philosophy.

> We need a theory of power that recognizes that our practical daily activity contains an understanding of the world – subjugated perhaps but present. Here I am reaffirming Gramsci's argument that everyone is an intellectual and that each of us has an epistemology.

This requires a careful analysis of the relations of force from the economic corporate and habitus to the ethico-political and back.

It is important, however, to be cautious here as well. This must not imply some utopian-Communist and romantic notion of 'transparent representation of everyday life.' As Habermas (1991) has pointed out, such conception of total consciousness is grounded in preindustrial romanticism that understates the importance of 'systems logics' defined by media such as law, money and administration. Such media, he argues, have proven to be essential to ensure the economies that have allowed at least societies of late modernity to develop the potentials of productive forces which are essential both to affluence and the sense that we have a contingent relation to absolute material constraints. Here we need to accept that social differentiation and social division of labor requires some degree of 'systems-world steering.' The challenge is to develop 'reflexive knowledge' which allows us to contain the logic of the systems-world in a way that ensures that the cultural capacities are generated to make mutual actualization, recognition and self-limitation at least a possibility.

Notes

1 I would like to thank my students in the *Advanced Political Analysis* seminar at the University of Birmingham for the inspiration that helped me write this chapter. It is dedicated to one of them: the late Joshua Beeby.

2 For a similar critique of Baudrillard, see Albritton (1992).

References

Albritton, R. (1986) *A Japanese Reconstruction of Marxist Theory*. London: Macmillan.

Albritton, R. (1992) 'Theorizing the Realm of Consumption in Marxian Political Economy: An Unoist Approach,' Unpublished Manuscript, Department of Political Science, York University, Toronto, Canada.

Archer, M., Bhaskar, R., Collier, A., Lawson, T. and Norrie, A. (eds) (1998) *Critical Realism: Essential Readings*. London: Routledge.

Barry, A. (1993) 'The European Community and European Government: Harmonization, Mobility and Space,' *Economy and Society* 22 (3): 314–26.

Baudrillard, J. (1981) *For a Critique of the Political Economy of the Sign*. St. Louis: Telos Press.
Braverman, H. (1974) *Labor and Monopoly Capital*. New York: Monthly Review Press.
Bourdieu, P. (1977) *Outline of a Theory of Practice*. Cambridge: Cambridge University Press.
Cox, R. W. (1987) *Production, Power and World Order*. New York: Columbia University Press.
Davies, M. and Ryner, M. (eds) (2006) *Poverty and the Production of World Politics: Unprotected Workers in the Global Political Economy*. Basingstoke: Palgrave Macmillan.
de Goede, M. (2001) 'Discourses of Scientific Finance and the Failure of Long-Term Capital Management,' *New Political Economy* 6 (2): 149–70.
de Goede, M. (2003) 'Beyond Economism in IPE,' *Review of International Studies* 29 (1): 79–97.
Eagleton, T. (1991) *Ideology: An Introduction*. London: Verso.
Elias, N. (1996) *The Germans*. New York: Columbia University Press.
Foucault, M. (1976 [1994a]) 'Two Lectures,' in Kelly, M. (ed.) *Power and Critique*. Cambridge, Mass.: The MIT Press.
Foucault, M. (1988 [1994b]) 'The Art of Telling the Truth,' in Kelly, M. (ed.) *Power and Critique*. Cambridge, Mass.: The MIT Press.
Giddens, A. (1979) *Central Problems in Social Theory*. London: Macmillan.
Gramsci, A. (1971) *Selections from the Prison Notebooks*. New York: International Publishers.
Habermas, J. (1984) *The Theory of Communicative Action* Vol. 1. Cambridge: Polity.
Habermas, J. (1991) 'What Does Socialism Mean Today? The Rectifying Revolution and the Need for New Thinking on the Left,' *New Left Review* 183: 3–21.
Haeusler, J. and Hirsch, J. (1989) 'Political Regulation: The Crisis of Fordism and the Transformation of the Party System in West Germany,' in Gottdiener, M. and Komninos, N. (eds) *Capitalist Development and Crisis Theory*. New York: St. Martin's Press.
Hall, S. (1988) '"The Toad in the Garden": Thatcherism among the Theorists,' in Nelson, C. and Grossberg, L. (eds) *Marxism and the Interpretation of Culture*. Urbana Ill.: University of Illinois Press.
Harrod, J. (1987) *Power, Production and the Unprotected Worker*. New York: Columbia University Press.
Hartsock, N. C. M. (1996) 'Community/Sexuality/Gender,' in Hirschmann, N. and de Stefano, C. (eds) *Revisioning the Political: Feminist Reconstructions on Traditional Concepts in Western Political Thought*. Boulder Colo.: Westview Press.
Harvey, D. (1982 [1999]) *The Limits to Capital*. London: Verso.
Harvey, D. (1990) *The Condition of Postmodernity*. Oxford: Blackwell.
Hay, C. (2002) *Political Analysis: A Critical Introduction*. London: Palgrave.
Jessop, B. (1990a) 'Regulation Theory in Retrospect and Prospect,' *Economy & Society* 19 (2): 153–212.
Jessop, B. (1990b) *State Theory: Putting Capitalist States in their Place*. Cambridge: Polity Press.

Jessop, B. (2004) 'Critical Semiotic Analysis and Cultural Political Economy,' *Critical Discourse Studies* 1 (1): 1–16.
Jessop, B. and Sum, N.-L. (2001) 'Pre-Disciplinary and Post-Disciplinary Perspectives,' *New Political Economy* 6 (1): 89–101.
Laclau, E. and Mouffe, C. (1985) *Hegemony and Socialist Strategy*. London: Verso.
Leborgne, D. and Lipietz, A. (1988) 'New Technologies, New Modes of Regulation: Some Spatial Implications,' *Environment and Planning D* 6 (3): 263–86.
Ling, L. H. M. (1996) 'Hegemony and the Internationalizing State: A Post-Colonial Critique,' *Review of International Political Economy* 3 (1): 1–26.
Ling, L. H. M. (1997) 'The Other Side of Globalization: Hypermasculine Developmentalism in East Asia,' Paper presented at the ISA Special Workshop 'The Political Economy of Regionalisms,' Research Centre of International Political Economy, University of Amsterdam, December.
Lipitetz, A. (1985) *Mirages and Miracles*. London: Verso.
Luxemburg, R. (1970) *The Mass Strike: the Political Party and the Trade Unions*. London.
Lyotard, J.-F. (1984) *The Postmodern Condition: A Report on Knowledge*. Manchester: Manchester University Press.
Marx, K. (1973) 'Introduction,' *The Grundrisse*. New York: Vintage Books.
Marx, K. (1977) *Capital* Vol. 1. New York: Vintage Books.
Moore-Lappe, F. and Collins, J. (1982) *Food First: The Myth of Scarcity*. London: Abacus.
Poulantzas, N. (1978) *Political Power & Social Classes*. London: Verso.
Ryner, M. (2002) *Capitalist Restructuring, Globalization and the Third Way: Lessons from the Swedish Model*, London: Routledge.
Ryner, M. (2003) 'Disciplinary Neo-Liberalism, Regionalization and the Social Market in German Restructuring,' in Cafruny, A. and Ryner, M. (eds) *A Ruined Fortress? Neoliberal Hegemony and Transformation in Europe*. Lanham Md: Rowman and Littlefield.
Sayer, A. (1992) *Method in the Social Sciences: A Realist Approach*, second edn. London: Routledge.
Simon, R. (1982) *Gramsci's Political Thought*. London: Lawrence and Wishart.
Taylor, C. (1985) 'Interpretation and the Sciences of Man,' *Philosophy and the Human Sciences: Philosophical Papers 2*. Cambridge: Cambridge University Press.
van der Pijl, K. (1998) *Transnational Classes and International Relations*. London: Routledge.
Walters, W. (2000) 'Governing the "Common Market": Towards a Genealogy of European Government,' Paper presented at the Annual Meeting of the International Studies Association, Los Angeles, March.

8

Towards a Cultural International Political Economy: Poststructuralism and the Italian School

Bob Jessop and Ngai-Ling Sum

This chapter seeks to overcome the one-sided emphasis on materiality at the expense of discursivity that plagues much work in critical international political economy (IPE). It does so by introducing the concept of cultural political economy (hereafter CPE) in an effort to avoid both the tendency towards soft economic and/or political sociology, in which the material specificity of economic and political categories is dissolved into a generic concern with the social or cultural, and the tendency towards hard political economy, in which economic and political categories are reified and their social construction and contingency are ignored (cf. Sayer 1998). Insofar as it emerged in part through critical engagement with structuralism, our approach can certainly be described as poststructuralist. However, because it is inspired by classical political economy and Gramsci's work on hegemony, it could also be described as prestructuralist. Thus, while we affirm the importance of neo-Gramscian contributions to IPE, we also criticize them for failing to exploit fully Gramsci's account of the coconstitution and coevolution of the material and the discursive. We also argue that this is best achieved through a combination of critical semiotic analysis and the critique of political economy in an approach that insists that both time and institutions matter to the overall dynamic of hegemonic struggles. This new approach has already been applied to 'the economy in its inclusive sense' – *l'economia integrale* (Jessop 1990, 2002, 2004) – and can be fruitfully extended to 'the capitalist world order in its inclusive sense' (Sum 2004) through an analysis of the relations between the production of hegemony and the hegemony of production.

An adequate exploration of 'the capitalist world order in its inclusive sense'[1] would identify the many social practices and emergent mechanisms that govern the interaction of (a) the structural dynamic of accumulation on a world scale and (b) the global hegemony of capital as a principle of social organization on a world scale. This means looking at the production of accumulation strategies, governance projects, and hegemonic visions as well as processes that operate 'behind the backs of the producers' and that shape other institutional orders and global civil society. In addition, we must recognize that these practices and mechanisms operate on different spatial and scalar horizons so that an adequate account of the world order in its integral sense must also be sensitive to issues of space, place and scale and, in particular, the question of how global hegemony is grounded in, and instantiated at, different sites and scales, each with its own specificities. In exploring these themes we seek to move beyond economism and idealism to provide a coherent set of concepts and mechanisms to study new forms of (dis)integration in the global political economy. We first address the 'cultural turn' in political economy and then discuss its application to IPE.

Cultural political economy (CPE)

CPE emerges from taking the 'cultural turn'[2] in political economy and thereby modifying both critical semiotic analysis and political economy. On the one hand, in contrast to most applications of critical discourse analysis, we explore the role of the three generic evolutionary mechanisms – variation, selection, and retention (Campbell 1969) – in shaping struggles for hegemony. On the other hand, in adopting the cultural turn, we highlight the role of the production of intersubjective meaning as a crucial moment in institutional evolution and in shaping economic and political crisis-tendencies and responses.[3] This general approach can be restated in terms of three broad claims about the role of discourse in the radical critique of political economy (cf. Jessop 2004; Sum and Jessop forthcoming).

First, ontologically, discourse contributes to the overall constitution of specific social objects and social subjects and, *a fortiori*, to their coconstitution and coevolution in wider ensembles of social relations. Orthodox political economy tends to naturalize or reify its theoretical objects (such as land, machines, the division of labor, production, money, commodities, the information economy) and to offer impoverished accounts of how subjects and subjectivities are formed and how different modes of calculation emerge, are institutionalized, meet resistance, and are transformed or overturned. In contrast, CPE views technical and economic objects as socially constructed, historically specific, more or less socially embedded in – or disembedded from – broader networks of social relations and institutional ensembles, more or less embodied and 'embrained' in individual actors, and in need of continuing social 'repair' work for their reproduction. The same holds for the objects of orthodox political science and (neo-)realist international relations (IR) theory. These tend to treat the state as an ensemble of governmental institutions with specific capacities and resources deployable by state managers and other political forces in pursuit of interests that are objectively grounded in their respective social positions or in a naturalized, (neo-)realist logic of state action. In contrast, our CPE approach follows Marx, Gramsci, and Poulantzas (among others) in examining the state in its inclusive sense ('political society and civil society') as a social relation. This regards state power as the institutionally-mediated condensation of a changing balance of forces and examines struggles to constitute the state apparatus in its inclusive sense as well as the identities and subjectivities of the forces engaged in political struggle. Moreover, in revealing the socially constructed nature of the phenomena of political economy, CPE involves a form of political intervention that goes beyond *Ideologiekritik* (which serves at best to uncover the ideal and material interests behind specific meaning systems and ideologies) and explores the mechanisms involved in selecting and institutionalizing the dominance and/or hegemony of these systems and ideologies over others (see below).

Second, epistemologically, CPE critiques the categories and methods of orthodox political economy and (neo-)realist IR theories and stresses the contextuality and historicity of all claims to knowledge. It rejects any universalistic, positivist account of reality, denies the facticity of the subject-object duality, allows for the coconstitution of subjects and objects, and eschews economic reductionism. In this sense, CPE is a form of political intervention into the field of knowledge production. For, in stressing the materiality of social relations and their emergent properties, it escapes both the sociological imperialism of pure social constructionism and the voluntarist vacuity of certain lines of discourse analysis, which suggest that agents can will anything into being in and through an appropriately articulated discourse (Laclau and Mouffe 1985). In short, CPE recognizes both the constitutive role of discourse and the emergent extra-discursive features of social relations and their conjoint impact on capacities for action and transformation.

Third, methodologically, CPE combines concepts and tools from critical discourse analysis with those from critical political economy. The 'cultural turn' includes a wide range of approaches but we use discourse to cover them all. For they all assume that discourse is causally efficacious as well as meaningful and that not only can actual events and processes and their emergent effects be *interpreted* but also, at least in part, *explained* in terms of discourse. Thus CPE examines the role of discursive practices not only in the continual (re-)making of social relations but also in the contingent emergence, provisional consolidation, and ongoing realization of their extra-discursive properties. However, if they are to prove more than 'arbitrary, rationalistic, and willed' (Gramsci 1971: 376–7), specific economic and political imaginaries and their associated discursive practices must have some significant, albeit necessarily partial, correspondence to real material interdependencies in the actually existing economic and political fields and their articulation with the wider ensemble of social relations. It is the interaction between the discursive and extra-discursive that gives relatively successful economic and political imaginaries their performative, constitutive force in the material world (see below).

A closer look at the Italian School

Having presented the basic features of CPE, we now address some specific issues for the development of a cultural international political economy that is consistent with general trends in poststructuralism. We begin with a sympathetic critique of the so-called Italian School pioneered by neo-Gramscian IPE theorists such as Cox (1987), Gill (1991), Rupert (1995), and Robinson (1996). These theorists do not belong to a unitary school with a common set of concepts but they do share a broad research program. This builds on three features that they identify, rightly or wrongly, in Gramsci's anti-economistic philosophy of praxis: (a) the grounding of class hegemony in political, intellectual, and moral leadership, albeit with a decisive economic nucleus, with the role of coercion confined to a last resort; (b) his interpretation of power blocs as long term strategic alliances of economic and political forces; and (c) his analysis of the relation between economic base and ethico-political superstructure in terms of a relatively stable, mutually constituting historical bloc.[4] In order to move from national to international political economy, the Italian School rescales these concepts from national states and class configurations to the field of international relations. Thus it gives a subordinate position to most national states *qua* institutional ensembles while paying increasing attention to international as well as national forces and to the internationalization of the state (compare Cox 1981 with Gill 1995 and Cox 1987). Thus the emphasis falls on the increasing scope for a transnational class to emerge and for one (or, at most, a few) national states to be dominant or hegemonic in regional or world orders, mediated through the internationalization of state apparatuses on different scales. It views 'production' and 'social forces' in terms of 'states' and inter-state relations in a 'world order' dominated by the expanding logic of capitalism and relates the formation of power blocs and historical blocs in late capitalism to the development of a transnational bourgeoisie. Although this approach is often insightful, its pioneers remain wedded to a rather traditional, state-centric view of class hegemony and domination and fail to develop the full implications of Gramsci's concern with civil society and its role in constituting power and hegemony. Moreover, in contrast to Gramsci, who saw discourse at work in the technological and economic fields as well as in struggles over political and ideological domination, it has a rather structuralist reading of the production orders.

We can demonstrate what is at stake here by distinguishing the 'hegemony of production' and the 'production of hegemony.' The former refers to the relative dominance of a given production and/or financial order (for example, Fordism) in structuring a social formation and to the structural mechanisms that secure its relative dominance in a historical bloc. Conversely, the 'production of hegemony' involves the processes and mechanisms through which 'political, intellectual, and moral leadership' is secured in and across the organizations and institutions of civil society and is successfully articulated with a specific economic configuration and state system. The Italian School tends to focus on the 'hegemony of production' and the formation of structured coherence between the economy, the state, and ideological domination rather than on the specific discursive and extra-discursive mechanisms involved in producing hegemony throughout a social formation. As such, despite its support for Gramsci's anti-economism and its emphasis on transnational historical blocs, early Italian School work had a residual 'economism' because it neglected the specific discursive processes and mechanisms involved in securing the dominance of a given economic order and historical bloc (Jessop and Sum 2001; de Goede 2003). This stands in marked contrast to Gramsci's own concerns with the always-already ideological character of economic practices and agents – witness his classic analysis of how hegemony in American Fordism was deeply rooted in the factory, the labor market, and the reordering of domestic life as well as in a broader array of social practices and institutions (Gramsci 1971).

Preliminary attempts to escape these limitations appear in second-generation neo-Gramscian work such as Gill on 'disciplinary neoliberalism' (1995), Rupert on common sense and resistance (1997; 2003), Davies on 'transnational hegemony' (1999), Egan on the movement against the Multilateral Agreement on Investment (2001), Steger on 'globalism' (2002), Amoore on 'flexible labour' (2002), and Cox on 'civilization and intersubjective meanings' (2002). Nonetheless we believe that this second-generation work can be further improved by integrating it with a neo-Gramscian analysis of the 'production of hegemony' in the world economic order. This helps us examine more directly the articulation among ideas, cultural hegemony and civil society and to examine corresponding forms of domination and resistance.

We refer to 'integral world capitalist order' by analogy with Gramsci's idea of the 'state in its inclusive sense' or the 'integral state' (political society and civil society) (1971) and Jessop's account of the 'economy in its inclusive sense' or '*l'economia integrale*' (accumulation regime and mode of regulation) (1990). Thus it can be understood as a world economic governance system formed through 'hegemony of production and production of hegemony in (trans-)national civil society.' As such it is characterized by a relative structured coherence based on the mutually supportive intermeshing of the 'hegemony of production' and the 'production of hegemony' so that they displace and defer capitalist contradictions and secure a limited measure of social integration. This can never be completely achieved at the level of the world market and world society because continuing capital accumulation always depends on the continuing displacement and deferral of contradictions into zones marked by instability and crisis that coexist with zones of relative coherence (cf. Jessop 2002). But we can certainly distinguish between periods when there is relative integration at the level of the world market and world society and periods when there is fragmentation and conflict.

The interdependence between hegemony of production and production of hegemony is vital to understanding the particular form, content and processes of the hegemony and resistance that typifies a specific historical epoch. Thus one should study closely the political, economic, and cultural relations between the discourses and practices of the 'production order' and those of groups and institutions of civil society. To show how this approach can be developed, we will briefly review how neo-Gramscians and neo-Foucauldians have undertaken the 'cultural' turn. This is useful because Gramsci is a prestructuralist and Foucault a poststructuralist thinker and their respective approaches therefore have different implications for (international) political economy.

The cultural turn in IPE: synthesizing Gramsci and Foucault

Gramsci and Foucault argue in their different ways that power operates 'within the systems and subsystems of social relations, in the interactions, in the microstructures that inform the practices of everyday life' (Holub 1992: 200). Both seek to move away from a strongly institutionalist, juridico-political, and state-centric account of power and its exercise without neglecting the role of institutions and apparatuses. Each is concerned, more or less explicitly, with discourse and discursive formations, with the articulation of power and knowledge, with hegemony and common sense, and with consent and coercion. And they also discuss the embedding and embodying of power in everyday routines. It is hardly surprising, then, that scholars have recently tried to enhance the contribution of Gramsci's concepts to IPE by incorporating Foucault's work, especially its concern with discursive practices, disciplinary normalization, and the role of governmentality. But this has not always been carried through coherently and consistently. For example, while Gill (1995) refers to 'disciplinary neo-liberalism', he neglects the 'micro-technologies of power' that promote and underpin the neoliberal project by normalizing certain objects/subjects of governance. And, although de Goede (2003) refers to the disciplinary and performative aspects of finance, she did not relate micropower back to the macrohegemony of consent/coercion. We believe that it is fruitful to combine the insights of Gramsci and Foucault, especially in terms of exploring technologies of power; but we also urge caution in doing so because of the important differences that exist between their respective meta-theoretical assumptions and overall approaches.

For Foucault, power is immanent and relational – it has no ultimate ground beyond specific technologies of power and their articulation to knowledge. This approach encourages researchers to open the 'black box' of hegemony and domination to explore specific technologies of power (cf. Dean 1999). Foucault analyzed these in different ways at different stages in his work and his later studies on biopower and governmentality are especially illuminating on the disciplinary force of specific normalizing processes and institutions at both the micro- and macro-levels (see Larner this volume). But Foucault's commitment to the 'death of the subject' means that the technologies of power have theoretical priority over their agential supports as well as over the subjects (or individual bodies and populations) who are formed and disciplined by them. Subjects rarely appear as agents, let alone as centered agents. Indeed, even though Foucault claims that, wherever there is power, there is resistance, he grounds this in a generic 'plebeian instinct' of resistance rather than in specific material positions, identities, or interests. In this sense, Foucault tends to focus either on the surface manifestations of power relations or their underlying technologies; he lacks a clear account of the actual effectivity of discourses or disciplines in specific situations. Thus, while his later lectures do note how the exercise of power in different sites may be strategically codified through the state and how capitalist relations privilege some disciplinary techniques over others, Foucault still focuses on the microdynamics of power in everyday life. Accordingly, as Marsden (1999: 149) has noted, Foucault can tell us something about the *how* of power but far less about the *why* of power and its role in reproducing particular forms of social domination (for a contrasting view, see introduction).

Whereas Foucault is more interested in 'diagrams' and technologies of power that can be applied across different social fields, Gramsci grounds the exercise of power in specific material apparatuses (political and ideological as well as economic) and specific social practices. His theory of hegemony is concerned both with particular modalities and apparatuses of power and with particular subjects with particular social identities and material interests. He rejects any transhistorical account of power and focuses on power in modern capitalist social formations where mass politics have developed. Moreover, whereas Foucault rarely concedes that there is an overall structural coherence to social formations apart from the general adoption of specific technologies of power, Gramsci asks how an inherently unstable and conflictual social formation acquires a certain degree of social order through the continuing achievement of unstable equilibria of compromise. This is why he puts so much emphasis on hegemony, power blocs, and historical blocs but also recognizes the role of force, fraud, and corruption in securing social order. Far from subscribing to the automatism of a mechanical base-superstructure relation, Gramsci adopts a more fluid and interactive understanding of the reciprocal relations among the economic, political, ideological and cultural spheres.

Given these differences, we should not attempt to combine Foucault to Gramsci as if their respective approaches were wholly commensurable and complementary. This does not preclude some form of synthesis. Indeed several attempts have already been made to combine Foucault and Gramsci – either to 'foucauldize Gramsci' or to 'gramscianize Foucault'[5] (see Figure 8.1). At the expense of ignoring other scholarly influences and mediations in the work of the following theorists, we can locate certain contributions of Stuart Hall along with the post-Marxist work of Laclau and Mouffe in the first group; and Fairclough, Jessop and de Certeau in the second. Those who attempt to foucauldize Gramsci aim to further reduce the risk of reductionism in Gramsci's Marxist philosophy of praxis by emphasizing the plurality and heterogeneity of identities and social forces and the inherent unfixity of micro- and macrosocial relations (for example, Hall 1981, 1982; Laclau and Mouffe 1985). Thus Foucault's work is invoked to emphasize the immanence of power in opposition to its economic determination in the last instance, to highlight the variety of mechanisms that produce and discipline subjects, and to insist on the inevitable plurality and contingency of identities and interests. However, while this creates the space for recognizing the diversity of identities at play in modern societies and to avoid class reductionism, it risks losing sight of materiality so that hegemony becomes little more than 'discursive idealism' or 'discursive totality' (cf. the critiques in Chouliaraki and Fairclough 1999: 117; and Brenans 1999: 19). It also misses the later Foucault's interest in the mechanisms and struggles involved in the strategic codification of power relations and the development of governmental rationalities that provide the basis for emergent and provisional macrosocial order. In short, 'foucauldizing' Gramsci leads to a conflationary form of theorizing that dissolves the distinction between the ideational and the material (McAnulla 1998: 8).

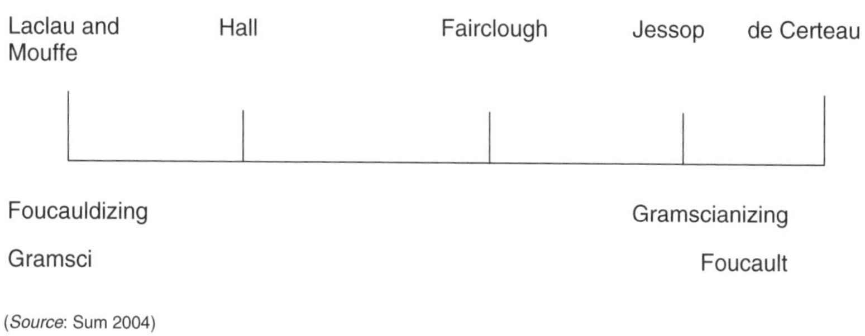

Figure 8.1 From Foucauldizing Gramsci to Gramscianizing Foucault
Source: Sum 2004

To escape this conflationary solution to the ideational versus structuralist trap, we follow those who, in order to produce a better understanding of the dialectic of materiality and discursivity, have tried to 'gramscianize Foucault.' Their approach stresses the contradictory and conflictual dynamic of capitalist social formations based on the reciprocal interweaving and interaction of the material and discursive. It takes seriously the ways in which dominance and social power are enacted in and through discourse but also recognizes that there are emergent structural properties to power relations that constrain the field of discursive practices and struggles. In this sense, then, it explores the mutually constraining, mutually transforming, mutually constitutive dialectic of discourse and social structuration at all scales from the microsocial to the emergent dynamics of a world order in the process of formation.

Jessop's strategic-relational approach (hereafter SRA), at least in its early stages (1982, 1990), is more material-discursive than discursive-material insofar as it highlights the ways in which structures may privilege some actors, some discourses, some identities, and some strategies over others (cf. Fairclough 1995: 6; Chouliaraki and Fairclough 1999: 24–6, 68). But the SRA also explores how specific actors orient their strategies in the light of their understanding of the current conjuncture, their strategic calculation about the 'objective' interests tied to specific 'subjective' identities, and, perhaps, the lessons they have learnt from previous rounds of strategic conduct or routine behavior. Thus the SRA sensitizes us to the reciprocal path-dependent and path-shaping nature of hegemonic transformation. Jessop's later work integrates discursive elements (for example, economic and political imaginaries) into the SRA so that he can explore the coevolution of discursive and extra-discursive processes and their conjoint impact in specific contexts (2004). Of particular interest here are the discursive and extra-discursive mechanisms that select and then institutionalize some discourses among the many that are continually produced. The SRA also implies that there is a coconstitution of subjects and objects in fields such as production, governance, and hegemony. Moreover, while eschewing reductionist approaches to economic and political analysis, it would stress the materiality of social relations and highlights the constraints involved in processes that operate 'behind the backs' of the relevant agents. As such, it would be especially concerned with the structural properties and dynamics resulting from such material interactions. Substantively, this approach takes economic and political imaginaries not as 'arbitrary, rationalistic, and willed' (Gramsci

1971: 376–7) but as corresponding, albeit partially, to real material forces in the existing IPE. In short, Jessop's work could mediate between the neo-Gramscian focus on the economic, political, and intellectual-moral bases of power and the neo-Foucauldian concern with specific technologies of individual and social power and locate both in a broader critique of political economy.

The strategic-relational analysis of the role of both structure and agency in struggles over hegemony rests on the general evolutionary distinction between variation, selection, and retention. First, there is continuing *variation* in discourses as actors intentionally or unintentionally redefine the sites, subjects, and stakes of action and articulate innovative strategies, projects and visions. This is especially likely during crises, which often produce profound strategic disorientation and a proliferation of alternative discourses. Second, while most of this variation is arbitrary and short-lived, with no long term consequences for overall social dynamics, some innovations are *selected* because they resonate discursively with other actors and social forces and/or because they are reinforced through various structural mechanisms. So we must explore the discursive and extra-discursive mechanisms that select some discourses for further elaboration and effective articulation with other discourses. Discourses are most powerful where they operate across many sites and scales and can establish and connect local hegemonies into a more encompassing hegemonic project. Third, these discourses will be *retained* (discursively reproduced, incorporated into individual routines, and institutionally embedded) when they can reorganize the balance of forces and guide supportive structural transformation.

Although any given economic or political imaginary is only ever partially realized, those that succeed, at least in part, have their own performative, constitutive force in the material world – especially when they correspond to (or successfully shape) underlying material transformations, can mobilize different elites to form a new power bloc, can organize popular support, disorganize opposition, and marginalize resistance. They will be most successful when they establish a new spatiotemporal fix that can displace and/or defer capital's inherent contradictions and crisis-tendencies in the international political economy. In short, discourses and their related discursive chains can generate variation, have selective effects – reinforcing some discourses, filtering others out, and contribute to the differential retention and/or institutionalization of social relation through the recursive selection of certain genres and knowledging technologies. These technologies of control operate at the

1. Discursively-selective moment
2. Structurally-inscribed strategic selective moment (as applied to discourse)
3. (Inter-)discursively-selective moment
4. Moment in remaking dominant subjectivities and practices
5. Moment in conditioning and reembedding social relations

(*Source*: Sum 2004)

Figure 8.2 The Five Discursively Selective Moments in the Production of Hegemony

microsocial level to normalize and discipline thoughts, aspirations, decisions, and common sense through mundane discursive practices (for example, metaphors, indexes, tables) and routine practices (for example, working, reading, managing, discussing, debating, advertising) of everyday life. Organic intellectuals have a key role here in giving meanings and constructing common sense knowledge to underpin consent. Inspired in their everyday lives by a wide range of influential figures such as industrial statesmen (and stateswomen), managers, lawyers, auditors, politicians, civil servants, academics, school teachers, pop stars and sport celebrities with a high-profile campaigning role, individuals and groups refashion subjectivities by reflecting on their circumstances, values, interests, and conduct. The greater the range and scale of sites in which resonant discourses and practices are selected and retained, the greater is the scope for them to condition everyday social practices, institutions and modes of governance. The resulting social forms are typically asymmetric in regard to economic resources, state capacities, gender, ethnicity, nature, place, and so on. This allows counter-hegemonic movements to develop and to promote alternative discourses, strategies and tactics. We can summarize these ideas by identifying six interrelated moments in the operation of discursive[6] and structural selectivity (see Figure 8.2).

Producing hegemony, sub-hegemony and counter-hegemony in everyday life

In order to highlight the complex relation between domination and resistance, we now explore how these processes cut across the hegemonic, sub-hegemonic and counter-hegemonic spheres of activity that are contested in everyday life.

Production of hegemony and sub-hegemony

The relative success of global actors (such as global institutions or transnational companies) in securing global governance depends on their mobilization of actors from other sites and scales. For present purposes, this includes the diffusion of discourses produced by these actors to other scales through intermediaries who speak the intended hegemonic 'language' and translate it into regional and local contexts. This is never a purely one-way, top-down or bottom-up process because the stability of hegemony rests on the capacity to absorb alternative meanings and marginalize resistances so that dominant discourses are adapted to more global or local circumstances and thereby strengthened through everyday practices. This involves an admittedly asymmetrical, multilateral adaptation and negotiation of circulating discourses concerned with transforming the capitalist order. Economic-corporate concessions play a key role here as they do on other scales so that local and regional elites align their interests with a transnational class – with material and symbolic rewards for those who are quick to relay and recontextualize hegemonic discourse. All of this depends in turn on appropriate intermediate technologies of power to anchor such discourses regionally and locally (Peet 2000; Sum 2004). Martin-Barbero (1993) refers here to the 'hegemonic echo' that legitimates, customizes, and recontextualizes ideological power in common sense and everyday practice. This indicates that continuing hegemony depends on a certain flexibility and fluidity, on the ability to combine values, ideas, identities, and interests from various sources and scales. In a more bottom-up manner, new discourses may also emerge from sub-hegemonic centers of power and reverberate back to the hegemonic sites, where they may be absorbed into the hegemonic codes (Peet 2000). These processes of ideological exchange reinforce the ties between hegemonic and sub-hegemonic nodes. Thus studies of hegemonic processes on a global scale must identify the multiscalar inter-discursive spaces where actors with different horizons of action produce an 'integral world capitalist order'. This new 'world order' and associated practices represent a dominant 'worldview' that has an underlying structural class relevance as well as being ethnic-, gender- and place-biased.

These processes of hegemony building gradually stabilize a kind of systemic power that cannot be reproduced mechanically but depends, as Gramsci emphasizes, on the prosaics of everyday life. Thus, hegemony is produced and reproduced in everyday cultural transactions that partly express and partly shape values, actions, and meanings (see Aitken this volume). These hidden forms of domination, which are embedded in everyday activities and experiences, are reflected in folklore and common sense. This can be reinforced through the normalization of the prevailing patterns of economic, political, and ethico-cultural domination so that the interests of dominant groups go largely unchallenged. This aspect of Gramsci's work was extended in Foucault's microtechnologies of control and related disciplinary practices.

The production of counter-hegemony and resistance in everyday life

Despite the appearance of social unity and consensus generated by successful hegemonic projects, this is always a temporary, if not illusory, unity. The gaps between discourses and practices at the microlevel open up spaces for alternative conceptions of society and counter-hegemonic subjectivities. Likewise, at the macrolevel, the very selectivity of hegemonic projects means that some identities and interests are excluded and suppressed. The latter involves not only those who lose out on class grounds but also those who are oppressed on gender, 'race', ethnic, territorial, and other grounds (Jessop and Sum 2001: 94–5; Bakker 2003: 66–82; Rupert 2003: 186). Thus hegemony remains vulnerable and there is a permanent potential for hegemonic instability as diverse social forces exploit these tensions and conflicts and offer alternatives and engage in counter-hegemonic mobilization. This has its own potential bases in class, social movements and popular culture and can deploy both 'wars of position' and 'wars of maneuver' to resist hegemonic control and organize action across different sites at different scales. Alternative social forums (for example, World Social Forum, European Social Forum) illustrate the potential of counter-hegemonic wars of position; some recent transnational protests (anti-globalization riots in Seattle and Genoa) illustrate the limits of wars of maneuver. The internet and alternative publishing media, watch groups, and agit-prop vehicles have become important in coordinating this 'post-modern prince' (Gill 2000) and providing alternative symbols and means of receiving and imparting information that guide efforts to promote social change.

These public forms of open opposition coexist with more subterranean forms of resistance and subversion in everyday life. Michel de Certeau's work (1984) on the polyvalence of tactics of resistance is useful here. He argues that dominant social forces operate primarily through 'strategies,' that is, practices that assume a stable base of operations; in contrast, marginal actors must use 'tactics' that do not depend on a secure locus from which to act continuously and legitimately. They operate in the space of the liminal, the outside, the other (see Coward this volume). Tactics involve a continuing trial-and-error search through the 'practice of everyday life' for weak points and angles of attack. Tactical action uses speed or time to throw entrenched powers off balance in order to gain what often prove to be merely temporary advantages – taking action on the wing and securing transient victories (de Certeau 1984: 35). This theory of strategies and tactics can help us theorize the relation of hegemonic and counter-hegemonic power and reveal tensions within and across different technologies of power. Indeed, according to Harris (1992: 156), de Certeau can be used to gramscianize Foucault by providing a more nuanced account of resistance to complement the latter's account of disciplinary power. De Certeau's concept of tactics sheds light on the prosaic forms of creativity that enable individuals and groups to escape the 'webs of discipline' by exploiting the affordances of mundane products and routine circumstances to subvert their disciplinary logic. Drawing on everyday practices such as reading, walking and cooking, he shows how people develop alternative uses of commodities and other objects in ways that may subvert their 'legitimate' or otherwise prefigured modalities of consumption. Such 'dispersed, tactical, and makeshift creativity' constitutes an 'anti-discipline' that Foucault's analysis overlooks (Langer 1988:123; see also Davies this volume).

De Certeau's work on the everyday, while providing important observations, lacks a coherent conception of capitalism. As such, Lefebvre's work on '*détournement*' (or diversion), which was appropriated from the French Situationists led by Debord, calls attention to cultural playfulness and protests (for example, 'culture jamming' or 'reclaim the streets') that subvert and dislocate commodification. Seen from these aspects of de Certeau's and Lefebvre's work, it can be said that everyday life is a continuing battle of wits and a site of microresistance in which the (un-)structured and covert activities of the liminal seek to accommodate power while simultaneously protecting their interests and identities. However, resistance must entail something more than a rewriting of culture within the symbolic space of capitalism. For Gramsci, resistance will last if it is followed by a 'war of position' mediated by the building of a counter-hegemonic historic bloc of cultural, economic and political structures and relations and articulated and organized by its own organic intellectual. In short, hegemony is unstable, contingent, and incomplete and is continually liable to challenge through crises in the power bloc, the disjunction between hegemonic and sub-hegemonic discourses and forces at key nodal points in the global order, and the emergence of resistance and counter-hegemonic projects.

There is a continual interplay of wars of position, wars of maneuver, and short term tactics of resistance as social forces seek to hegemonize, form sub-hegemonic linkages, and neutralize the counter-hegemonic. Hegemony (as opposed to domination) is typically (re-)produced through accommodating a broad coalition of interests compatible with the continued reproduction of existing social relations. Where this is threatened, then we must also consider the possibilities of passive revolution and increased resort to force, fraud, and corruption (cf. Gramsci 1971). The flexibility required to maintain hegemony can be seen in an increasingly important response to current challenges to neoliberal globalization, namely, recent attempts to define and construct a new kind of 'moral leadership' under the general rubric of the 'globalization with a human face.' Thus, if a 'new constitutionalism' was the means of institutionalizing 'disciplinary neoliberalism' in the 1990s (Gill 1995), this is now being complemented by a 'new ethicalism' (see also Daly on new business ethics, this volume). This variation in response to the crisis of neoliberalism has been selected and promoted by transnational elites as an ethico-managerial strategy to reconnect economic policies with moral norms and to reconfigure them into managerial visions and practices (for example, corporate social responsibility, accountability and transparency) (Sum 2004, 2005; Sum and Pun 2005). These changes do not suspend the contradictions between capital and labor or the rivalries inherent in capitalist competition but they do seek to give them a 'human face' that can mobilize trade unions and social movements as well as individuals behind corporate social responsibility and to defuse the growing resistance to unfettered capitalism at the micro- and macroscales. This passive revolution combines 'war of maneuver' and 'war of position' in the search for a more stable social basis for global capitalism based on civil society as well as the labor movement and state authorities. Nonetheless the underlying contradictions and rivalries remain. Thus, just as capital seeks to escape its 'social responsibilities' where they hurt profitability, marginal forces continue to resist at individual sites of production up to the organization of social movements on a global scale (for example, the World Social Forum).

Conclusion

We have proposed a CPE approach to overcome the recurrent and complementary temptations of (a) economism versus culturalism and (b) structuralism versus voluntarism. CPE makes two theoretical innovations to address these temptations. First, while it affirms the 'cultural turn' in political economy and the performative power of the imaginary, it applies some of the tools of evolutionary economics (derived in part from evolutionary theory more generally) to discourse analysis. Second, it adopts a SRA to structure and agency (Jessop 1990). This aims to avoid the 'agencyless structuralism' of earlier IPE and the 'structureless agency' of neo-Foucauldian approaches. But this contribution goes beyond a general presentation of the SRA. For, in building on neo-Foucauldian analyses, we have noted some technologies of power that are critical in helping to secure global hegemony (Sum 2004). Such technologies are never neutral but have their own selectivities. They often have a key role in establishing nodal points of local or regional equilibria of compromise and in linking sub-hegemonies at different sites and scales of action into the broader world order through everyday activities. In this sense hegemony is necessarily produced and reproduced in everyday transactions. Their production and reproduction depend on complex interlinkages and intertextualities across different sites and scales of economic, political, and social organization. Thus hegemony is achieved through recurrent molecular phases and interactions that, together with material concessions and the judicious use of force, produce an 'unstable equilibrium of compromise' from which there emerges a 'collective will of a certain level of homogeneity'.

We have also highlighted the interaction between (sub-)hegemonic and counter-hegemonic forces in cultural IPE. The formation of a 'popular collective will' can never be complete because there are always excluded or marginalized forces, both within a given social formation and beyond it. This provides a permanent reservoir of resistance and a permanent potential for the development of counter-hegemony on different scales and sites. This is most noticeable in periods of crisis, especially when the crisis involves more than limited economic issues and is translated into the political and ideological spheres. The complex interactive achievement of building consensus and moral leadership is central to Gramsci's thinking and can be enriched by referring to Foucault, de Certeau, and so on, and integrating their analyses into a strategic-relational CPE and its application in IPE.

Notes

1 This essay focuses on the capitalist world order, that is, the tendential development of a world society dominated by the logic of capital accumulation. The same basic approach can be applied to the tendential development of a world society dominated by other principles of societal organization (see Jessop 2002).
2 On the cultural turn, see Bonnell and Hunt (1999).
3 For more general reviews of evolutionary and institutional economics, see Hodgeson (1988; 1993) and Lawson (1997).
4 Some Italian School theorists equate power bloc, historical bloc, and the social bases of stable orders of production and political power – we have distinguished these in order to identify the three key themes that the 'School' derives from Gramsci.
5 The term 'gramscianizing Foucault' was first used by Harris (1992: 156).
6 On 'discursive selectivity,' see Hay (1996).

References

Amoore, L. (2002) *Globalization Contested: an International Political Economy of Work*. Manchester: Manchester University Press.

Bakker, I. (2003) 'Neo-Liberal Governance and the Reprivatization of Social Reproduction,' in Bakker, I. and Gill, S. (eds), *Power, Production and Social Reproduction*. Basingstoke: Palgrave.

Bonnell, V. and Hunt, L. (1999) *Beyond the Cultural Turn*. Berkeley: University of California Press.

Brenans, D. (1999) 'Historical Materialism and Ordinary Language: Grammatical Peculiarities of the Class Struggle "Language Game,"' *Rethinking Marxism* 11 (2): 19–37.

Campbell, D. T. (1969) 'Variation and Selective Retention in Socio-Cultural Evolution,' *General Systems* 14: 69–86.

Chouliaraki, L. and Fairclough, N. (1999) *Discourse in Late Modernity*. Edinburgh: Edinburgh University Press.

Cox, R. (1981) 'Social forces, states and world orders: Beyond international relations theory,' *Millennium*, 10 (2), 126–55.

Cox, R. (1987) *Production, Power and World Order*, New York: Columbia University Press.

Cox, R. (with Schechter, M.) (2002) *The Political Economy of a Plural World*. London: Routledge.

Davies, M. (1999) *International Political Economy and Mass Communication in Chile*. New York: St. Martin's Press.

de Certeau, M. (1984) *Practices of Everyday Life*. Berkeley: University of California Press.

de Goede, M. (2003) 'Beyond Economism in IPE,' *Review of International Studies* 29 (1): 79–97.

Dean, M. (1999) *Governmentality: Power and Rule in Modern Society*. London: Sage.

Egan, D. (2001) 'The Limits of Internationalization: A Neo-Gramscian Analysis of the Multilateral Agreement on Investment,' *Critical Sociology* 27 (3): 1–42.

Fairclough, N. (1995) *Media Discourse*. London: Edward Arnold.

Gill, S. (1991) *American Hegemony and the Trilateral Commission*. New York: Cambridge University Press.

Gill, S. (1995) 'Globalization, Market Civilization, and Disciplinary Neoliberalism,' *Review of International Studies* 16 (4): 369–81.

Gill, S. (2000) 'Toward a Postmodern Prince? The Battle of Seattle as a Moment in the New Politics of Globalisation,' *Millennium* 29 (1): 131–40.

Gramsci, A. (1971) *Selections from the Prison Notebooks*. London: Lawrence and Wishart.

Hall, S. (1981) 'Notes on Deconstructing "The Popular,"' in Samuel, R. (ed.) *People's History and Socialist Theory*. Boston: Routledge and Kegan Paul.

Hall, S. (1982) 'The Rediscovery of "Ideology": The Return of the Repressed,' in Gurevitch, M., Bennett, T., Curran, J. and Woolacott, J. (eds) *Culture, Society and the Media*. London: Methuen.

Harris, D. (1992) *From Class Struggle to the Politics of Pleasure: the Effects of Gramscianism on Cultural Studies*. London: Routledge.

Hay, C. (1996) 'Narrating Crisis: the Discursive Construction of the "Winter of Discontent,"' *Sociology* 30 (2): 253–77.

Hodgeson, G. M. (1988) *Economics and Institutions*. Cambridge: Polity.

Hodgeson, G. M. (1993) *Economics and Evolution*. Cambridge: Polity.

Holub, R. (1992) *Antonio Gramsci: Beyond Marxism and Postmodernism*. London: Routledge.

Jessop, B. (1982) The Capitalist State: Marxist Theories and Methods, Oxford: Martin Robertson.

Jessop, B. (1990) *State Theory*. Cambridge: Polity.

Jessop, B. (2002) *The Future of the Capitalist State*. Cambridge: Polity.

Jessop, B. (2004) 'Critical Semiotic Analysis and Critical Political Economy,' *Critical Discourse Studies* 1 (1): 1–16.

Jessop, B. and Sum, N.-L. (2001) 'Pre-Disciplinary and Post-Disciplinary Perspectives,' *New Political Economy* 6 (1): 89–102.

Jessop, B. and Sum, N.-L. (2006) *Beyond the Regulation Approach: Putting Capitalist Economies in their Place*. Cheltenham: Edward Elgar.

Laclau, E. and Mouffe, C. (1985) *Hegemony and Socialist Strategy*. London: Verso.

Langer, B. (1988) 'Review of Practices of Everyday Life,' *Contemporary Sociology* 17 (1): 122–3

Lawson, T. (1997) *Economics and Reality*. London: Routledge.

Marsden, R. (1999) *The Nature of Capital: Marx After Foucault*. London: Routledge.

Martin-Barbero, J. (1993) *Communication, Culture and Hegemony*. Newbury Park CA: Sage.

McAnulla, S. (1998) 'The Structure-Agency Debate and its Historiographical Utility,' http://www.psa.ac.uk/cps/1998%5Cmcanulla.pdf, accessed on 10 August 2004.

Peet, R. (2000) 'Geographies of Policy Formation: Hegemony, Discourse and the Conquest for Practicality,' Paper for the Geographies of Global Economic Change Conference, October 12–14, Clark University, http://www.clarku.edu/leir/Peet.htm, accessed on 6 July 2004.

Robinson, W. (1996) *Promoting Polyarchy: Globalization, US Intervention and Hegemony*. Cambridge: Cambridge University Press.

Rupert, M. (1995) *Producing Hegemony*. Cambridge: Cambridge University Press.

Rupert, M. (1997) 'Globalization and American Common Sense,' *New Political Economy* 2 (1): 105–16.

Rupert, M. (2003) 'Globalizing Common Sense: A Marxian-Grasmcian (Re)Vision of the Politics of Governance/Resistance,' *Review of International Studies* 29 (S1): 181–98.

Sayer, A. (1998) 'Critical and Uncritical Turns,' http://www.lancs.ac.uk/fss/sociology/papers/sayer-critical-and-uncritical-truns.pdf, accessed on 28 April 2005.

Steger, M. (2002) *Globalism*. Latham: Rowman & Littlefield.

Sum, N.-L. (2004) 'From "Integral State" to "Integral World Economic Order": Towards a Neo-Gramscian Cultural International Political Economy,' Working Paper No. 7, Institute for Advanced Studies Working Paper Series, Lancaster University, (http://www.lancs.ac.uk/ias/polecon/index.htm), accessed on 28 April 2005.

Sum, N.-L. (2005) 'From "New Constitutionalism" to "New Ethicalism": Global Business Governance and the Discourses and Practices of Corporate Social Responsibility,' *Paper prepared for the European Consortium of Political Research. Workshop 24, Transnational Private Governance in the Global Political Economy, Granada, Spain, April 14–19.*

Sum, N.-L. and Jessop, B. (forthcoming) *The Economic Institutions of Culture: Towards a Cultural Political Economy*. Cheltenham: Edward Elgar.

Sum, N.-L. and Pun, N. (2005) 'Globalization and Paradoxes of Transnational Ethical Production,' *Competition and Change*, 9 (2): 225–44.

9
The Political Economy of (Im)Possibility

Glyn Daly

The very term 'political economy' is something that already names an ambiguous, even impossible, relationship. Derived from the Greek *oikonomia* (i.e. matters of household management and regulation), economy is something that designates a certain *domestication*; the keeping of good order. The political, on the other hand, is always that which upsets/challenges the order of 'the household' in the broadest sense of the term. The political not only bears witness to the impossibility of any ultimate Household, it is also – and as a consequence – that which liberates the very possibility for developing new forms of social organization, identity and belonging. This is the paradox to which Lefort (1989) refers: the political establishes the authenticity of every institution only to the extent that it shows the essential historicity and contingency of their inauguration. Every institution depends for its being on a political process of institutivity which it cannot incorporate or domesticate within it. Every household depends upon a certain impossible excess that is always 'promised' to something beyond what currently exists; to something Other.

This chapter has two central objectives. The first comprises an exploration of the aspect of the political in political economy. It will do this primarily through a critique of Luhmann's systems theory which has become increasingly influential in contemporary approaches to (international) political economy. This critique will be developed mainly through a post-Marxist and poststructuralist approach in which the emphases are on discourse, negativity and antagonism. Whereas many of the traditional perspectives on political economy – of both liberal and Marxist persuasions – have tended to view the economy in terms of an extra-discursive or extra-political infrastructure, this paper affirms the opposite: the economy is fully a discursive construction and as such is essentially prone to political subversion and recomposition in respect of other discursive positions.

Second, however, the paper is concerned with the development of an analytical approach that also addresses the opposing register: that is to say, the economy of the political. With its compelling emphasis on contingency (the 'primacy of the political') both poststructuralism and post-Marxism have arguably tended to overlook, or downplay, the way in which the political becomes economized in a given conjuncture. This is not to endorse any kind of return to a back-to-basics economism. On the contrary, the point is rather that through a critique of economism we should not then embrace the opposite fetish of a pure politicism; *both* registers need to be taken into account precisely on the basis of their mutual interplay and subversion.

There are two main aspects to this economization of the political. The first comprises the standard ideological attempt to present the economy in thoroughly depoliticized and naturalistic terms in which the keeping of economic order is viewed as a purely pragmatic and technocratic enterprise; as Blair has put it, there is 'no left or right in economic policy only good and bad' (1998). On this view modern globalization is a spontaneous and irrepressible force of integration that is leading progressively to the ontological society: the final utopian order of humankind synthesized through a mature, sympathetic and responsible liberal capitalism. But secondly, there is a deeper and more subtle aspect to this economization. Today's conjuncture does not simply repress the political, rather it engages reflexively with the latter and in such a way that it attempts to channel and compose it in paradigmatic fashion. There is in this sense a certain glamoring of the political that endeavors to bind and convey its energies in and through certain key incantations and watchwords: difference, consensus, inclusivity, tolerance, multiculturalism and so on. To change the metaphor, the political is something that tends to be recruited to, and configured within, a characteristic 'grammar' that allows for the development of certain lines of questioning, indictment and critique but crucially not others. In these broader terms the economization of the political is something that stakes out *historically* the realm of the possible against that which is deemed impossible. There exists, in tendential terms, a kind of (non-Hegelian) dialectical totality in which a particular order already takes into account its own failures and deficiencies and calls for its own 'transformation' in typically specious, and grammatical, ways.

This paper represents a speculative contribution to the development of a broader approach to political economy – both in terms of an analysis of the functioning of the political in the economy and the economization of the political – that focuses on the way in which the very sense of the possible is circumscribed through markers of impossibility.

The persistence of the political

The history of Marxist thought reveals a progressive undermining of the idea of the economy as an autonomous entity with endogenous laws. With the likes of Hilferding, Gramsci and the later post-Marxists, what begins to emerge is a new type of perspective in which the political itself becomes increasingly apparent as an object of theoretical reflection. To this effect, the economy has been shown to depend on more and more conditions of possibility that, far from expressing any cosmic decree, are themselves the result of contingent political practices. Yet the tension between naturalism and the logic of the political is already revealed within Marx's own thought.

One of the great achievements of Marx consists in what Hesse (1980) might call his metaphoric redescription of the economy; a redescription that, for the first time, sought to analyze economic relations in terms of social context. Marx was vehemently opposed to those conventions of political economy that attempted to derive economic meaning, and to justify vast inequalities of wealth, on the grounds of a mythical state of origins.

In contrast to abstract ideals, Marx affirmed the *social* character of labor such that the individual's potential for production and self-development is always dependent upon a given framework, or mode of production, that in turn reflects certain power relations; a balance of forces between classes. This enabled Marx to advance a powerful critique against naturalistic conceptions of capitalism that have persisted from Smith and Locke right through to Friedman and the dominant forms of neoclassical economics. Against such pieties concerning 'free' labor contracts in an open market, Marx demonstrated how workers are *forced* to sell their labor power as, under capitalism, they are denied access to the means of production and subsistence. For Marx, the classical liberal paradigm turned precisely on the attempt to finesse the power basis of capitalism.

A logic of contingency is already apparent within Marx insofar as there is a fundamental emphasis on the economy as a human construction rather than an underlying form waiting to be discovered. By deobjectifying the economy and showing its reality to be the result of wider power relations that generates its principles of construction, there is a clear sense in which Marx expanded the dimension of the political. At the same time, this expansion is limited as, in a contrary movement, there is a reabsorption of the political within a new form of objectivism. For Marx the problem was not positivity itself but rather the liberal version of it. Accordingly he sought a restoration of the modernist enterprise through the affirmation of a metaphysical law of history foretelling of an ultimate resolution.

The political shone all too briefly in Marx. Yet it was not something that could be extinguished. Indeed the subsequent history of the Marxist imagination is characterized by a tendential ebbing and flowing between the idealist search for certainties and their persistent denial by the political. This is reflected in an increasing destabilization of the traditional economic/noneconomic distinction. Rejecting the view of the economy as a self-enclosed order Hilferding (1985), for example, focused on the way that the modern economy developed within the terms of a nationalist framework. Gramsci (1976), of course, developed this line of enquiry even further. For Gramsci, the economy cannot be separated from ideological and cultural practices but is articulated with these phenomena in a characteristic historic bloc. By developing a radically contextualist approach, Gramsci showed that nothing automatically follows from economic relations and that we cannot predict whether they will be articulated in nationalist, liberal or social democratic terms (or other terms). A basic undecidability exists whose resolution will depend upon the outcome of concrete forces in political struggle. And the types of resolution that result will have crucial consequences for the construction and functioning of the economic space.

In his emphasis on the undecidable and political character of structuring principles, Gramsci may be said to render visible the political as a basic dimension of all social ordering and identification. We might reasonably argue that Gramsci is distinguished in modern thought not so much as a political theorist but as a theorist of the political. In his critique of economism, Gramsci provides the theoretical resources for politicizing political economy and thereby for a new imagination of actively radicalizing economic practice.

Yet it would be mistaken to think that theoretical reflection on the political has developed only within Marxism. One could cite examples of various thinkers, from other traditions, whose interventions have also served to undermine objectivist-naturalist approaches to the economy: Weber's analysis of economic development in terms of religious-cultural context; Simmel's argument that the value of money cannot be referred to an absolute foundation but depends on a broader network of symbolic exchange; Polanyi's emphasis on the social conditions of possibility for a 'market economy'; Keynes' demonstration of the artificial constitution and manipulation of the economic 'ground' through state intervention. More recently the French Regulation School has shown that the functioning of the economy is not an endogenous matter (as in classical models) but depends on the construction of an entire mode of social regulation that transcends the economy as such. Each of these perspectives move away from the idea of the economy as a closed autonomous order and towards a view that considers the latter in far more contextual and discursive terms (see Daly 1991; 1999).

The envisioning of the political, however partial or incomplete, is not exclusive to any one tradition, but reflects a synergy of all those themes and tendencies that have led to a weakening of idealist thinking about economic reality. On this basis a new approach is enabled that affirms the nonnatural character of all economic order and identity. Such an approach would begin from an analysis of the ways in which all economic systems attempt to conceal their essential *lack* of ground through artificial power processes of discursive constitution. It is in this context that the work of Luhmann makes an important contribution.

From autonomy to autopoiesis – beyond the positivity of systems

Contemporary political economy has drawn increasingly on the work of Luhmann and, in particular, his notion of autopoiesis (for example, Lash and Urry 1994; Leyshon and Thrift 1997; Jessop 1990, 2002). The general tendency has been to link autopoiesis with a certain endogeny in the development of complex systems of exchange and production. Jessop, for example, enlists autopoiesis to underscore his view that the economy (specifically, the capitalist market economy) exhibits a radical operational autonomy (Jessop 1990, 2002). Notwithstanding this autonomy, Jessop maintains that a market economy is further sustained by interdependent forms of regulation and what he refers to as 'social embeddedness' within the lifeworld of a society (2002).

While I am in general agreement with this approach I think that there are two potential problems that should be addressed. First, Jessop tends to use the notions of autonomy and autopoiesis interchangeably and in doing so, I would argue, loses sight of the distinctiveness of the latter. Second, and related, there is sometimes an inclination in Jessop to present the idea of economic autonomy in terms of a rather traditionalist economy/society division. The point that should be emphasized is not that economic practices cannot achieve a certain (relative) autonomy, but that this is entirely a matter of politico-discursive constitution in a particular context and is not something that can be universalized. The ambiguity surfaces at those points where Jessop insists on an analysis that secures a basic distinction between the discursive and the extra-discursive (1990: 302; 1999: 2; also Jessop and Sum, and Ryner this volume). This clearly runs the risk of reproducing a standard formulation whereby the economy is implicitly identified with the 'extra-discursive' dimensions of material reproduction, structural conditions and so on (as if the latter were independent of discursive reality and stood outside history). There is thus the potential danger that 'social embeddedness' could be perceived as a simple process of adjustment to, and the legitimization of, an underlying autonomous economic reality.

Luhmann's perspective allows for a different approach. Through his theory of autopoiesis, Luhmann's central innovation concerns his problematization of autonomy conceived as extra-discursive foundationalism. At the same time, Luhmann's position is highly ambiguous. If, on the one hand, Luhmann demonstrates the nongrounded character of all systems, on the other, he is drawn towards a new type of idealism in which society is presented as a positivity of systems that progressively masters all distortion. I will argue, in contrast, that the radicalism of Luhmann's autopoietic theory can be developed further by linking it with the post-Marxist affirmation of the ineradicability of power, negativity and antagonism: that is, by linking it to the notion of the political and a transcendence of all positivism.

Luhmann begins from the position that 'the world is constituted by the differentiation of meaning systems, by the difference between system and environment' (1995: 208). What Luhmann demonstrates is that systems can never be grounded in anything solid. It is because of the essential absence of any (extra-discursive) ground that we have systems in the first place. If an ultimate ground was reachable then the logic of systematization would cease to have any meaning: we would simply have infinite presence – a final domestication of the real.

A system establishes its consistency by differentiating itself from its 'environment': that is, that which designates the negative correlate of the system, or 'simply "everything else"' (Luhmann 1995: 181). This is achieved through processes of self-referral or autopoiesis.[1] A system is autopoietic insofar as it manifests the 'recursive application of its own operations' (Luhmann 1988: 336). The coherence of a system depends upon its ability to differentiate itself from, but also to engage with and interpret, its environment in terms of its code of organization.

The system of law, for example, no longer appears arbitrary because of the numerous sedimentations of case study, constitutional interpretation, preceding judgments and so on; all of which help to reinforce coherence and patterning. Such sedimentations serve to repress the fact that there exists no clear point of origin – autopoietic routinization is precisely the illusion of foundation – and that the legal system cannot be based on any absolutist conception of Law.

A system of law requires, in the first place, a basic code for distinguishing what is lawful and what is not. But this immediately presents a paradox because the legal/illegal distinction is not something that can be determined outside the system of law. Furthermore, the question as to whether the legal system *itself* is legal or illegal is strictly unthinkable and undecidable (see Esposito 1991). And this applies to the formation of every system. Where a system's code encounters itself – as in the legality/illegality of an existing system of law, the value of a system of valuation, the representativeness of a system of representation and so on – the system is confronted with a fundamental lack of ground: in short, it is confronted with the political. No system is capable of systematizing its own principle(s) of construction.

What autopoiesis shows is that the 'ground' of any system is merely the artifice of its recursivity. Every foundation is ultimately a phantom of a system's tautological (self-referring) constitution. This is why for Stäheli the 'self-referential system functions as a metaphor for the impossibility of the origin' (Stäheli 1995: 19). The more a system refers to itself the more it serves to underline an essential lack of foundation. Autopoiesis is precisely that which acts as a stand-in for the absent foundation.

From this perspective, the idea of autopoiesis has to be strictly separated from traditionalist conceptions of autonomy and independence. It is precisely because the latter cannot be formed that autopoiesis comes into being. The 'closure' of any system is purely an artificial effect that depends upon the discursive-contingent practices of inclusion/exclusion. On these grounds we can infer the basic paradox governing all systematicity: that the lack of origins/foundations makes systems both necessary and impossible.

This paradox, I would argue, is not sufficiently developed by Luhmann. He appears to be irresistibly drawn to an idealist position and his extensive analysis of differential system formation becomes simultaneously a major weakness. This is particularly apparent in his functionalist account of contradictions and conflict. For Luhmann, conflicts and contradictions 'function as an alarm in society's immune system' (1995: 387): that is, as a kind of signaling in which '(t)he signal merely warns, merely flares up, is merely an event – and suggests action in response' (*ibid.*: 373). The problem here is that while he explicitly rejects such totalizing notions as Centre and Subject, his alternative conception of social reality – as a perpetual differentiation of systems – runs the risk of becoming equally totalizing.

The development of systematization is one that is regarded as capable of tendentially resolving social negativity and opacity. By conceiving society in terms of an immune system, he effectively reduces the notion of the political to one of simple adjustment (or 'noise abatement'). Politics becomes a mere problem of perturbation that can be neutralized within the basic framework of the societal system and in such a way that autopoiesis proceeds undisturbed (*ibid.*: 373).

System failure – reintroducing the political

The essential question that begs to be answered in Luhmann's analysis is what are the conditions of possibility for system formation as such? In addition, how should the frontiers of a system be conceived?

For Luhmann systems exist as a basic phenomenalism. As in a complex organism, systems develop through processes of differentiation that augment coherence and regularity and each system functions as difference within an overall process of differentiation (*ibid.*: 208). By basing his analysis on a pure logic of differentiation (a logic that embodies systematicity as such), Luhmann advances a vision of the social universe in terms of a constant, and in principle limitless, expansion of systems; an expansion that constantly resolves its problems (negativity) along Hegelian lines.

From a post-Marxist perspective this vision is defective. In the first place, the formation of systems depends fundamentally on the construction of frontiers of antagonism against an irreducible negativity. Systems can only be systems in relation to what they are not: as orders of intelligibility carved out against that which would overwhelm them. And it is because frontiers are always precarious in the face of such negativity that they may be said to establish the conditions of possibility and impossibility for all systems.

Luhmann is correct in his observation that any attempt to represent what is beyond 'meaning-constituting' systems is ultimately interior to those systems and merely leads to their extension: put in other terms, the significance of any 'beyond' always involves a system of signification. Within the Luhmannian paradigm of a continuous logic of (positive) differentiation limits become strictly unthinkable. A differential approach to limits is evidently self-defeating as it would mean transforming the latter into a difference *within* the system – thereby rendering ineffectual their function as limits.

The effectivity of a true limit derives from an entirely opposing register – that of negativity. A limit is only instituted as the result of the *failure* of a system and a radical interruption/suspension of its differential logic. The limit of a system emerges precisely at the point where a system *cannot* incorporate or represent a set of elements and in consequence excludes the latter as Other. Limits, therefore, are produced as orders of *equivalence* and not difference (see Laclau 1996). Every limit depends upon a certain dichotomy between an equivalential order of those elements perceived as belonging to a system and a corresponding equivalential exclusion of those elements identified as a 'threat' to that system. In short, limits are always of the type system/anti-system.

This evidently does not mean that limits remain fixed in a once-and-for-all manner. Limits can always be subverted and redrawn precisely because they are penetrated by negativity. In this sense limits are always historically defined. Yet what is transhistorical is the fact that limits *per se* cannot be eradicated (see also Coward this volume, on the limits of Empire). For example, a moral system that is designed to maximize tolerance in respect of cultural differences is one that is also compelled 'violently' to exclude its Other: racial bigotry, xenophobia, cultural chauvinism and so forth. The very possibility of a system of differential tolerance is one that depends on, and grows out of, the equivalential negation of that which is deemed to be intolerable.

Three points should be emphasized. First, a system can only be instituted through logics of exclusion and antagonism that in providing the sense of limits are constitutive and affirming of its positive content (a 'not-system' in order for a 'system'). Accordingly every system is a *power construction* that relies upon the repression of its Other. This insight is decisive in turning foundationalism on its head. Systems do not possess positive grounds but are shown to grow out of negativity and antagonism. It is not that systems are foundation-*less*, but rather that 'foundations' are *made* (not discovered) through political processes of exclusion and delimitation.

This means – second point – that the political can be seen to be a fundamental dimension of every system. In the absence of preexisting grounds or generative principles, all systems are ultimately political to the extent that they are constituted through acts of violence and exclusion. A legal system, for example, cannot be *legalized* in an external or absolutist sense, but depends upon discursive fiat and contexts of social power: 'these commandments and not those.' This is precisely what Derrida means when he speaks of the 'violence of the law before the law' (1994: 31): that is, a political intervention that sustains the possibility of a legal system only to the extent that it shows its impossibility as a natural positivity.

Every system is marked by an originary discursive violence, an arbitrary 'line in the sand,' that seeks to establish a certain territorial coherence *vis-à-vis* radical undecidability. Through processes of routinization and sedimentation, systems typically attempt to finesse their artificiality by concealing the political nature of their origins behind a particular idealism. In search of authenticity, the violence of a system tends to be disavowed through reference to an external and tautological principle – destiny, divinity, dynasty ('the way it is/always has been') – and, more especially, through the invocation of certain mysterious laws of history, nature, the market, God and so forth. We might say that what is missing is the psychoanalytic insight into the *obscene* supplement (of violence and repression) that necessarily accompanies every system and upon which the latter implicitly relies (see also Gammon and Palan this volume). This gives rise to an irresolvable tension: (i) autopoietic mechanisms seek to gentrify systems through artificially inducing closure and by presenting them as natural and universal; but (ii) the repressed-excessive dimension, which is constitutive of a system, is something that can never be mastered and thus all 'closure' and 'universality' is inherently compromised. It is in this tension between systems and their ungovernable excesses that the political is continuously reborn.

In consequence, and as a final point, systems are *essentially* prone to failure and can always be challenged and subverted by precisely those forces that are antagonized/excluded by a system. An important corollary of this is that failure cannot be reduced to an internal moment of autopoietic readjustment. Rather failure designates the eruption of those events and antagonisms that are *external* to the system in the sense that they cannot be managed or represented within the terms of the latter.[2] Moreover, there exists a fundamental gap between the failure of a system and the processes of recomposition; a gap through which the ontological possibility of the political emerges. Whether a failure will be resolved through fascist, socialist, social democratic or some other means, is not something that can be derived from the failure in and of itself: this will depend on the outcome of a hegemonic struggle in a particular context. Failure is not merely a transition in the unfolding of a pregiven principle of intelligibility but rather the very degeneration of the latter.

System failure is one that leads to a widening of the realm of the possible – a reactivation of the political – in which a diversity of social forces will compete to establish new principles of ordering and intelligibility that will in turn affect the dimensioning of systems and the nature of their autopoietic functioning. What post-Marxism enables us to grasp is the susceptibility of autopoiesis itself to hegemonic reformulations; reformulations that are essentially possible because of the central impossibility of mastering failure and negativity.

Casino capitalism

Luhmann's perspective may be said to reflect a particular tension in contemporary thought between what might be called the epistemological and aspirational dimensions of modernity. The modernist paradigm can be understood as a series of rationalist attempts to subordinate the political within an overall system of integration where basic antagonisms have been eliminated. In the contemporary era, there has been a clear distancing from such rationalism and its totalitarian propensities. At the same time, writers like Bell (2000), Fukuyama (1992) and Rorty (1989) – who would endorse this distancing – nevertheless affirm the tendential emergence of a new holistic order: global liberal capitalism. In this way, a certain embodiment of the modernist aspiration – an ultimate systematization – is presented as having somehow survived the epistemological ruination of modernism as such. From this point of view, liberal capitalism and human destiny are seen to comprise a synchronicity that is being historically realized.

More recently, this tendency is reflected in the fashionable, and increasingly influential, thesis of 'natural capitalism' developed by Hawken *et al.* For these authors natural capitalism is concerned with the creation of a new industrial revolution that accords with planetary ecosystems and responds to the 'basic principles that govern the earth' (1999: 313). Production should be developed in terms of 'bio-mimicry' and a holistic system of valuation should be established:

> To make people better off requires no new theories, and needs only common sense. It is based on the simple proposition that *all* capital

> be valued. While there may be no 'right' way to value a forest, a river, or a child, the wrong way is to give it no value at all. (Hawken *et al.* 1999: 321)

What the natural capitalists envisage is a steady process of bringing the 'house' of capitalism into good order; of establishing an (ontological) economic harmony that fulfills the promise of capitalism as the true human paradigm. Socio-environmental problems can be resolved by factoring them into the economic calculus of capitalism and in such a way that the latter can achieve its full potential. This idea of a progressive overcoming of all distortion and exclusion is paradigmatic of the dominant liberal approach to globalization. The liberal think tank, the *Globalization Institute*, sees the matter this way:

> Globalization is the increasing integration of the global economy to bring together rich and poor countries...Only by integrating the poorest into the world economy can we put an end to the poverty that still blights much of the world today (http://www.globalizationinstitute.org)

What the liberal myth disavows is the fact that capitalism *of necessity* is a power system of exclusion. While capital works ceaselessly to transform and commodify all existing social relations, what it refuses to bargain with (in fact, *cannot* bargain with) is precisely its exploitative conditions of possibility. What, for example, would happen if the cost of exploitation – the extraction of surplus value from workers, the immiseration of vast sectors of the world's population (one in every five are condemned to live on less than US$1 per day) – was actually factored into the economic calculus of capitalism? Confronted with its own code of organization it would simply implode. Within the strict terms of the capitalist paradigm what cannot be valuated are its very symptoms of global privation and social injustice. Capitalism cannot ingest the excesses upon which it relies for its constitution. One of the most striking features of this constitutive excess is the so-called foreign debt. This debt is now so extreme, so permanent, that it cannot properly be *accounted* within existing conventions. The quantification of this debt appears increasingly arbitrary and absurd. In the modern age, the foreign debt – a debt which, in practical terms, is beyond calculation and is exorbitant in relation to any possibility of actually being met – is rather the name (or one of the names) for the structural dislocation, the traumatic failure, of global capitalism as a universal system.

What Marx sought to disclose was precisely the pathological element (of power and exclusion) behind the 'neutral' calculus of capitalism. While the latter is a radical universal force (bursting every provinciality asunder), at the same time it is manifestly parochial in its social tendentiousness. Through processes of gentrification (or autopoiesis) capitalism strives to institute itself as *the* global order through a disavowal of its politico-discursive violence.

It is interesting in this context to look at the type of (implicit) critique that Scorsese develops in his excellent *Casino*. In this film, Scorsese explores the dual-edged nature of capitalism through his two main characters: Sam 'Ace' Rothstein (Robert de Niro) and Nicky Santoro (Joe Pesce). As in Marx's notion of primitive accumulation, Nicky may be said to reflect the primitive, or foundational, violence of capitalism; a violence that is integral to the construction of a casino system in the deserts of Los Angeles and to sustaining a power base for its operation ('pre-legal' reliance on corruption, money-laundering, extortion and so on). As time progresses, however, Nicky becomes an increasing liability as he constantly seeks to reinforce his position through crude acts of gangsterism. What Nicky fails to appreciate, and what the character of Ace is all too aware of, is that the power of the casino resides precisely in it being a self-reproducing autopoietic system. It naturalizes its violence through its obscene calculations of 'chance' such that the house always, ultimately, wins. In this context, we might say that Nicky represents the excessive drive, the monstrous face, of capitalism; an ugly reminder of the casino system's origins who must be disavowed and consigned to the periphery. And thus on the orders of certain corporate interests (that remain anonymous) he is taken to the desert to meet the gruesome fate of being buried alive.

In a similar way, we could say that the contemporary system of capitalism endeavors to gentrify itself through a disavowal of the crude reality of exploitation/privation and by pushing its necessary measures of violent repression to the internal and external peripheries of the world. In this way, neoliberal ideology attempts to naturalize capitalism by presenting its outcomes of winning and losing as if they were simply a matter of chance and sound judgment in a neutral marketplace (see also Peterson this volume).

It could further be argued that today's model of hospitality is the casino itself. The casino is, in principle, open to all those who have money and are prepared to play by the rules. At the same time there are significant categories of exclusion: those who win excessively – consistently successful gamblers tend to be banned for playing the game(s) too well; those who lose excessively – gamblers who take the game(s) *too* seriously and risk all to beat the house system; those who are excessively proximate – local people are typically banned from gambling in the casinos.

The hospitality of contemporary capitalism can be seen to function along similar lines: (i) the constant reproduction of a demographic of debt – the endless invitations to take out loans to deal with existing loans (rather than escape the cycle of debt altogether); (ii) the withdrawal of participatory credit from those who take it too literally – those who in a sense embody the very nature of fictitious capital; (iii) the maintenance of a critical distance from the Other – a kind of postmodern culture of neighborliness without having to deal with real neighbors as such (for example, the migrant who wants to take up residence, the inert presence of the poor, and so on).

In contrast to Kant's affirmation of an open and cosmopolitan approach to hospitality, the increasing tendency in contemporary capitalism is towards a far more conditioned hospitality that we might characterize as megalopolitan:[3] that is a hospitality whose fate and frontiers of belonging/nonbelonging are determined and coordinated through the key megalopolises – New York, Berlin, London, Hong Kong and so on – of a global power structure that endeavors to domesticate the universal and, by extension, the political itself.

The economy of the political

It is in this context that we should address the economy of the political: that is, the historical determination of the parameters of possibility. The central emphasis here is on the way in which the play of the political tends to be conditioned by a meta-political logic (which itself is a thoroughly political construction); in post-Marxist terms, it stresses the way in which hegemony itself can become effectively hegemonized by certain key themes and rules of political engagement that govern its economy.

Let's take the voguish development of 'business ethics' and the way that this is becoming increasingly standardized in terms of a postmodern political correctness – respecting difference, valorizing the personal and so on. The British inventor and entrepreneur, James Dyson, has been acclaimed as a role model for a new type of business culture both in terms of his development of innovative 'green' forms of technology (especially the vacuum cleaner) and through a hands-on leadership/managerial approach that encourages participation and creativity among employees. At a critical point of expansion, however, it was decided in 2004 that the majority of his plant would have to move to Malaysia. Breaking out of the old mode of industrial relations, the response of the company was to set up a series of 'listening committees' to deal with the resultant eight hundred redundancies and to provide personalized advice and support. While this management-with-a-human-face approach was widely accepted as both positive and responsible, what remained beyond question was the legitimacy of the decision to export production – this was simply accepted as a *fatum*. Thus what we have is the political development of a new form of business ethical practice but only to the extent that it represses a more radical and substantive form of politico-ethical engagement.

This implicit acceptance of what is possible is emblematic of mainstream political culture. From New Labour to the 'third way' and even Beck's (1992) 'new enlightenment' there is a paradigmatic tendency towards the pragmatic in addressing what is viewed as the 'common problems' of the economy, environment, technology and so on. Lyotard (1984) is fully justified in his characterization of the contemporary attitude as one of incredulity towards radical forms of political engagement. The global vision of a New World Order is seen very much in terms of a mere expansion of liberal capitalism where the megalopolitan power structures remain firmly in place. Any real transformation – power sharing and a meaningful redistribution of wealth (as opposed to the relatively superficial idea of 'debt' cancellation) – is viewed with the utmost scepticism and is quickly consigned to the domain of the 'unrealistic.' In this way the political tends to become economized; subject to a logic of autopoietic reflexivity that provides a kind of elementary grid for its functioning.

It is against this background that the distinctive theoretical attitudes towards the notion of class can be situated. In much of post-structuralist and post-Marxist thought the analytical use of class has been rejected on the grounds that it presupposes a unified and incomplex agency that is preprogrammed for social revolution. Laclau, for example, rightly points out that the socially more cohesive forms of industrial working class are tending to disappear from the developed economies and that the political orientation of the popular classes (as Gramsci knew well) cannot be predicted in advance or independently of historical context (Laclau in Butler *et al.* 2000: 296–301). For Žižek, by contrast, class is something that connotes the primary form of social antagonism under capitalism (see Žižek and Daly 2004: 146–50).

While there is no simple 'third way,' I think that the merits of both positions can be in fact maintained by changing the terms of debate. That is to say, class should not be regarded, in the traditional 'scientific Marxist' sense, as a positive identity but rather the opposite: a signifier of embodied negativity; something that again bears witness to the traumatic failure of megalopolitan capitalism. In this sense of the embodied negativity or symptoms of capitalism, class designates the socially excluded, the outcast, the destitute and today's figure of the 'migrant'.

In this respect we might say that class is approximative of Lacan's use of the alchemical term *caput mortuum* (death's head). The *caput mortuum* is the residue, the indivisible remainder, after all that is of value has been extracted in a particular process. It is that which is excluded from the sphere of positive value and yet is integral to its production – it represents the (negativized) truth of such a sphere. Fink explains its functioning in the context of a numerical chain of signification:

> The *caput mortuum* contains what the chain does not contain; it is in a sense the other of the chain. The chain is as unequivocally determined by what it excludes as by what it includes, by what is within as by what is without. The chain never ceases to *not* write the numbers that constitute the *caput mortuum* in certain positions, being condemned to ceaselessly write something else or say something else which keeps avoiding this point, as though this point were the truth of everything the chain produces as it beats around the bush (Fink 1995: 27).

Class would seem to have the same paradoxical status *vis-à-vis* today's emphasis on the identitarian chain of 'alliance politics.' That is to say, class functions as something that cannot be positively 'named' within the chain as if it were one more difference and yet is the very (negativized) sticking point – a kind of existential tort – that renders the latter possible.

A central imperative of a radical politics must be the development of a defining solidarity with the abject classes; one that faces up to our ethical implication in the production of global abjection in systemic terms (see also Amoore this volume). This solidarity of excess would mean moving beyond the current postmodern economy of the political and its identitarian logic – precisely because, as with the *caput mortuum*, the symptoms of social negativity are constitutively debarred from, and excessive to, such an economy. It would be a solidarity based upon a fundamental disclosure of the constitutive preconditions of this economy.

The perspective that has been outlined here is one that seeks a broader approach to political economy and in such a way that it enables us to critique and to confront the economy (the historical circumscription) of the possible. In this context it affirms a politics that does not defer to house rules but which is prepared to take on directly today's silently accepted markers of impossibility.

Notes

1 Literally meaning self-creation – from the Greek *poiesis* (creation). Autopoiesis first achieved currency with the thought of Maturana and Varela (Maturana and Varela 1980, 1987; Varela 1979), where it was applied to the field of biology. In this context, autopoiesis refers to a cybernetic description of cell metabolism whereby a cell establishes its coherence and consistency (its 'inside') through the mutual interaction and reinforcement of its components against its 'outside'.

2 For example, the popular mobilizations against the system of apartheid. The externality here clearly does not imply an 'extra-discursive' but rather a deformation of the existing system from a position of equivalential resistance to it.

3 The distinction that I am using between the cosmopolitan and the megalopolitan is tendential rather than absolute.

References

Beck, U. (1992) *Risk Society: Towards a New Modernity*. London: Sage.

Bell, D. (2000) *The End of Ideology*. Harvard: Harvard University Press.

Blair, T. (1998) Address to French Assembly.

Butler, J. *et al.* (2000) *Contingency, Hegemony, Universality*. London: Verso.

Casino (1995) directed by Martin Scorsese.

Daly, G. (1991) 'The Discursive Construction of Economic Space,' *Economy and Society* 20 (1): 79–102.

Daly, G. (1999) 'Marxism and Postmodernity,' in Gamble, A. *et al.* (eds) *Marxism and Social Science*. London: Macmillan.

Derrida, J. (1994) *Specters of Marx*. New York: Routledge.

Esposito, E. (1991) 'Paradoxien als Unterscheidungen von Unterscheidungen,' in Gumbrecht, U. H. and Pfeiffer, K. L. (eds), *Paradoxien, Dissonanzen, Zusammenbruche: Situationen offener Epistemologie*. Suhrkamp: Frankfurt.

Fink, B. (1995) *The Lacanian Subject: Between Language and Jouissance*. Princeton: Princeton University Press.

Fukuyama, F. (1992) *The End of History and the Last Man*. Harmondsworth: Penguin.

Gramsci, A. (1976) *Selections from the Prison Notebooks*. London: Lawrence and Wishart.

Hawken, P. *et al.* (1999) *Natural Capitalism: Creating the Next Industrial Revolution*. Boston: Little, Brown & Co.

Hesse, M. (1980) *Revolutions and Reconstructions in the Philosophy of Science*. Brighton: Harvester Press.

Hilferding, R. (1985) *Finance Capital*. London: Harvester Wheatsheaf.

Jessop, B. (1990) *State Theory*. Cambridge: Polity.

Jessop, B. (1999) 'Narrating the Future of the National Economy and the National State' (draft), published by the Department of Sociology, Lancaster University at: http://www.lancaster.ac.uk/sociology/soc014rj.html.

Jessop, B. (2002) 'The Social Embeddedness of the Economy and its Implications for Economic Governance,' in Adaman, F. and Devine, P. (eds) *Economy and Society: Money, Capitalism and Transition*. Montreal: Black Rose Books.

Laclau, E. (1996) *Emancipation(s)*. London: Verso.

Lash, S. and Urry, J. (1994) *Economies of Signs and Space*. London: Sage.

Lefort, C. (1989) *Democracy and Political Theory*. Minneapolis: University of Minnesota Press.

Leyshon, A. and Thrift, N. (1997) *Money/Space: Geographies of Monetary Transformation*. London: Routledge.

Luhmann, N. (1988) 'Closure and Openness: On Reality in the World of Law,' in Teubner, G. (ed.) *Autopoietic Law: A New Approach to Law and Society*. New York: de Gruyter.

Luhmann, N. (1995) *Social Systems*. Palo Alto: Stanford University Press.

Lyotard, J. (1984) *The Postmodern Condition*. Manchester: Manchester University Press.

Maturana, H. and Varela, F. (1980) *Autopoiesis and Cognition*. Dordecht, Holland: Reidel.

Maturana, H. and Varela, F. (1987) *The Tree of Knowledge*. Boston, MA: Shambhala Publications.

Rorty, R. (1989) *Contingency, Irony and Solidarity*. Cambridge: Cambridge University Press.

Stäheli, U. (1995) 'Latent Places of the Political in Niklas Luhmann's Systems Theory', Working Paper No. 5, Centre for Theoretical Studies, University of Essex, February 1995.

Varela, F. (1979) *The Principles of Biological Autonomy*. New York: North Holland.

Žižek, S. and Daly, G. (2004) *Conversations with Slavoj Žižek*. Cambridge: Polity.

Part III

Politics of Dissent

What critical political economy shares in its poststructuralist as well as its Gramscian guises, is its analysis and encouragement of dissent and transformation. The introduction already discussed the ways in which perspectives on transformation are rearticulated through poststructural interventions that emphasize performativity, contradictory subject-positions, and the contingency of political struggle. Rethinking the politics of dissent through an engagement with poststructural thinking is an important future direction of critical IPE, and the chapters in this section offer promising starting-points for such engagements.

First, Wendy Larner's analysis of discourses of neoliberalism demonstrates that the way in which neoliberalism is conceptualized has effects on the ways in which it is to be *resisted*. If seen as policy project, strategies of resistance tend to take the form of arguments over the success or failure of policy programs. If neoliberalism is seen as an ideological formation, attention is focused on resistance as a discursive and ideological struggle that centers on articulations of interests and identities. If neoliberalism is seen as a practice of governmentality, resistance comes to hinge even less on a specific political program for reform, but is enabled through a destabilization of the assumed inevitability of restructuring and an attentiveness to the complexity, ambiguity, and contingency of contemporary political formations. Larner's analysis of the messy actualities of neoliberalism in New Zealand makes visible the compromises, contradictions and inconsistencies that inevitably characterize neoliberal political projects, thus revealing neoliberalism to be a more tenuous, insecure and *vulnerable* phenomenon than is commonly assumed.

Secondly, Matt Davies explores the concept of everyday life, as developed by Lefebvre, and its promise as a site of resistance. Everyday life is becoming increasingly important to IPE, and is frequently conceptualized as a privileged site of resistance (for example in Jessop and Sum this volume). According to Davies, however, everyday life cannot automatically be prioritized as a site of resistance, as it is also the site in which capitalist governance is reproduced and bears down heavily. According to Davies, 'everyday life is a burden, it is mundane, routine, repetitive, boring.' What is needed, then, in order to think resistance in IPE, is a *critique* of everyday life. Davies examines critically three IR/IPE authors who have engaged with everyday life, in order to draw out the insight that everyday life is neither a site where power is reproduced, nor where it is resisted, but a site that must be theorized through its ambiguities. Davies concludes the chapter by exploring Lefebvre's concept of inhabitation as a practice that transforms space as a site of resistance.

Thirdly, Bice Maiguashca explores the working of power by analyzing its points of resistance, in this case, the work of Women's Reproductive Rights Movement. Drawing upon Gramscian and poststructural concepts of power, Maiguashca offers an empirical reading of the diverse strategies of resistance deployed by this movement. She demonstrates the twin importance of challenging both policy and the normalized narratives of population and sexuality on which development policy has been based. One of the areas in which the Women's Reproductive Rights Movement has been active, is in challenging the sexist and racialized neo-Malthusian population discourses that represent poor people as irresponsible and unable to control their sexual urges. However, effects of political resistance are unpredictable, and apparent victories of the movement in rearticulating women's rights have been appropriated by campaigners with more conservative agendas. It is important, then, according to Maiguashca, that in this shifting discursive field, women activists continue to struggle to re-appropriate, redefine and repoliticize these terms.

Finally, Louise Amoore's chapter offers a radical rethinking of resistance through a poststructural lens. Amoore starts with the premise – also noted in the introduction – that there is no clear and unambiguous distinction between 'the world we are against and the world we seek to secure.' For Amoore these contradictory subject positions should not be denied or resolved, because it is precisely here that important points of politicization are possible. The insecure and incomplete nature of identities – in contrast to the settled, secured self – contain the potential for recognition of the intimate connections between self and other. Amoore thus builds upon Foucault's insight that 'there is no Locus of great refusal,' in order to explore the multiple and contradictory sites in which contemporary political dissent can be seen at work. She explores, amongst other practices, art and literature as practices that are able to question and disturb what have become ordinary experiences, and that are able to confront us with our radical dependence on others.

10
Neoliberalism: Policy, Ideology, Governmentality

Wendy Larner

Introduction

The term 'neoliberalism' denotes new forms of political-economic governance premised on the extension of market relationships. In critical social science literatures the term has usurped labels referring to specific political projects (Thatcherism, Regeanomics, Rogernomics), and is more widely used than its counterparts including, for example, economic rationalism, monetarism, neoconservatism, managerialism and contractualism.[1] Indeed, Jane Jenson (1999) recently used 'neoliberal' as a general descriptor for postwelfare state citizenship regimes. It is in this context that I reassess existing analyses of neoliberalism. The imperative for this examination arises from my growing conviction that many critical commentators have underestimated the significance of neoliberalism for contemporary forms of governance and, as such, have been largely unable to engage in the formulation of an effective 'post-social politics.'[2]

At first glance the object of my enquiry appears self-evident. Internationally, conservative and social democratic governments alike are involved in debates over welfare state processes. Whereas under Keynesian welfarism the state provision of goods and services to a national population was understood as a means of ensuring social well-being, neoliberalism is associated with the preference for a minimalist state. Markets are understood to be a better way of organizing economic activity because they are associated with competition, economic efficiency and choice. In conjunction with this general shift towards the neoliberal tenet of 'more market,' deregulation and privatization have become central themes in debates over welfare state restructuring.

This chapter claims that neoliberalism is a more complex phenomenon than may have been recognized by many participants in these debates. In order to address this claim, the first part of the paper identifies three different interpretations of neoliberalism. I distinguish between analyses that understand neoliberalism as a policy framework, those that portray neoliberalism as an ideology and those who conceptualize neoliberalism through the lens of governmentality. I show that each of these interpretations of neoliberalism has different implications for understandings of the restructuring of welfare state processes and for the envisaging of political strategies that might further aspirations for social justice and collective forms of well-being. In this context, it should be immediately apparent that this delineation of the different interpretations of neoliberalism is not simply an academic exercise; our understandings of this phenomenon shape our readings of the scope and content of possible political interventions.

I argue that analyses that characterize neoliberalism as either a policy response to the exigencies of the global economy, or the capturing of the policy agenda by the 'New Right,' run the risk of underestimating the significance of contemporary transformations in governance. Neoliberalism is both a political discourse about the nature of rule and a set of practices that facilitate the governing of individuals from a distance. In this regard, understanding neoliberalism as governmentality opens useful avenues for the investigation of the restructuring of welfare state processes. At the same time, however, I suggest that the insights of the governmentality literature should be enhanced by those from feminist and other critical theorizing in which the contested nature of discursive practices is centered. In this regard:

> Those whose aim it is to create knowledge that will assist social contestation should take on the difficult work of understanding actual and possible contests and struggles around rule, and our theories should enable rather than prevent such projects (O'Malley, Weir and Shearing 1997: 512).

Neoliberalism as policy

The most common conceptualization of neoliberalism is as a policy framework – marked by a shift from Keynesian welfarism towards a political agenda favoring the relatively unfettered operation of markets. Often this renewed emphasis on markets is understood to be directly associated with the so-called 'globalization' of capital. The argument is a familiar one. New forms of globalized production relations and financial systems are forcing governments to abandon their commitment to the welfare state (Schwartz 2001; Teeple 1995). Rather than formulating policies to ensure full employment and an inclusive social welfare system, governments are now focused on enhancing economic efficiency and international competitiveness. One consequence is the 'rolling back' of welfare state activities, and a new emphasis on market provisioning of formerly 'public' goods and services.

Analysts tend to attribute this shift in policy agendas to the capture of key institutions and political actors by a particular political Ideology (with a capital 'I'); a body of ideas or a worldview (Purvis and Hunt 1993). This body of ideas is understood to rest on five values: the individual; freedom of choice; market security; laissez faire; and minimal government (Belsey 1996). These values underpin the new institutional economics (built on public choice theory, transactions cost theory and principal-agency theory) which, together with a new emphasis on managerialism, comprise the intellectual basis of the neoliberal challenge to Keynesian welfarism, and provide the theoretical impetus for deregulation and privatization. In turn, this new intellectual agenda has been popularized by think tanks and corporate decision makers, backed by powerful international organizers such as the IMF and the World Bank (Marchak 1991).

The widespread adoption of this system of ideas, which has resulted in a free market version of restructuring, is attributed to the influence of key politicians and/or political organizations. Politicians such as Thatcher and Reagan are most often mentioned, together with their counterparts elsewhere, such as Mulroney and Douglas. Other analyses focus on the importance of Finance Departments and Treasury advisers (Boston 1995; Considine 1994). Finally, a wide set of both public and private interests, particularly those representing multinational capital, are identified as supportive of market liberalism (Martin 1993). In each analytical case, however, it is assumed that neoliberalism is a policy reform program initiated and rationalized through a relatively coherent theoretical and Ideological framework.

Of course there is a healthy internal debate amongst those who understand neoliberalism as a policy agenda. Public choice theory, to give just one example, has been challenged on numerous grounds (Dunleavy 1991; Hood 1991). It is also clear that neoliberal policies are differentially applied. In their discussion of New Zealand's model of public management, for example, Jonathon Boston (1996: 40) and his colleagues stress that, 'As is often the case, broad overarching terms, such as the NPM, can shelter within them a wealth of policy diversity.' However, my point is that despite debate and diversity within this literature, the key actors are understood to be politicians and policy makers, and component parts of the neoliberal policy agenda are seen as mutually reinforcing. Indeed, the very use of the word agenda denotes a coherent program of 'things to be done' (Teeple 1995: 169).

Such analyses constitute the vast majority of popular interpretations, as well as many academic commentaries on neoliberalism. Understandably, for many such observers the extension of market relations is highly problematic. More specifically, deregulation and privatization are identified as transferring power away from democratically elected governments with a mandate to ensure universal service provision, towards private capital concerned primarily with furthering opportunities for accumulation. In turn, this shift from public to private sector is understood to erode the foundations of both national economies and traditional social solidarities. As Susan Strange (1995: 289) has observed, 'that these changes have to a large extent emasculated state control over national economies and societies has almost become a journalistic platitude.'

In these analyses the response to neoliberalism tends to take the form of arguments over the success, or otherwise, of policy programs. Consequently the outcomes of neoliberal policy reforms predominate in these debates. In New Zealand, for example, quantitative research based on macroeconomic indicators is used to dispute the efficacy of the shift towards 'more market' (Dalziel 1997; Evans *et al.* 1996). Social policy analysts have demonstrated that increased social and spatial polarization is amongst the consequences of neoliberal reform (Boston *et al.* 1999; Stephens 1996). It is also argued that neoliberalism has exaggerated swings in the business cycle. The most common response to the shift to a minimalist noninterventionist state is an argument for the reintroduction of forms of state control that will attenuate the power of the market and prioritize the reestablishment of national control. Thus a change in the policy agenda, involving a return to the more protectionist stance associated with Keynesian welfarism, is seen as the primary solution to the problems generated by neoliberalism.

My argument is that while accounts of neoliberalism as policy serve a useful purpose in terms of elaborating the consequences of welfare state restructuring, as an explanation of the phenomenon itself they may raise more questions than they answer. It is notable that, for example, while very few political parties explicitly identify themselves as neoliberal, adherence to market based policy options characterize the current policy programs of social democratic and conservative governments alike. Assuming a critical distance from the tenets of neoliberalism, in particular the preference for market mechanisms as a means of ensuring social well-being, how is it that such a massive transformation in the policy making agenda has been achieved?

Moreover, given the tenuous empirical claims and lack of intellectual rigor on which this policy agenda appears to be based, how is it possible to explain the tenacity of ideas associated with neoliberalism? For as political scientist Janine Brodie (1996a: 131) has observed, 'changing public expectations about citizenship entitlements, the collective provision of social needs, and the efficacy of the welfare state has been a critical victory for neo-liberalism.' It is noticeable in New Zealand, for example, that despite the apparent unpopularity of the so-called 'free market revolution,' many political claims are now framed in the language of choice, flexibility and the market (see Larner 1997a). In short, how do we account for the apparent success of neoliberalism in shaping both political programs and individual subjectivities?

Neoliberalism as ideology

Neo-Marxist and socialist-feminist theorizations of neoliberalism provide useful means of addressing these questions, and thus constitute the second interpretation of neoliberalism to be discussed in this chapter. This might be seen as a more 'sociological' approach to neoliberalism in which a wider range of institutions, organizations and processes are considered. Best known of these are the analyses of Thatcherism associated with British theorist Stuart Hall. Rejecting the 'classic variant' of the Marxist theory of ideology, namely the idea that the ruling ideas are the ideas of the ruling class, Hall argues that the power of Thatcherism was its ability to constitute subject positions from which its discourses about the world made sense to people in a range of different social positions (Hall 1988). In doing so Thatcherism 'changed the currency of political thought and argument' and marked the consolidation of a new ideological hegemony based on the tenets of neoliberalism (Hall 1988: 40).

In arguing that Thatcherism was an ideological transformation, Hall makes explicit three points: first, that neoliberalism is not simply a system of ideas, nor a lurch to the Right in the formulation of policy agendas; second, that power is not constituted and exercised exclusively on the terrain of the state; third, that hegemony is only achieved through an ongoing process of contestation and struggle. Strongly influenced by Gramsci, his claim is that Thatcherism is best understood as a 'struggle to gain ascendancy over the entire social formation, to achieve positions of leadership in a number of different sites of social life at once, to achieve the commanding position on a broad strategic front' (Hall 1988: 52).

Most immediately, the strength of this work is that it does not underestimate the contradictions and complexities of Thatcherism as a concrete political phenomenon. In particular, Hall was concerned with the fact that Thatcherism had managed to articulate the interests of a wide range of groups in Britain, thereby clearing the way for the reassertion of market forces. Moreover, rather than understanding the ideology of the 'New Right' as a coherent corpus, he emphasized the different threads of this ideological formation; in this case the tensions between a 'pure' neoliberal ideology premised on the individual and free market, and a more traditional conservative ideology based on family and nation. Finally, his work opens the crucial question of identity. Rather than dismissing the attraction of the English working class to Thatcherism as 'false consciousness,' he explored the ways in which individual and group understandings were reconstructed through and against these ideological processes.

Hall's analysis of Thatcherism was, in part, an intellectual response to apparent political acquiescence of the British working class to neoliberal tenets. However, as the articles in Morley and Chen (1996) suggest, it was also a response to the rise of the so-called 'social movements' (including feminism, gay and lesbian politics, and ethnic struggles) and the subsequent extension of politics into 'lifestyle' issues such as health, food, sexuality and the body (also Hall 1989). More generally, as social heterogeneity and cross-cutting axes become increasingly visible, social theorists have been forced to take questions of identity and subjectivity more seriously. Indeed, it is noticeable that identity has become a 'keyword' for the social sciences, and that a more capacious Gramscian conception of ideology is now commonplace.[3]

In the work of Jane Jenson (1993; 1995), the question of identity formation is central. Jenson is concerned to explore the 'universe of political discourse' within which identities are socially constructed. Her emphasis is on political agency; how it is that groups of people mobilize around particular collective identities in order to represent their interests and intervene in the process of restructuring. Her primary emphasis is on oppositional identities, in particular those of social movements, rather than those constituted through official institutions and narratives. In the context of the argument made in this paper, the strength of Jenson's work is that she alerts us to the idea that the 'universe of political discourse' is not monopolized by hegemonic groups.

Innovative accounts of neoliberalism and welfare state restructuring emerge out of these neo-Gramscian literatures, most notably in the work of socialist-feminist analysts. Janine Brodie (1996a: 386), for example, argues that the contemporary shift in governing practices is 'a historic alteration in state form which enacts simultaneous changes in cultural assumptions, political identities and the very terrain of political struggle.' Her work interrogates new discourses of social welfare, marking shifts in understandings of citizenship, and exploring how these articulate with new understandings of gender relations. Moreover, she stresses that social movements are part of this complex matrix of discursive construction and reconstruction (Brodie 1996b). Likewise, in an analysis of the 'politics of post-welfare state arrangements' in the Ministry of Health and Social Services in Quebec, Dominique Masson (1997: 26) explicates the role of women's organizations in shaping new state forms, emphasizing that restructuring is a contested process; 'a complex, messy and contingent historical phenomena.'

These analyses show that new political configurations are more multivocal than we might previously have understood. Most immediately, we are alerted to the possibility that there are different configurations of neoliberalism, and that close inspection of particular neoliberal political projects is more likely to reveal a complex and hybrid political imaginary, rather than the straightforward implementation of a unified and coherent philosophy. Moreover, in making visible the claims of those all too often portrayed as the 'victims' of welfare state restructuring, these studies emphasize that new welfare state arrangements emerge out of political struggle, rather than being imposed in a top down manner. Finally, and not unrelatedly, we are forced to explore the notion that power is productive; that the articulations between hegemonic and oppositional claims give rise to new political subjectivities and social identities which then enter into the 'discourse of restructuring' (Yeatman 1990).

Neoliberalism as governmentality

As will be apparent from the discussion above, it is a short step from ideology to discourse, and thus to the third reading of neoliberalism to feature in this paper. However, this step requires us to move from Gramsci to Foucault, and from neo-Marxism to poststructuralism. In poststructuralist literatures discourse is understood not simply as a form of rhetoric disseminated by hegemonic economic and political groups, nor as the framework within which people represent their 'lived experience,' but rather as a system of meaning that constitutes institutions, practices and identities in contradictory and disjunctive ways (Fairclough 1992). Indeed, Hall himself has taken this step, with a self-identified shift from a 'base-superstructure ideology model' to a 'discursive model' (Terry 1997: 46).

The most influential poststructuralist theorization of neoliberalism is that associated with the neo-Foucauldian literature on governmentality.[4] This literature makes a useful distinction between government and governance, and argues that while neoliberalism may mean less government, it does not follow that there is less governance. While on one hand neoliberalism problematizes the state and is concerned to specify its limits through the invocation of individual choice, on the other hand it involves forms of governance that encourage both institutions and individuals to conform to the norms of the market. Elsewhere I have used the term 'market governance' to capture this point (Larner 1997b).

The governmentality literature has inspired innovative analyses of welfare state restructuring, which show that social policy reform is linked to a new specification of the object of governance. The conception of a national community of citizens, made up of male breadwinners and female domestic workers, has been usurped by a new understanding in which not only are firms to be entrepreneurial, enterprising and innovative, but so too are political subjects. Neoliberal strategies of rule, found in diverse realms including workplaces, educational institutions and health and welfare agencies, encourage people to see themselves as individualized and active subjects responsible for enhancing their own well-being. This conception of the 'active society' can also be linked to a particular politics of self in which we are all encouraged to 'work on ourselves' in a range of domains, including the 'counter cultural movements' outside the purview of traditional conceptions of the political (Dean 1995).

Nikolas Rose (1993) elucidates the process by which this new formula of rule has usurped that of the 'welfare state.' He argues that it was the linking of the critiques of the welfare state (from both sides of the political spectrum) to the political technologies associated with marketization, that provided the basis for 'advanced liberal' rule. Welfare agencies are now to be governed, not directly from above, but through technologies such as budget disciplines, accountancy and audit. In association with this 'degovernmentalization' of the welfare state, competition and consumer demand have supplanted the norms of 'public service.' Correspondingly, the citizen is respecified as an active agent both able and obliged to exercise autonomous choices. In his research on unemployment William Walters (1996; 1997) has explicated how this new understanding forms the basis for active labor market policies, and is associated with the 'desocialization' of unemployment and poverty.

The political implications of these analyses are perhaps more subtle than those discussed previously. As O'Malley, Weir and Shearing (1997: 504) explain, 'the broad aim of the approach is to generate a "post-social politics" that provides a successor to socialism, but which nonetheless is more than a simple condemnation of neo-liberal and neo-conservative thinking.' At the same time, those working within this tradition are clear that they wish to avoid generating a specific political program. Rather they aspire to 'fragment the present'; 'the received fixedness and inevitability of the present is destabilized, shown as just sufficiently fragile as to let in a little glimpse of freedom – as a practice of difference – through its fractures' (Barry, Osborne and Rose 1996: 5). This politics stresses the complexity, ambiguity and the contingency of contemporary political formations to maximize possibilities for critical responses and interventions.

As yet, however, the governmentality literature has not paid a great deal of attention to the politics surrounding specific programs and policies (although see Dean and Hindess 1998). This is particularly the case *vis-à-vis* theorizations of neoliberalism in that the emphasis has been on broad governmental themes rather than specific neoliberal projects. This programmatic orientation is reflected in the distinction made by Rose (1996) between 'advanced liberalism' as a governmentality and 'neo-liberalism' as a political ideology. Yet it is obvious that without analyses of the 'messy actualities' of particular neoliberal projects, those working within this analytic run the risk of precisely the problem they wish to avoid – that of producing generalized accounts of historical epochs. Indeed, this is precisely the criticism made of this literature by Boris Frankel (1997), who argues that 'advanced liberalism' is a totalizing concept, despite attempts to distance the governmentality literature from other 'grand theories.'

Moreover, in the few instances where the emphasis has been on neoliberal projects, the analysis has tended to focus on official discourses, as read through government policy documents. As Pat O'Malley (1996) explains, this means that this body of work privileges official discourses, with the result that it is difficult to recognize the imbrication of resistance and rule. My point is that despite its origins in Foucauldian formulations, remarkably few of these analyses draw from the discourses of oppositional groups as well as those of hegemonic groups (although see Weir 1996). It is in this context that I argue for a formulation that draws on the insights of both the neo-Marxist and socialist-feminist analyses discussed in the second section of the paper, and the governmentality literature examined herein.

Theorizing the 'New Zealand experiment'

The 'New Zealand experiment' is a particularly challenging case through which to work my argument. International attention has focused on this country not only because of the depth and rapidity of the reforms instituted by successive governments since 1984, but also because this case appears to involve the direct application of a clearly delineated theoretical model. For example, John Gray (1998: 39) observed:

> The neo-liberal experiment in New Zealand is the most ambitious attempt at constructing the free market as a social institution to be implemented anywhere this century. It is a clearer case of the costs and limits of reinventing the free market than the Thatcherite experiment in Britain.

While these comments may be somewhat exaggerated, even more nuanced commentators agree the 'New Zealand experiment' was an early and extreme example of the now widespread transition from social democracy to neoliberalism in welfare state societies (for example Schwartz 1994; Neilson 1988).

In most discussions of the 'New Zealand experiment' neoliberalism is understood as a coherent, top down, state initiated policy agenda based on a unified political philosophy. Indeed there is such a tight identification between neoliberalism and the state that in the most recent edited collection on the political economy of New Zealand they are referenced together (Rudd and Roper 1997: 309). There is also a widespread assumption that this policy agenda has 'programmatic coherence' (Hindess 1997: 22), despite the diversity of political perspectives and ideological standpoints from which concepts such as devolution, community and empowerment are disseminated. Even when the resonance between hegemonic and oppositional claims is acknowledged, the explanation tends to be in terms of 'their' cooption of 'our' language. One consequence of this formulation is that many of those who would contest this policy agenda unwittingly reinforce the coherence of neoliberalism.

It is the 'programmatic coherence' of neoliberalism that this paper seeks to challenge. My claim is that in constructing neoliberalism as a monolithic apparatus that is completely knowable and in full control of the 'New Right,' such analyses inadvertently reconstruct its hegemony. In this regard I am persuaded by Wendy Brown's (1995) argument that many well-intentioned contemporary political projects and theoretical postures inadvertently redraw the very configurations and effects of power they seek to vanquish. Both neo-Marxist and socialist-feminist literatures on the 'politics of restructuring' and the poststructuralist literatures on governmentality open up possibilities to theorize the 'New Zealand experiment' in ways that emphasize its historically contingent and internally contradictory aspects, rather than its coherence. In this regard, it will be apparent that I take seriously the poststructuralist admonition to recognize the consequences of our theories, and to make visible 'contested representations within what are putatively singular or common cultures' (Yeatman 1994: 30).

What then might we see if we were to take such an approach? Most immediately, the analysis needs to be grounded in detailed investigations of the case in order to make visible the 'messy actualities' of new forms of governance; the contradictions, complexities and inconsistencies that inevitably characterize neoliberal political projects, including the 'New Zealand experiment.' Moreover, whereas a more orthodox account might analyze these differences as simply permutations on a more general theme; stressing, for example, the similarities between Rogernomics and Thatcherism, an approach grounded in the literatures explored herein would stress the specificity of these political projects (Larner and Walters 2000). Such an approach understands that different formulations of neoliberalism emerge out of a multiplicity of political forces always in competition with another, producing unintended outcomes and unexpected alignments. Moreover, the emergence of new political projects is never a complete rupture with what has gone before, but rather is part of an ongoing process involving the recomposition of political rationalities, programs and identities.

In terms of substantive research projects, the differing strands of thought that come together under the label of neoliberalism in New Zealand can be identified and explored. Reviving the distinction between neoconservatism and neoliberalism, and then identifying variants within each of these formulations, may be a critical first step. In this regard, the work of Bruce Jesson *et al.* (1988) and Anne Else (1992) is notable, and can be used to inform contemporary concerns. Both were concerned to emphasize two different strands of 'New Right ideology' – libertarianism and authoritarianism – and argued the fourth Labour government was dominated by libertarians. This argument could be extended. For example, whereas Hall argued that Thatcherism managed to articulate neoliberalism with neoconservatism, it could be argued that the achievement of the fourth Labour government was that it was able to articulate a libertarian version of neoliberalism with social democratic aspirations (Larner 1997a). This point also alerts us to the importance of exploring the contradictions between social justice and economic agendas during the 1980s. This is an often noted, but rarely investigated, aspect of existing commentaries on the 'New Zealand experiment.'

In contrast, the policies and programs of the National government of the 1990s involved an articulation between a more authoritarian version of neoliberalism and neoconservatism, and was thus a more recognisable 'New Right' configuration. However, even during the 1990s there were diverse and sometimes contradictory formulations. There were, for example, clear tensions between 'market governance' in the economic realm premised on individualistic and entrepreneurial economic subjects who could be 'governed from a distance,' and the increased visibility of the state in the area of social policy. These tensions were most notable in the 1998 proposal to develop a 'Code of Social and Family Responsibility.' This Code was premised on the assumption that direct monitoring of New Zealand families could be used to foster self-reliant and enterprising neoliberal subjects. Rather than conflating these tensions under broad claims about the 'New Right,' the contradictions within and between these political rationales can be made explicit and explored (Larner 2000).

It follows that greater attention should be paid to the contestations within and between hegemonic (neoliberal?) groups. Already there is work that alerts us to the existence of such tensions; for example the debates within the Labour party (Oliver 1989; Wilson 1989), or the well publicized clashes between the Employers Federation and the Manufacturers Federation. Closer attention to the specificities of neoliberalism would also encourage 'de-centered' approaches to the state, with an emphasis on the detail of the restructuring of different government departments and state agencies.

Inevitably such projects multiply the social locations from which new formulations emerge. Social movements become visible in these analyses, not simply as victims, but as active agents in the process of political-economic change. At the same time it needs to be recognized that political 'resistance' is figured by and within, rather than being external to, the regimes of power it contests (Brown 1995). Again, signposts exist for such work. Denese Henare (1995) and Brenda Tahi (1995), for example, emphasize that in New Zealand public sector restructuring has been significantly shaped by attempts to institutionalize biculturalism. As Mason Durie (1998: 11) observes:

> Positive Maori development, with its focus on tribal responsibilities for health, education, welfare, economic progress, and greater autonomy, fitted quite comfortably with the free market philosophy of a minimal state, non-government provision of services, economic self-sufficiency and privatisation.

This is not to suggest that the discourses of neoliberalism and *tino rangatiratanga* can be reduced to each other, nor is it to deny neoliberal hegemony. However it is to take seriously the idea that new welfare state arrangements emerge out of political struggle, rather than being simply imposed in a top down manner. In New Zealand demands from Maori for the right to deliver services in culturally appropriate forms constitute a very significant critique of the postwar welfare state. Moreover, as Elizabeth Rata argues, in the last two decades there has been a dialectical interaction between state actors and Maori as both have attempted to reposition themselves in a wider global context. During this process neoliberals and some Maori found themselves in unexpected agreement on a key theme: namely, the dangers of continued dependency on the state (Rata 1997: 11). In this case, therefore, we see very clearly that the claims of social movements are part of the discursive construction and reconstruction associated with welfare state restructuring.

Similarly, while the economic restructuring program initiated by the fourth Labour government is often seen as detrimental for women, there were also important feminist victories during this period. An active women's council and a feminist party president meant that broader feminist struggles were reflected in both Labour party organization and policy proposals. Once elected, the fourth Labour cabinet was notable for the inclusion of several 'stroppy women' (Sheppard 1999: 10). The presence of these women provided the impetus for important initiatives, including the establishment of a Ministry for Women's Affairs. Equal Employment Opportunities (EEO) programs were also advanced, becoming mandatory in the public sector with the passing of the State Sector Act 1988. In her analysis of the EEO initiative, Alex Woodley (1993) argues its success could be attributed to a general appreciation of the merits of the case, together with widespread political support from women in parliament, the bureaucracy, community groups and trade unions. Homosexual Law Reform and the short-lived Employment Equity Act[5] were amongst the other important initiatives. Thus, whereas neoliberalism is often associated with an anti-feminist backlash (see David 1986, for example, on the UK and the US), the contrary was the case in New Zealand during the 1980s.

Understanding neoliberalism through these lenses also encourages investigation of the reformulation of identities, not simply as the outcome of rhetoric or political manipulation, but rather as an integral part of the process of restructuring. It would center on the recognition that political power does not just act on political subjects, but constructs them in particular ways (Marshall 1994). This would help us understand the processes by which the subjectivities of New Zealanders have become more closely aligned with the individualistic assumptions that underpin neoliberalism, and how economic identities have come to be posited as a new basis for political life, usurping those associated with social citizenship. Elsewhere, for example, I have shown that the restructuring of the telecommunications industry was integrally associated with a move away from governmental conceptions of the 'public' and the concomitant centering of the 'consumer' as the hegemonic political-economic identity. The analysis demonstrated that this change was a consequence of the contestation between dominant and oppositional claims, rather than being simply imposed from above (Larner 1997b).

This attention to identity can be extended to consider how new gendered, racialized and classed subjectivities are also emerging out of the articulations between hegemonic and oppositional claims in the 'discourse of restructuring' (Yeatman 1990). It is notable, for example, that the new 'consumer-citizen' is degendered (Probyn 1998). The concept of the male breadwinner has also been eroded, manifest in a more gender-neutral model of the citizen worker (O'Connor *et al.* 1999). Government agencies and documents now recognize diverse family forms, rather than insisting on a culturally specific nuclear model of the nuclear family, and more often use the gender-neutral term 'parents,' rather than the gender specific terms 'mothers' and 'fathers.' Indeed, one of the striking aspects of the proposed Code of Social and Family Responsibility was that despite the emphasis on the family as a self-supporting site of social well-being, it explicitly referred to mothers only when discussing pregnancy and child bearing, and exhorted fathers to assume more responsibility for childcare and family life.

Of course, it is easy to be cynical about these changes. Certainly, when second wave feminists demanded the rights to economic independence and labor force participation for women on the same terms as men, they did not anticipate increasing numbers of men being employed in jobs and under terms and conditions once associated only with women (Armstrong 1996). Moreover, women who opt for motherhood now find their labor devalued in a context where paid work appears to be all (Copas 1999), whereas those who choose not to have children contend with the legacy of earlier formulations and are seen as 'un-natural women.' My point, however, is that there is an articulation between feminist claims for gender neutrality premised on the assumption that women have the right to autonomous personhood, and neoliberal claims for possessive individualism. As O'Connor, Orloff and Shaver (1999: 53–4) remind us, neoliberalism emerged in a period when increasing numbers of women entered into the labor market, and during which liberal feminists have forcefully asserted women's personhood in law and the market. The consequence is that neoliberals are thus more willing to recognize women as individuals in their own right than their postwar political counterparts.

Conclusion

Most immediately, I am making a claim for a more detailed engagement with contemporary changes in governance, rather than dismissing them as the prerogative of the 'New Right.' Such investigations may reveal that neoliberalism is a more tenuous phenomenon than is commonly assumed. By focusing attention on the historically specific and internally contradictory aspects of neoliberalism, and the shaping of specific neoliberal projects by articulations between both hegemonic and nonhegemonic groups, it will become apparent that neoliberalism, like the welfare state, is 'more an ethos or an ethical ideal, than a set of completed or established institutions' (Dean 1997: 213). The emergence of new forms of political power does not simply involve the imposition of a new understanding on top of the old. The transformation of a polity involves the complex linking of various domains of practice, is ongoingly contested, and the result is not a foregone conclusion. Consequently, contemporary forms of rule are inevitably composite, plural and multiform.

Thus, while fully recognizing the distinctiveness of the contemporary forms of political-economic life, it will become possible to move past the either/or debates that currently structure political life. If neoliberalism cannot be reduced to a single set of philosophical principles or a unified political ideology, nor is necessarily linked to a particular political apparatus, this will encourage us to think about different versions of neoliberalism, and allow exploration of the possibilities that might enhance social well-being. As O'Malley, Weir and Shearing (1997: 503) explain:

> Not only does (the governmentality literature) provide a theoretical elaboration which potentially opens everyday and institutional programmes and practices for critical and tactical thinking, it also provides a considerable array of empirical work in terms of which interventions can be examined and thought out.

Obviously these claims challenge many orthodoxies. Yet without such an engagement, we restrict our potential to imagine political alternatives. Only by theorizing neoliberalism as a multivocal and contradictory phenomenon can we make visible the contestations and struggles that we are currently engaged in. Moreover, the alternatives, premised on monolithic conceptions of the 'New Right,' or neoliberal capitalism, are both politically disempowering and intellectually unsatisfying. As academics, we need to pay careful attention to the reasons why the so-called 'rhetoric' of programmers resonates, parodies and complicates our analyses, if only because in acknowledging the complexity of neoliberalism we stand a better chance of identifying possibilities to advance social justice aims in a new context.

Notes

1. Barry Hindess argues that the existence of different labels suggests we should regard contemporary political-economic changes as the outcome of several distinct lines of development. As will become apparent later in the paper, I am sympathetic to this point although my focus herein is slightly different. See Hindess 1997.
2. The term 'post-social' refers to the idea that we are no longer governed through unitary conceptions of society. New forms of social governance assume cultural and political difference. See Dean 1999.
3. Thanks to Phil Ryan for stressing this point.
4. Burchell, Gordon and Miller (1991); Barry, Osborne and Rose (1996); Rose (1999); Dean (1999).
5. The repeal of this act was one of the first actions of the new National government.

References

Armstrong, P. (1996) 'The Feminization of the Labour Force: Harmonizing Down in a Global Economy,' in Bakker, I. (ed.) *Rethinking Restructuring: Gender and Change in Canada*. Toronto: University of Toronto Press.

Barry, A., Osborne, T. and Rose, N. (eds) (1996) *Foucault and Political Reason: Liberalism, Neo-liberalism and Rationalities of Government*. Chicago: The University of Chicago Press.

Belsey, A. (1996) 'The New Right, Social Order and Civil Liberties,' in Levitas, R. (ed.) *The Ideology of the New Right*. Cambridge: Polity Press.

Boston, J. (1995) 'Origins and Destinations: New Zealand's Model of Public Management and the International Transfer of Ideas,' in Weller, P. and Davis, G. (eds) *New Ideas, Better Government*. Sydney: Allen and Unwin.

Boston, J., Martin, J., Pallot, J. and Walsh, P. (1996) *Public Management: The New Zealand Model*. Auckland: Oxford University Press.

Boston, J., Dalziel, P. and St John, S. (1999) *Redesigning the Welfare State in New Zealand: Problems, Policies, Prospects*. Auckland: Oxford University Press.

Brodie, J. (1996a) 'Restructuring and the New Citizenship,' in Bakker, I. (ed.) *Rethinking Restructuring: Gender and Change in Canada*. Toronto: University of Toronto Press.

Brodie, J. (1996b) 'New State Forms, New Political Spaces,' in Boyer, R. and Drache, D. (eds) *States Against Markets: the Limits of Globalisation*. London: Routledge.

Brown, W. (1995) *States of Injury: Power and Freedom in Late Modernity*. Princeton: Princeton University Press.

Burchell, G., Gordon, C. and Miller, P. (eds) (1991) *The Foucault Effect: Studies in Governmentality*. Hemel Hempstead: Harvester Wheatsheaf.

Considine, M. (1994) *Public Policy: A Critical Approach*. Melbourne: Macmillan Education.

Copas, S. (1999) '(Over)Working Women; Gendered Discourses of Market Governance in New Zealand,' MA thesis, Department of Sociology, University of Auckland.

Dalziel, P. (1997) 'New Zealand's Economic Reforms 1984–95: Comment,' *Victoria Economic Commentaries* 15 (1): 1–6.

David, M. (1986) 'Moral and Maternal: The Family in the New Right,' in Levitas, R. (ed.) *The Ideology of the New Right*. Oxford: Polity Press.

Dean, M. (1995) 'Governing the Unemployed Self in an Active Society,' *Economy and Society* 24 (4): 559–83.

Dean, M. (1997) 'Sociology after Society,' in Owen, D. (ed.) *Sociology after Postmodernism*. London: Sage.

Dean, M. (1999) *Governmentality*. London: Sage.

Dean, M. and Hindess, B. (eds) (1998) *Governing Australia: Studies in Contemporary Rationalities of Government*. Cambridge: Cambridge University Press.

Dunleavy, P. (1991) *Democracy, Bureaucracy and Public Choice*. Brighton: Wheatsheaf.

Durie, M. (1998) *Te Mana, Te Kawanatanga: The Politics of Maori Self-Determination*. Auckland: Oxford University Press.

Else, A. (1992) 'To Market and Home Again: Gender and the New Right,' in du Plessis, R. *et al.* (eds) *Feminist Voices: Women's Studies Texts for Aotearoa/New Zealand*, Auckland: Oxford University Press.

Evans, L., Grimes, A., Wilkinson, B. with Teece, D. (1996) 'Economic Reform in New Zealand 1984–1995: The Pursuit of Efficiency,' *Journal of Economic Literature* 34 (4): 1856–902.
Fairclough, N. (1992) *Discourse and Social Change*. Cambridge: Polity Press.
Frankel, B. (1997) 'Confronting Neo-liberal Regimes: The Post-Marxist Embrace of Populism and Realpolitik,' *New Left Review* 226: 7–92.
Gray, J. (1998) *False Dawn: The Delusions of Global Capital*. London: Granta Publications.
Hall, S. (1988) 'The Toad in the Garden: Thatcherism among the Theorists,' in Nelson, C. and Grossberg, L. (eds) *Marxism and the Interpretation of Culture*. London: Macmillan Education.
Hall, S. (1989) 'Introduction,' in Hall, S. and Jacques, M. (eds) *New Times*. London: Lawrence and Wishart.
Henare, D. (1995) 'The Ka Awatea Report: Reflections on its Process and Vision,' in Wilson, M. and Yeatman, A. (eds) *Justice and Identity: Antipodean Practices*. Wellington: Bridget Williams Books.
Hindess, B. (1997) 'A Society Governed by Contract?' in Davis, G., Sullivan, B. and Yeatman, A. (eds) *The New Contractualism?* Melbourne: Macmillan Education.
Hood, C. (1991) 'A Public Administration for All Seasons?' *Public Administration* 69 (1): 3–20.
Jenson, J. (1993) 'All the World's a Stage: Ideas, Spaces, and Time in Canadian Political Economy,' in Jenson, J., Mahon, R. and Bienefeld, M. (eds) *Production, Space, Identity: Political Economy Faces the 21st Century*. Toronto: Canadian Scholars Press.
Jenson, J. (1995) 'Mapping, Naming, and Remembering: Globalization at the End of the Twentieth Century,' *Review of International Political Economy* 2 (1): 96–116.
Jenson, J. (1999) 'Changing Citizenship Regimes: Concepts and Applications,' Paper presented at a Symposium on Citizenship, Representation and Neo-liberalism held at the University of Auckland on 24 July 1999.
Jesson, B. *et al.* (eds) (1988) *Revival of the Right*. Auckland: Heinmann Reed.
Larner, W. (1997a) 'A Means to an End: Neo-liberalism and State Processes in New Zealand,' *Studies in Political Economy* 47: 7–38.
Larner, W. (1997b) 'The Legacy of the Social: Market Governance and the Consumer.' *Economy and Society* 26 (3): 373–99.
Larner, W. (2000) 'Post-Welfare State Governance: Towards a Code of Social and Family Responsibility,' *Social Politics* 7 (2): 244–65.
Larner, W. and Walters, W. (2000) 'Privatisation, Governance and Identity: the United Kingdom and New Zealand compared,' *Policy and Politics* 28 (3): 361–77.
Marchak, P. (1991) *The Integrated Circus: The New Right and the Restructuring of Global Markets*. Montreal: McGill Queens Press.
Marshall, B. (1994) *Engendering Modernity: Feminism, Social Theory and Social Change*. Boston: Northwestern University Press.
Martin, B. (1993) *In the Public Interest? Privatisation and Public Sector Reform*. London: Zed Books.
Masson, D. (1997) 'Constituting "Post-Welfare" Welfare Arrangements: The Role of Women's Movement Service Groups in Quebec,' Paper presented at the

Canadian Sociology and Anthropology Association, Learned Societies of Canada, St Johns, Newfoundland, 10 June 1997.

Morley, D. and Chen, K.-S. (1996) *Stuart Hall: Critical Dialogues in Cultural Studies*. London: Routledge.

Neilson, D. (1988) 'State Autonomy and the Mode of Political Regulation: Neo-liberal Restructuring in New Zealand,' *Studies in Political Economy* 57: 45–72.

O'Connor, J., Orloff, A. and Shaver, S. (1999) *States, Markets, Families: Gender, Liberalism and Social Policy in Australia, Canada, Great Britain and the United States*. Cambridge: Cambridge University Press.

Oliver, H. (1989) 'The Labour Caucus and Economic Policy Formation 1981–84,' in Easton, B. (ed.) *The Making of Rogernomics*. Auckland: Auckland University Press.

O'Malley, P. (1996) 'Indigenous Governance,' *Economy and Society* 26 (3): 310–26.

O'Malley, P., Weir, L. and Shearing, C. (1997) 'Governmentality, Criticism, Politics,' *Economy and Society* 26 (4): 501–17.

Probyn, E. (1998) 'McIdentities: Food and the Familial Citizen,' *Theory, Culture and Society* 15 (2): 155–73.

Purvis, T. and Hunt, A. (1993) 'Discourse, Ideology, Discourse, Ideology, Discourse Ideology...,' *British Journal of Sociology* 44 (3): 473–99.

Rata, E. (1997) 'The Theory of Tribal Capitalism,' Paper presented to SAANZ, Massey University, Albany, December.

Rose, N. (1993) 'Government, Authority and Expertise in Advanced Liberalism,' *Economy and Society* 22 (3): 281–300.

Rose, N. (1996) 'Governing "Advanced" Liberal Democracies,' in Barry, A., Osborne, T. and Rose, N. (eds) *Foucault and Political Reason: Liberalism, Neo-liberalism, and Rationalities of Government*. London: UCL Press.

Rose, N. (1999) *Powers of Freedom: Reframing Political Thought*. Cambridge: Cambridge University Press.

Rudd, C. and Roper, B. (eds) (1997) The Political Economy of New Zealand. Auckland: Oxford University Press.

Schwartz, H. (1994) 'Small States in Big Trouble: State Reorganization in Australia, Denmark, New Zealand and Sweden in the 1980s,' *World Politics* 46 (4): 527–55.

Schwartz, H. (2001) 'Round up the Usual Suspects! Globalization, Domestic Politics and Welfare State Change,' in Pierson, P. (ed.) *New Politics of the Welfare State*. Oxford: Oxford University Press.

Sheppard, S. (1999) *Broken Circle: The Decline and Fall of the Fourth Labour Government*. Wellington: Publishing Solutions Limited.

Stephens, B. (1996) 'Social Services,' in Silverstone, B., Bollard, A. and Lattimore, R. (eds) *A Study of Economic Reform: the Case of New Zealand*. Amsterdam: New Holland.

Strange, S. (1995) 'The Limits of Politics,' *Government and Opposition* 30 (2): 291–311.

Tahi, B. (1995) 'Biculturalism: The Model of Te Ohu Whakatupu,' in Wilson, M. and Yeatman, A. (eds) *Justice and Identity: Antipodean Practices*. Wellington: Bridget Williams Books.

Teeple, G. (1995) *Globalisation and the Decline of Social Reform*. Toronto: Garamond Press.

Terry, L. (1997) 'Travelling "The Hard Road to Renewal,"' *Arena* 8: 39–58
Walters, W. (1996) 'The Demise of Unemployment?' *Politics and Society* 24 (3): 197–219.
Walters, W. (1997) 'The "Active Society": New Designs for Social Policy,' *Policy and Politics* 25 (3): 221–34.
Weir, L. (1996) 'Recent Developments in the Government of Pregnancy,' *Economy and Society* 25 (3): 373–92.
Wilson, M. (1989) *Labour in Government 1984–1987*. Sydney: Allen and Unwin.
Woodley, A. (1993) 'One Step Forward, Two Steps Back – The Pay Equity Campaign: A Study of Political Strategy,' MA research essay, Department of Sociology, University of Auckland.
Yeatman, A. (1990) *Bureaucrats, Technocrats, Femocrats*. Sydney: Allen and Unwin.
Yeatman, A. (1994) *Postmodern Revisioning of the Political*. New York: Routledge.

11
Everyday Life in the Global Political Economy

Matt Davies[1]

Calls to ground the study of international relations in everyday life have found increasing salience among critical approaches to the field. Feminists, poststructuralists and historical materialists have all sought to address problems in international relations theory by breaking down conceptual divisions between the domestic and international, between the local and the global, or between the private and the public. Everyday life is not a new concern among sociologists or philosophers and a variety of approaches to it, ranging from positivist descriptions of daily routines to speculative accounts of the lifeworld, have been posited and explored in these disciplines. However, for International Relations (IR), and particularly for International Political Economy (IPE), everyday life remains largely under- or untheorized, with damaging consequences for the concept's contribution to critique.

The impetus behind the call to ground IR in everyday life stems from the ongoing sense that the shape and the trends of global politics result not only from those actors who have been the concern of traditional IR theory, especially the state-as-actor, but also from actors usually understood to 'act' only at the local or national level. The oft-criticized notion of 'global civil society' was an example of such an effort to think global politics 'from the bottom up.'[2] For IPE, however, the question remains: how do marginalized groups, such as the global poor, become political protagonists at a global or international scale? This is an urgent question for approaches to IPE that take normativity seriously, which would suggest the need for a transformation or an emancipatory project and for understanding the possibilities for political resistance in the context of the processes characteristic of the global political economy.

This chapter argues that the political possibilities for the global poor are shaped by carrying out a *critique* of everyday life – which is thus necessary in order for critical theories of IPE to develop their normative potential. The critique of everyday life is not the sole province of intellectuals and scholars. It is also carried out in the conduct of everyday life itself. As will be seen, this understanding of critique highlights the reasons that the 'level' of the everyday is important for understanding resistance – as well as for understanding the reproduction of the fragmented and hierarchically ordered social formations constituting the global political economy. The capacity to realize transformational or emancipatory projects is too often short-circuited by analyses that locate resistance as an automatic response on the part of the oppressed to the development of contradictions within the political projects of the powerful; or by asserting that the poor are a static, inert or passive mass; or by analyses in which the indeterminacy of the notion of resistance can indicate any nonelite gesture as an act of resistance, without the conceptual tools to specify 'resistance to what' or in what ways resistance is different from compliance.

To avoid this theoretical short-circuiting, this chapter outlines a critical account of everyday life drawing primarily from the work of Henri Lefebvre.[3] Lefebvre distinguished the everyday from daily life (Lefebvre 1988: 87, fn. 1). Daily life has always existed; it is merely what we do day-to-day and is often what IR theorists mean when they write about everyday life. For Lefebvre, in contrast, the everyday is what we get when the imperatives of capitalism or capitalist modernity begin to transform daily life to fit its patterns and needs. The historical forces driving the invention of everyday life include the mental-manual division of labor, upon which the separation of 'specialized activities' from the 'residue' of daily life is based; and it also includes urbanization, which paves the way for the transformation of space into abstract space and the fragmentation of experience into, for example, work, leisure, and family life.

The chapter then turns to a discussion of some important contributions to thinking about everyday life for the field of IPE from three theorists: Timothy Sinclair, Paul Langley, and David Campbell. This discussion focuses on how each conceptualizes (implicitly or explicitly) everyday life, and how each understands the relations between global or international forces and everyday life. Each contribution is discussed in the light of the critique of everyday life outlined in the previous section so that the chapter can conclude with a reconsideration of what and how a critique of everyday life can contribute to critical IPE.

What is everyday life?

Henri Lefebvre, as a theorist of how capitalism and modernity homogenize, fragment and create hierarchies in social life, considered the concept of 'everyday life' to be his most important contribution to Marxist thought. He defined it in a number of differing ways. It is the 'reality without truth,' counterpoised to the 'truth without reality' of philosophy (Lefebvre 1984: 14). It is the 'soil' in which the 'flowers and trees' of creative human activity grow (Lefebvre 1991a: 87). It is the object of programming in a 'bureaucratic society of controlled consumption' (Lefebvre 1984). 'In appearance, it is the insignificant and the banal. It is what Hegel called "the prose of the world," nothing more modest' (Lefebvre 1988: 78).

Lefebvre summarizes the historical emergence of the everyday into three stages. In the first, daily life remains connected to the rhythms of nature: '[t]he rhythms of life could be only poorly distinguished from the rhythms of nature: night and day, weeks and months, seasons and years' (Lefebvre 1988: 79). But, for example in France after World War II, industrialization and urbanization take off and France enters the second stage: '[e]xchange value prevails over use value. The commodity, the market, money, with their implacable logic, seize everyday life. The extension of capitalism goes all the way to the slightest details of ordinary life...' (Lefebvre 1988: 79).

The third stage, for Lefebvre, comes with the penetration of the media into the details of ordinary life and the consequent mediation and mass-mediation of everyday life. Elsewhere, Lefebvre develops this pessimistic view of everyday life into a description of late capitalist social order as a 'bureaucratic society of controlled consumption.' This description is itself historical, bound by its own time and place – Lefebvre was writing in Paris in 1967 when he elaborated this conception – and one we may wish to critique today. Nevertheless, it signals everyday life as an object for technocratic planning and programming – or we might say 'governance' in terms familiar to IPE.

The key to understanding the historical emergence of the everyday lies with the ways in which the development of capitalism and modernity fragment social life. The technical and social divisions of labor create specialized activities and spatial differentiations to support social fragmentation. Of course, such processes are not peculiar to capitalism and have indeed been part of the social world for a very long time. Lefebvre traces philosophy's turning away from the everyday back to the Greeks; for example, Plato's equation of daily life with vulgar, public opinion (*doxa*) (Lefebvre 1988: 78). This disdain persists through the Middle Ages and into the modern era. However, these diverse criticisms of ordinary life rest on:

> a common element: they were the work of particularly gifted, lucid and active *individuals* (the philosopher, the poet, etc.). However, this individual lucidity or activeness concealed an appearance or an illusion, and therefore a hidden, deeper reality. In truth their work belonged to a time and a class whose ideas were thus raised above the everyday onto the level of the exceptional and the dominant. Hence the criticism of everyday life was in fact *a criticism of other classes*, and for the most part found its expression in contempt for productive labour [...] (Lefebvre 1991a: 29, emphasis in original).

Lefebvre goes on to discuss the relationship between philosophy and everyday life in terms of leisure: 'As an activity, philosophy used to be precisely one of those exceptional and superior activities through which men who could devote their lives to leisure could step outside of everyday life, and which involved criticism of everyday life, implicitly or explicitly' (Lefebvre 1991a: 85). That the capacity to philosophize is tied to leisure is not coincidental. Everyday life is a burden: it is mundane, routine, repetitive, boring. To develop the perspective to criticize this burden, as well as the personality to do so, required a separation of the critic from productive labor: 'the man who was able to develop himself never worked' (Lefebvre 1991a: 30). Or, at least, so he thought. For, 'whether they were aristocrats, clerks still tied to feudalism, or bourgeois *honnêtes hommes*, such men only *appeared* to remain outside the social division of labour and social practice. In reality they were prisoners of the separation of manual and intellectual work' (Lefebvre 1991a: 30, emphasis in original).

Labor in any kind of social formation is divided in multiple ways but one of the fundamental and structuring divisions is between mental and manual labor (Sohn-Rethel 1978). This division underlies the emergence of ruling groups and the foundations of states. As the technical and social divisions of labor develop and specialization accelerates under capitalism, specialized activities organized in the linear rhythms of the ever-shortening time horizons of capital accumulation become increasingly separated from and dominant over the cycles of production and reproduction in everyday life.

The division of labor must also be linked to the separation of production from reproduction and the consequent dominance of the latter by the former. Lefebvre argued infamously that the burdens of everyday life are borne more heavily by women. Part of the basis for this claim – for which he was justly criticized – was his depiction of his wife's observation about a box of detergent: '*This* is an excellent product' (cited in Highmore 2002: 113). Lefebvre's suggestion here was that women were more vulnerable to having the commodities speak through them. However, Lefebvre was at the same time sensitive to the ways in which the fragmentation of life distributes the burdens of everyday life unevenly. The separation of production functions – labor – from reproduction – domesticity and family life – not only enables a division between waged and unwaged work, but also the domination and exploitation of the unwaged labor of social reproduction (see Peterson this volume).[4]

The domination of manual labor by the intellect, of everyday life by technique, planning or philosophy, and of reproduction by production also expresses itself in space. The lives of peasants or crafts people in precapitalist social formations differ from industrial workers in part in terms of the way that productive activity inheres in people's living spaces. There are social and spatial differentiations in peasant villages but the way work, domestic life, and festivals are organized and regulated belongs to the group as a whole. Urbanization, at the outset of the development of capitalism when urbanization was driven by industrialization, separates productive labor from leisure and domestic life and sets aside particular spaces for each. It also contributes to the increasing fragmentation of labor itself, situating individuals into increasingly complex social relations while isolating the individual and splitting consciousness between private and social or public consciousness.

The depiction of the everyday in such terms as have been discussed so far point to the suppression of diversity and difference, class domination and the means by which it is imposed and sustained, and the production of the everyday as a practically invisible burden. The description of everyday life in such terms, however, was not Lefebvre's project. In three separate volumes, and in numerous other works besides, Lefebvre set out to elaborate a *critique* of everyday life. 'Critique' must be understood here both in terms of the radical denunciation of the oppressive character of everyday life, that is, a sociological critique, *and* of the investigation of the conditions making everyday life possible, that is, a philosophical or immanent critique, in order to spell out the possibilities for overcoming or surpassing it.

Thus for Lefebvre, everyday life does not have a given character; rather it is shaped by its contradictions. To describe the contradictory character of everyday life, Lefebvre uses the metaphor of a diptych:

> where the first panel represents the *misery of everyday life*, its tedious tasks, humiliations reflected in the lives of the working classes and especially of women, upon whom the conditions of everyday life bear heaviest – child-bearing and child-rearing, basic preoccupations with bare necessities, money, tradesmen, provisions, the realm of numbers, a sort of intimate knowledge of things outside the sphere of material reality: health, desire, spontaneity, vitality; recurrence, the survival of poverty and the endlessness of want, a climate of economy, abstinence, hardship, repressed desires, meanness and avarice (Lefebvre 1984: 35).

However, there is another panel in Lefebvre's diptych, one that 'portrays the *power of everyday life*, its continuity, the permanence of life rooted in the soil, the adaptation of the body, time, space, desire; ... the unpredictable and unmeasurable tragedy forever lurking in everyday life; the coincidence of need with satisfaction and, more rarely, with pleasure; ... the ability to create in terms of everyday life from its solids and its spaces – to make something lasting for the individual, the community, the class ...' (*ibid.*). Lefebvre's description of this panel of the possibilities of everyday life is much longer, but the point is that even in this burden one can glimpse moments – moments understood by Lefebvre in terms of glimpses of the possible within the present – of potential for something beyond it. Indeed the elements Lefebvre refers to here are the material conditions for the transformation of life.

IPE and everyday life

Before considering how a critique of everyday life can inform a project for a critical IPE, we should examine some of the ways that the notion of everyday life has already been taken up in the field of IR. Three efforts to theorize the everyday in this field will be discussed here. Timothy Sinclair (1999), writing from an historical materialist perspective, advocates an 'international political economy of the commonplace.' Paul Langley (2003), developing a critical political economy of finance, seeks a conception of global finance grounded in everyday practices. David Campbell's poststructuralist arguments for 'transversal relations' and 'prosaic politics' indicate the everyday as a site where the *politics* in global politics takes place (1996). All of these share certain problems in their conceptualization of everyday life. In particular, each faces difficulties theorizing resistance due in part to the ways each understands the everyday as a level of social life. Conceiving social life in terms of its levels tends to treat everyday life as a ground upon which global forces act. This is often empirically true, but such an ahistorical conception reifies everyday life as a realm *separate* from the global. However, some conception of the levels of social life may be needed; in a critique of everyday life, the fragmentation of life into global and everyday levels, along with the consequences of this fragmentation, is what needs to be theorized.

Sinclair, writing from a perspective inspired by Robert Cox, argues that in order to grasp recent changes in the governance of the global political economy it will be necessary to link those global processes to transformations in everyday life: 'A central argument of this chapter is that the substance of global governance ... is also about everyday phenomena in our lives which support the incursions of processes of change ... This new international political economy will be one that links the changes at the broadest level with transformations in the lives of workers, consumers, and citizens' (Sinclair 1999: 157). Sinclair conceptualizes the everyday primarily as the material upon which changes in the global political economy are experienced or felt (Sinclair 1999: 158), or as an 'infrastructure' for the broad changes in global governance he maps out (Sinclair 1999: 164). This separation between the world as governance and the world as feeling or experience does resonate with Lefebvre's understanding of the historical emergence of everyday life as the 'residue' remaining when 'specialized' activities are separated out.

However, Sinclair's conception derives from Braudel's description of everyday life as a level beneath capital accumulation or market activity, and as static and resistant to change.

> The homogeneity of the messages that constitute global governance compete with longer-standing but less organized sets of practices and habits, in which at least fragments of economic and political life remain embedded in pre-existing social arrangements, where time horizons are longer, concrete situations are deemed specific rather than interchangeable, and the emphasis is on generating growth through production rather than extracting profits by market trading. Of crucial importance to this contest between global governance and what I term local governance is the dialectical

> potential of the commonplace arena in which these pressures compete. Global governance is challenged because of the contradictions and crises which develop from time to time in everyday experience, reflecting the failure, thus far, of global governance to become hegemonic in the Gramscian sense of combining coercive power with a measure of consensus (Sinclair 1999: 158).

Braudel's conception of capitalism as a level of the economy, specifically the parasitic level of accumulation through finance, is a matter of great controversy in political economy; in any case, his extensive studies of everyday life focus on an historical period before capitalist social relations were pervasive throughout the societies he examined. To transpose the precapitalist forms of everyday life to contemporary social and political life can have highly misleading implications.

For example, Sinclair rightly points to the crisis in social reproduction that is flowing from the changes he identifies in global governance. He argues that the situation of a society divided between privileged information workers and a vast pool of vulnerable service workers, 'is unstable and prone to fall into crisis as victims express their discontent. [...] This failure to attend to the basic reproduction of the population is one of the most significant vulnerabilities of synchronic global governance. An IPE of the commonplace is best placed to reveal the sorts of work-based tensions suggested here' (Sinclair 1999: 168). Sinclair is suggesting that there is a contradiction between the promotion of a neoliberal model of social order and the more confused and chaotic – but resistant to change – world of everyday life. The political crisis for global governance would thus flow inevitably from the crisis in social reproduction in everyday life occasioned by neoliberalism.

Such an understanding of everyday life misses the capacities developed under capitalist modernity to 'colonize' everyday life, as Lefebvre and also the Situationists put it.[5] For Lefebvre, the transformations of social life in France after World War II not only made everyday life the sphere or level of social life where the reproduction of the social relations had to take place, but also made of it an object for programming (*objet d'une programmation*) (Lefebvre 1984: 68–109). This is not simply a matter of convincing people to buy the goods advertised in the media. Lefebvre goes so far as to characterize a society extending control and compulsion to such an extent as a 'terrorist' society (Lefebvre 1984: 143–93). The crisis of reproduction experienced in everyday life by, for example, displaced workers, does not necessarily imply a crisis in the reproduction of a capitalist social formation precisely because of these diffuse and generalized compulsions. While such a society of maximum repression cannot maintain itself indefinitely, its transformation depends on identifying specific openings and contradictions in everyday life itself.

Paul Langley is more sensitive to the question of how everyday life can become an object for capitalism. He argues that the requirement for a 'new IPE' rests on 'a shift in the focus on inquiry, then, from finance that is global to finance in the global' (Langley 2003: 18). He thus goes beyond Sinclair's linking of levels in his account of the everyday life of finance. Indeed, by calling into question the distinctions that political economy draws between the financial and the real economy and between global and national economies, Langley begins to make possible an analysis of global finance from the perspective of everyday life: 'It is not simply that global finance has implications and consequences for everyday credit practices, but that global finance in part rests upon the restructuring of everyday life' (Langley 2003: 4).

Langley examines how the financial practices of consumers, shaped by the expansion of credit for household borrowing and the individualization and privatization of risk, are related to the practices of disintermediation, liberalization, and financialization in the global financial political economy. Indeed, this represents a profound rethinking of not only the subject matter for IPE, but also of the ways in which its object is constituted. 'The story of the emergence of global finance is not just a discrete tale of what is happening "out there" and its consequences for states and societies. Rather, contemporary transformations in social relations and practices of the everyday are important constitutive material, institutional and discursive features of global finance. The emergence of global finance has been "lived" in the changing experiences of everyday credit practices' (Langley 2003: 9).

Langley's rethinking of the relation between the global and the everyday has important implications for the study of the global political economy. The 'levels' of the global and the everyday appear as parts of a social totality reconstituted through critique, rather than distinct and autonomous spheres impacting one another. In political terms, while Langley could find opposition to the political economic processes and policies of global finance in the everyday, he also finds the mechanisms whereby global financial practices are made possible in the everyday. However, Langley does not problematize the notion of everyday life as thoroughly as he does that of global finance. The implications of the 'everydayness' of consumer and household credit practices are not explored.

One of the problems that need to be addressed is that routine activities will tend to be performed unreflectively. The ability of credit agencies and credit rating bureaus to program routine consumption practices depended on *not* revolutionizing everyday spending behavior. The radically new forms of global financial practice emerged from the *normalization* of new lending practices in everyday life. If the longer term implications of these changes are that everyday financial and credit practices have been radically altered, this has depended upon such changes taking place in the routines of everyday life upon which we have relatively little opportunity or reason to reflect. The burdens placed upon everyday life by unbearable household debt loads, for example, may indeed represent a crisis in the capacity of households to continue to bear the costs of reproduction. But the capacity of global finance to deal with decades of crisis at the global level through such programming indicates that the crisis of the household will not *of itself* produce a crisis in the reproduction of the social relations or, more pointedly, a political crisis. Langley's analysis of the everyday life of global finance provides crucial insights into how a political economic critique of the global or of globalization is necessary for IPE, but it must be supplemented by a critique of everyday life.

Like Langley and Sinclair, David Campbell is concerned with rethinking the possibilities for the study of world politics in the context of transformations in the global political economy. The problems he identifies with the 'billiard ball' image – that is, of world politics as interstate relations between sovereign national states – are remarkably persistent, even among critical international theorists. Campbell argues that a more appropriate way of thinking about global life must examine and problematize a series of assumptions shared by most conceptions of IR. In particular, theories of IR have trouble escaping the problematics imposed by the logic of sovereignty and anarchy, an uncritical conception of agents as autonomous and self-present, and an economistic conception of power as a fungible resource or 'commodity' (Campbell 1996: 11).

Campbell's criticisms of the sovereignty and anarchy problematic, the naturalization of agency, and an economistic conception of power – as well as his criticisms of the timidity of IR theorists – are devastating. However, the approach he proposes in this article has significant problems that limit its ability to theorize political resistance. Beginning with Campbell's critique of agency, recognizing that agency is constructed and that autonomy is achieved and not given does not *necessarily* establish discourse as the site and force constituting agency or autonomy. Indeed, the Russian anti-structuralist linguists, such as Bakhtin and even more pointedly his colleague Valentin Voloshinov, put forward a specifically materialist theory of language and discourse that is not disembodied from the producers of language themselves (see McNally 2001).

Embodiment is a crucial issue for the development of a critical theory of IPE drawing from the critique of everyday life. Campbell takes Alexander Wendt to task for his claim that the body is a '"material substrate of agency"' once the constitutive properties of the self are stripped away' (Campbell 1996: 13). Campbell objects in part that recent feminist political theory has thrown into question the existence of prediscursive material bodies as the ground for identity and politics (Campbell 1996: 13). Wendt does indeed seem to have a curious commitment to a base-superstructure model of agency; however, that the body is problematic does not negate the materiality of agency and, ultimately, of discourse itself. David McNally (2001) argues that the notion of discourse taken up in poststructuralist theory derives from (structuralist) Saussurean linguistics. Saussure separated *langue* from *parole* precisely in order to be able to discuss language in terms not dependent on the practical and embodied instances of language in everyday speech. Such a conceptual separation of *langue* and *parole* resonates with the mental/manual division of labor and its consequences. It is this disembodied – and fetishized – notion of *langue* that informs the poststructuralist move to assert the priority of discourse over the material. Once the body is reduced to an object or effect of discourse, there is no way to theorize the resistance of the body to the effects of discourse.

Campbell's critique of the economistic conception of power in the sovereignty problematic highlights another issue that critical theories of IPE must address. Campbell points out that one of the common assumptions of IR theory is that the 'capacity to wield power as a (usually material, though sometimes symbolic) resource over other agents is an important proviso of agency' (Campbell 1996: 11) – that is, power is a fungible 'commodity to be wielded by agents' (Campbell 1996: 18). Such a conception of power as a 'commodity' that can be used or accumulated does indeed undergird the sovereignty problematic that Campbell so effectively criticizes. Following cues from Michel Foucault, Campbell opposes this conception with an understanding of power as centrifugally circulating through networks or a 'net-like organization' (Campbell 1996: 18). However, this alternative conception is no less economistic than that of the sovereignty problematic: indeed, the priority of circulation in determining social relations is typical of liberal and neoliberal political economy. Whether understood as a model of liberal freedom – the circulation of power throughout the social network enables individual agents to pursue their indeterminate ends – or more darkly – the power relations that precede them presuppose all acts of resistance – the circulation of power in networks does not provide a ground to theorize resistance (but see the introduction and Amoore this volume for an alternative view).

Theorizing resistance is also clouded by Campbell's rejection of the idea of levels (Campbell 1996: 22). Campbell is quite correct to reject the 'rigid segmentarity' of the levels-of-analysis problem – it is this kind of conception of levels that limits Sinclair's account of the 'grounding' of the global in the everyday. His conception of 'transversal relations' permits Campbell to rethink the politics of the global through the politics of the everyday without relying on this idea of levels of politics. This is in some ways similar to Langley's project of locating everyday practices of finance 'in the global.' However, by abandoning a conception of the everyday and the global as levels, it becomes more difficult in Campbell's conception to retain a view of global political and social life as fragmented and hierarchical than it is in Langley's approach. And it is precisely the fragmentation of the social, the body, and the relations of power in social hierarchies that are the targets of the forms of resistance that any conception of the protagonism of the global poor must address.

To sum up, all of these theorizations of everyday life share certain problems. In particular, each faces difficulties theorizing resistance due in part to the ways each understands the everyday as a level of social life. Social life conceived in terms of its levels tends to treat everyday life as a ground upon which global forces act. This is often empirically true, but such an ahistorical conception reifies everyday life as a realm *separate* from the global. How can a *critique* of everyday life, elaborated along the lines suggested in the previous section, contribute to a critical approach to IPE in a way that addresses these problems?

IPE and the critique of everyday life

Each of these approaches to the problem of grasping the everyday in the global political economy responds to a common concern: the arbitrary and rigid separation of the 'levels of analysis' in the predominant approaches to IR and IPE truncates their analyses, blocking out – even more than bracketing – from their considerations any discussion of how people live their lives. In the mainstream approaches, resistance is not only futile and irrational but also literally inconceivable. Sinclair, Langley and Campbell each reconceptualizes the global political economy in order to discover the interactions and flows between the everyday and the global – in Campbell's case, going so far as to reject the notion of levels outright – in order to connect the ways of life of people with global political processes and forces.

Is everyday life a 'level' of the global political economy? Lefebvre (2003: 77–102) suggested that with regard to theorizing urban phenomena, three levels could be distinguished. He defines the global level not as planetary in scope, but as the level of state power and technocratic planning, the level of the most general and abstract relationships. For the bureaucrat, the state official or the technocrat (whether public or private), this level appears to be crucial, the position from which will is projected onto the world. The urban is a mediating level: it is on this level that plans and policies are projected and realized – or, crucially, resisted or not realized – in practice. The third level, designated by Lefebvre as the 'private,' is the level of habitation. To inhabit is more than merely to occupy: in habitation, human beings shape their spaces and are shaped by them.

For the study of IPE, the global level can be seen to correspond to the bureaucratic and technocratic planning of states, corporations, and international organizations – such as international financial institutions. Sinclair is correct to highlight the impact of global governance in this light. This level, however, should not be equated with 'globalization.' Planning is effected and executed at varying scales of localization.

The urban should not be seen as corresponding to the level of the state as understood in IR theory. As a mediating level, this conception of the urban specifically addresses the problems that Campbell finds in the rigidly segmented levels of IR. Studies in IPE have begun to investigate the implications of the city for accumulation, regulation and control.[6] Langley's arguments implicitly make use of the idea of mediation, as he investigates the ways that the strategies of financialization, disintermediation, and the like are themselves enabled by changes in everyday financial practices. Langley does not examine whether such practices are best conceived as specifically urban phenomena; however, in the context of the existing studies on cities in the global political economy this would certainly be an interesting question.

Sinclair, Langley and Campbell share the intuiting that the level of what Lefebvre calls the 'private' – the commonplace, everyday, ordinary, prosaic practice of living in the world and thereby producing the world – is decisive. This is also what Lefebvre argues. However, this intuition seems paradoxical. How can the level of the everyday be decisive when it is the level of the global that is identified with state power, or when it is on the level of the urban that plans are realized or not? We have indicated three elements for theorizing everyday life that will help us clarify this issue. First, as we have seen, the everyday emerges only with the development of the division of labor. Second, as an historical artefact, it carries with it the residues and traces of its past – for example, the festival, to which Bakhtin and Lefebvre looked for evidence of the world turned upside down (again), where the cruelties of peasant life were visited upon the powerful even if only in a manner that secured the social hierarchy. The everyday is misery *and* power, a burden *and* a resource, the programming of social demands *and* the possibility for social command. And third, we have Lefebvre's suggestion that the body is a site of resistance.

According to Lefebvre, the fragmentation of urban reality into three hierarchically ordered levels is organized by the same social processes corresponding to the mental/manual division of labor and the development of capitalism linked to the emergence of everyday life. The domination of the everyday by technique and specialization, the domination of reproduction by the demands of the organization of production, and the domination of habitation by technocratic and bureaucratic planning (whether state or corporate), all correspond to the domination of manual labor by intellect.

The reason that these dominated levels are decisive has to do with the distinction between inhabiting and occupying. The quotidian inhabiting of a space produces that space and things do not always go according to plan. To inhabit a space requires work, that is, the transformation of the space through the effort of its inhabitants. Work is fundamental to life, both in the sense that Cox (1987) and Harrod (1987) argued that all social life depends on the effort of provisioning goods and services to satisfy human needs, and also in the sense that it is through this transformational effort that humans realize themselves.

The production of space though inhabiting takes place over and through existing urban space. This is as axiomatic for the young professional in a gentrifying urban neighborhood shopping at the DIY store as it is for the squatter community occupying land on the outskirts of a Third World city. Through inhabiting, people transform their lived spaces to better suit their wants and needs. Of course, urban space is not infinitely pliable but it is here that we can begin to see how the burdens of everyday life are also resources. It is through the everyday, through the imperatives of social and biological reproduction, that the beginning of the articulation of needs occurs. For the crisis in social reproduction occasioned by neoliberal restructuring to take the political form of a 'double movement,' such as that supposed by Sinclair, or for the irruptions of transversal politics discussed by Campbell to take the form of political resistance, political subjects must emerge from the concrete everyday practices of the people who must bear the burden of production and reproduction (Davies 2005).

This returns us to the body. Lefebvre sought glimpses of the transformation of everyday life in numerous places, for example, in the body. As he argued, the body:

> will not allow itself to be dismembered without a protest, nor to be divided into fragments, deprived of its rhythms, reduced to its catalogued needs, to images and specializations. The body, at the very heart of space and of the discourse of Power, is irreducible and subversive. It rejects the reproduction of relations which deprive it and crush it. [...] The foundation of needs and desire, of representations and concepts, the philosophical subject and object, and what is more (and better), the basis of all praxis and reproduction: this human body resists the reproduction of oppressive relations – if not frontally, then obliquely. It is of course vulnerable. But it cannot be destroyed without destroying the social body itself: the carnal, earthly Body is there, every day. It is the body which is the point of return, the redress – not the Logos, not 'the human' (Lefebvre 1976: 89).

The mental/manual division of labor fragments not only the social world, but also the body itself as production is separated in time and in space from reproduction and as work is separated from life in the family or from the satisfaction of wants and needs in consumption. The oppression of the body and its rhythms in the work process is partly a function of the disciplining of the laboring body by time (Thompson 1993), and partly a function of the repression or appropriation of the creative initiatives taken by the worker – including in the workers' resistance to the discipline of production.[7] For example, as Michael Niemann and I pointed out, 'post-Fordist' management techniques can be understood as the reappropriation of the creative resistance of the worker to the discipline of the assembly line: if one worker 'doubles up' the tasks at one point of production, this frees up another worker to take time back for a cigarette break, to look after children, and so on. The workers' knowledge of the production process exceeds that of the managers. Corporations instituted concepts such as 'team work' to reappropriate that knowledge (Davies and Niemann 2002; see Hamper 1986 for other examples). The worker, as a laboring body, resists appropriation and disciplining in myriad ways but this fragmented resistance can be reappropriated into a function of the production process.

Where the laboring body resists 'obliquely,' in Lefebvre's term, such as in the pursuit of leisure, resistance can also lead back to alienation. Lefebvre characterized leisure as part of a dialectical unity with work in everyday life. The worker craves a 'sharp break' from work, practising leisure as the 'non-everyday' in the everyday (Lefebvre 1991a: 40). But everyday life organizes leisure just as it does work (Lefebvre 1991a: 30). The need for equipment and specialized skills reinserts many leisure activities into social relations mediated by the market and thus by the ideology of consumerism (Davies and Niemann 2002: 573). In any case, despite the enormous wealth and affluence produced in the modern world, very few people live in what could be described as a 'leisure society.' Lefebvre speculated that leisure time would not increase as quickly as 'compulsive time,' that is, the time given over to the compulsions of work, such as commuting (Lefebvre 1984: 53). His observation was borne out by Teresa Brennan, who argued that deregulation contributed to a significant increase in commuting time for affluent suburb dwellers as well as for city dwellers, along with significant increases in international migration for the purpose of finding work (Brennan 2003: 22–9).

While everyday resistance is important for IPE, great care must be taken with assertions that the everyday is a privileged site of resistance. Analysis must focus on the tendencies and the impetus to transform everyday resistances into political projects for transformation. Lefebvre offered one vision, which may seem nostalgic but which nevertheless resonates with the efforts of such political movements as Argentina's *piqueteros*.[8] Lefebvre preserves the distinction between work or works (*oeuvres*), the singular outputs of creative impulses, and products that are the programmed and repeatable outcomes of the organization of production under capitalism. Lefebvre recognizes that notions such as creativity and self-realization through works or work have been discredited along with the concepts of 'man' and of 'humanism.' However, he continues:

> One of the first and most essential conditions for the realization of a cultural revolution is that the concepts of art, creation, freedom, adaptations, style, experience, values, human being, be restored and re-acquire their full significance; but such a condition can only be fulfilled after a ruthless criticism of productivist ideology, economic rationalism and economism, as well as of such myths and pseudo-concepts as participation, integration and creativity, including their practical application, has been performed (Lefebvre 1984: 199; cf. Amoore this volume).

The importance of this assertion for the global political economy lies in understanding that the demands of the poor, marginalized or excluded are not merely those articulated in terms of attacks on the symbols of power and wealth in the West, but also and crucially include demands for a transformed everyday life, for example for the *piqueteros'* demand for *laburo digno*, labor with dignity.

Thus for Lefebvre, everyday life is *both* the part of social life where reproduction – biological, social, and of the social relations – takes place *and* the place where irreducible and materially embodied resistances to the repressive relations can come about. The critique of everyday life culminates in the political project of revolutionary transformation but such transformation is not possible unless it is a project to change life.

Notes

1 Earlier drafts of this chapter were presented at the International Studies Association conference in Honolulu, Hawaii, 4 March 2005, and at the Workshop Gender, Security and Insecurity held at the Centre d'études des politiques étrangères et de sécurité, Université du Québec à Montreal, 1 April 2005. I gratefully acknowledge the generous comments and criticisms of Marieke de Goede, Fred Dufour, Gigi Herbert, Michael Niemann, and Marcus Taylor, as well as of the participants in the ISA panel and the CEPES/UQAM workshop.

2 For important critiques of the concept of global civil society and summaries of the debates, see Pasha and Blaney (1998), and Amoore and Langley (2004).

3 Lefebvre has an ambiguous relation to poststructuralism. He was resolutely hostile to structuralism from the start – he identified it with technocracy. Along with Deleuze, he was an early defender of Nietzsche. He destroys the Cartesian cogito along with the Cartesian notion of space. At the same time,

he remained committed to Marxism throughout his life, and thought that the analytical privileging of language was a thin kind of idealism.

4 For a provocative historical account of primitive accumulation as a 'war on women' that produces this subordination of reproduction to production, see Silvia Federici's *Caliban and the Witch* (2004). For a theoretical account of the patterns of social power relations in production and reproduction, see Harrod (1987), especially Chapter 7 on the household.

5 Or for political forces to weather crises, as Gramsci argued. For some of the affinities between Gramsci and Lefebvre, see Kipfer (2002).

6 See Sassen (1991); Brenner (1998, 2000); and Palan (2003).

7 This discussion focuses on the laboring body but this should not be seen as a form of reductionism. See also McNally (2001) for a discussion of the maternal body alongside analysis of the laboring body.

8 The *piqueteros* are a political and social movement that emerged in the wake of the privatization and deregulation of the Argentine economy. Unemployed people, pensioners, youth, workers, and many others have adopted the strategy of cutting off crucial routes into and out of Argentina's cities with blockades (in Spanish, *piquetes*). They have defended worker-occupied factories and have also set up autonomous economic zones for self-provisioning and barter. Many of their demands are targeted on the state, such as demands for increases in the unemployment benefit, but their demands have a distinctively normative and ethical component.

References

Amoore, L. and Langley, P. (2004) 'Ambiguities of Global Civil Society,' *Review of International Studies* 30 (1): 89–110.

Bakhtin, M. (1968) *Rabelais and His World*, translated by Helene Iswolsky, Bloomington: Indiana University Press.

Brennan, T. (2003) *Globalization and Its Terrors: Daily Life in the West*. London and New York: Routledge.

Brenner, N. (1998) 'Global Cities, ('Glocal') States: Global City Formation and State Territorial Restructuring in Contemporary Europe,' *Review of International Political Economy* 5 (1): 1–37.

Brenner, N. (2000) 'The Urban Question as a Scale Question: Henri Lefebvre, Urban Theory, and the Politics of Scale,' *International Journal of Urban and Regional Research* 24 (2): 361–78.

Campbell, D. (1996) 'Political Prosaics, Transversal Politics, and the Anarchical World,' in Shapiro, M. J. and Alker, H. R. (eds) *Challenging Boundaries: Global Flow, Territorial Identities*. Minneapolis and London: University of Minnesota Press, pp. 7–31.

Cox, R. (1987) *Production, Power and World Order: Social Forces in the Making of History*. New York: Columbia University Press.

Davies, M. (2005) 'The Public Spheres of Unprotected Workers,' *Global Society* 19 (2): 131–54.

Davies, M. and Niemann, M. (2002) 'The Everyday Spaces of Global Politics: Work, Leisure, Family,' *New Political Science* 24 (4): 557–77.

De Saussure, F. (1983) *Course in General Linguistics*. London: G. Duckworth.

Federici, S. (2004) *Caliban and the Witch: Women, the Body and Primitive Accumulation*. Brooklyn, NY: Autonomedia.

Hamper, B. (1986) *Rivethead: Tales from the Assembly Line*. New York: Warner Books.
Harrod, J. (1987) *Power, Production and the Unprotected Worker*. New York: Columbia University Press.
Highmore, B. (2002) *Everyday Life and Cultural Theory: An Introduction*. London: Routledge.
Kipfer, S. (2002) 'Urbanization, Everyday Life and the Survival of Capitalism: Lefebvre, Gramsci and the Problematic of Hegemony,' *Capitalism, Nature, Socialism* 13 (2): 117–49.
Langley, P. (2003) 'The Everyday Life of Global Finance,' IPEG Papers in Global Political Economy No. 5, http://www.bisa.ac.uk/groups/ipeg/papers/PaulLangley.pdf
Lefebvre, H. (1976) *The Survival of Capitalism: Reproduction of the Relations of Production*, Translated by Frank Bryant. London: Allison and Busby.
Lefebvre, H. (1984) *Everyday Life in the Modern World*. New Brunswick, NJ and London, UK: Transaction Publishers, 1984.
Lefebvre, H. (1988) 'Toward a Leftist Cultural Politics: Remarks Occasioned by the Centenary of Marx's Death,' in Nelson, C. and Grossberg, L. (eds) *Marxism and the Interpretation of Culture*. Urbana and Chicago: University of Illinois Press, pp. 75–88.
Lefebvre, H. (1991) *Critique of Everyday Life Volume I: Introduction*. London: Verso.
Lefebvre, H. (2003) *The Urban Revolution*. Minneapolis and London: University of Minnesota Press.
McNally, D. (2001) *Bodies of Meaning: Studies on Language, Labor, and Liberation*. Albany: State University of New York Press.
Palan, R. (2003) *The Offshore World: Sovereign Markets, Virtual Places, and Nomad Millionaires*. Ithaca: Cornell University Press.
Pasha, M. K. and Blaney, D. L. (1998) 'Elusive Paradise: The Promise and Peril of Global Civil Society,' *Alternatives*, 23 (3) 417–50.
Sassen, S. (1991) *The Global City: New York, London, Tokyo*. Princeton, NJ: Princeton University Press.
Sinclair, T. J. (1999) 'Synchronic Global Governance and the International Political Economy of the Commonplace,' in Hewson, M. and Sinclair, T. J. (eds) *Approaches to Global Governance Theory*. Albany: State University of New York Press, pp. 157–71.
Sohn-Rethel, A. (1978) *Intellectual and Manual Labour: A Critique of Epistemology*. London and Basingstoke: Macmillan.
Thompson, E. P. (1993) 'Time, Work-Discipline and Industrial Capitalism,' in *Customs in Common: Studies in Traditional Popular Culture*. New York: The New Press, pp. 352–403.

12
Rethinking Power from the Point of View of Resistance: The Politics of Gender

Bice Maiguashca

The central aim of this chapter is to explore in what ways the work of Robert Cox and that of Ernesto Laclau and Chantal Mouffe can help us think about the nature of power relations in the context of social movements. More specifically, the chapter asks two sets of questions: 1) what forms of power relations are social movements resisting and how are they manifested, and 2) how can we conceptualize these power relations and what would the implications be of such an effort for our understanding of politics in the discipline?

This chapter tackles these questions in three parts. The first part examines the work of Robert Cox and Ernesto Laclau and Chantal Mouffe critically assessing their respective conceptions of power. The second part suggests an alternative perspective that draws on Foucault and emphasizes the importance of tracing power from its point of impact rather than its point of origin. It goes on to illustrate how this reorientation enables an empirical reading of the power relations that conditioned the rise of one particular social movement, that is, the global women's reproductive rights movement. The concluding part of the paper reflects on the insights gained from this particular example for theorizing power relations more generally.

Conceptualizing power and the tug-of-war between the 'material' and the 'discursive'

Let us turn first to the work of Cox for whom the unambiguous center of power is production relations. As he states,

> The system of power that emerges from these linked historical structures begins with the way the world's work is done through a series

> of connected *structures of production relations*, each of which is a power relationship, some more dominant and oppressive, others more equitably balanced. Production not only takes place through a power relationship, but also creates resources that can be transformed into other forms of power – financial, administrative, ideological, military and police power (Cox 1987: 5).

Thus, according to Cox, world politics must be conceptualized in terms of three interrelated historical social structures – *modes of social relations of production, forms of state*, and *world orders* – that emanate from the global relations of production, that produce unequal social relations and that give rise to social classes and 'class power.' Each social structure in turn is comprised of objective, subjective and institutional dimensions so that patterns of collective behavior are understood to be sustained by a combination of material resources as well as shared beliefs and ideas.

Within this framework, at least two implicit characterizations of power come to the fore: the material and the ideological. While the former refers to the technical productive capacities, natural resources and the coercive forces of the state, or what Cox alternatively refers to as 'political power,' the latter includes both the prevailing intersubjective beliefs or 'common sense' of a particular order as well as the contrasting ideologies of particular groups. This dual conception of power is exemplified by Cox when he states, 'Where ideological and policy hegemony is not sufficient to protect the structure of global governance, then military force is available' (Cox 1999: 109).

From the point of view of understanding the emergence of social movements, there are two main strengths to this framework. First, Cox highlights the ways in which ideas can be understood as 'powerful.' As 'inter-subjective beliefs,' ideas set out the parameters for thought and action and thereby serve to constrain behavior. As the collective images of specific groups, on the other hand, they provide an important site of resistance and are seen as potentially enabling. Second, by situating these forms of power within historical structures he requires us to examine how power relations are reproduced through the intended and unintended actions of collective social agents over time. Thus, Cox seeks to hold on to both an agent and structural conception of power.

Despite these strengths, however, there are limitations to Cox's framework. In terms of ideological power, his understanding of intersubjective beliefs as the efforts of a particular class to legitimize, sustain and reproduce their rule is limiting. In this vision, ideas are understood as the *means* by which class interests are expressed and solidarity is constructed and not as a *sui generis* modality of power that has a dynamic and causal logic of its own. To this extent, Cox maintains a structure/superstructure dichotomy between the material and the ideological that becomes evident when Cox writes:

> There is always a tension between a widely held conception of the world and the realities of existence for particular groups of historical people. Gaps develop between changing material conditions and old intellectual schemata. Such gaps suggest latent conflict, the actualising of which depends on a change of consciousness on the part of the potential challengers and their adoption of a contrasting image of society. (Cox 1976: 183)

The predominant line of causality is clear: here the material 'realities' of existence are juxtaposed to our 'conceptions' of it with changes in the former creating the impetus for changes in the latter.

Turning to his understanding of material power, while at times he veers close to the notion of the 'forces of production,' at others he implies a broader concept which includes the coercive and administrative capabilities of the state. Whether it be understood in its narrow or broad sense, however, Cox's concept of material power does not help us identify or conceptualize manifestations of power not enacted by the state, but by one social group against another. For example, violence against women, such as wife battery, cannot be captured conceptually within his notion of material power.

If Cox gives undue causal weight to material power, he also narrows its point of origin to one social sphere, that is, production relations. This is not to say that an exploration of the impact of changing production relations is unimportant to understanding the rise of contemporary social movements. Indeed, social movements such as the women's reproductive rights movement have responded to the spread of capitalist relations across the globe. It is to say that by privileging relations of production as the central site of power relations and class as the dominant form, Cox curtails the ability of his critical theory to speak to the experiences of a number of marginalized peoples who have mobilized against power relations generated within other social spheres. As we shall see, while it is certainly necessary to trace the subordination of women's reproductive rights to changes in global production relations, it is not sufficient; a comprehensive picture of the power relations at work here requires us not only to go beyond the economic sphere (to the exploration of the private sphere for example), but also to identify a different form of power relation altogether, that is, *gender*.

In their book *Hegemony and Socialist Strategy*, Ernesto Laclau and Chantal Mouffe, argue for the need to reconceptualize power within the broader context of what they term *discursive relations* (Laclau and Mouffe 1985). By discursive they mean the totality of discourses – which include written documents, speech, ideas, concrete practices, rituals, institutions and empirical objects – that constitute our social world and that provide it with meaning. These discourses cannot be seen as emanating from a 'sovereign center' – either in the form of a dominant class or a political institution, such as the state – but instead must be understood as the product of a complex array of 'articulatory practices' which are historically specific and contingently constructed. Thus, for Laclau and Mouffe we are embedded in and constituted by these 'discursive relations' which, in turn, structure our understanding of the world and establish the ways in which we reproduce it. By shifting our gaze from the autonomous speaking subject to discursive practices, Laclau and Mouffe bring to light the systemic and pervasive nature of power.

Despite this nonfoundational conception of power, however, Laclau and Mouffe (1985: 112) tell us that 'any discourse is constituted as an attempt to dominate the field discursively, to arrest the flow of differences, to construct a centre.' To this extent, every society is constructed around a particular set of 'hegemonic' discourses which have become institutionalized and serve as the 'political glue' for that specific social formation. These 'nodal points,' as Laclau and Mouffe call them, act as 'discursive centers' through which counter discourses increasingly become defined. As such, 'nodal points' play a crucial role in structuring the network of meaning within a society and in establishing the predominant frameworks for social and political identification.

This conception of power clearly differs from that of Cox. First, power must be understood in a nonfoundational, nonessentialist way so that it cannot be seen as stemming from one social sphere (the economic) or from one particular social agent (state or classes). Second, by defining 'discursive relations' in terms of discourses, institutions and concrete material practices, Laclau and Mouffe reject the distinction between material and nonmaterial modalities of power as well as the structure and superstructure matrix implied in the Gramscian approach. Third, power cannot be conceived as an entity wielded by specific agents. Rather it is relational in nature and operates in impersonal, covert and unpredictable ways that exceeds the intentions of those who seek to enact it. Finally, Laclau and Mouffe conceptualize power as both productive and constraining. In other words, in its productive capacity power must be understood not only as reproducing a particular social order through the organization of consent, but also as the very condition of possibility for the construction of any social agent and any social identity. Power is thus not conceived as something external to be overcome through resistance; it is rather the very terrain on which we are constituted as social agents.

This poststructuralist conception of power is helpful to understand social movements in at least three ways. First, it draws our attention to the particular role of language in the reproduction of our social order and to discourses as an important site of meaning construction. Second, Laclau and Mouffe dislodge power relations from the economic sphere and see social movements as responding to a variety of interwoven power relations that emerge within different social spheres and operate in varying modalities. In other words, they encourage us to be far more curious about where and how power operates. Third, power is not understood as a property of an agent or groups of agents but rather understood as permeating all levels of a social order. Unlike Cox's intersubjective meanings, discourses are not reducible to class consciousness and must be seen as having a logic of their own. Finally, Laclau and Mouffe require us to acknowledge the contingent dimension of power and its unpredictability; politics is not a response to a disjuncture between the ideational and material, as it is for Cox, but a spontaneous, creative and contingent process with no predetermined end.

Despite these strengths, this poststructuralist conception of power raises some questions. While Laclau and Mouffe are right to call our attention to the role of discourses in the construction and politicization of identities, their conflation of material and nonmaterial power under the label of 'discursive relations' makes it hard to explore how different modalities of power manifest themselves and develop a logic of their own. In other words, they do not provide us with the conceptual tools to explore whether the material dimensions of discursive relations are qualitatively different from the nonmaterial dimensions. In a similar vein, they conflate the *ideas* and intersubjective meanings we hold about the world and the *discourses* we use to express them; in this view, our understandings of who we are and who we can become is entirely constructed through these discourses. Without distinguishing between the realm of intersubjectivity and the realm of language/discourse, however, it becomes hard to imagine self-reflexive agents who can reach beyond the discourses that construct them in order to critique them.

A second potential limitation is that their approach is fundamentally 'formal' in orientation and highly abstract in nature. Rather than derive their theory of power from the substantive explorations of what they term 'nodal points,' Laclau and Mouffe develop their ideas in the light of linguistic theory. Thus, unlike Gramsci, who was concerned with the historical specificity of structural power relations, Laclau and Mouffe provide us with little insight into the concrete social processes that give rise to these 'nodal points,' and their attendant hegemonic discourses, or their effects. A final problem is that given their emphasis on contingency, they implicitly suggest that the 'nodal points' suturing a particular society together can be unwoven by means of alternative articulatory practices. The weight and embeddedness of historically reproduced patterns of behavior are minimized by the flux and flow of contingency (but see introduction and Daly and Amoore chapters for a contrary view).

In sum, despite their strengths, I suggest that both perspectives examined here are constrained in their ability to aid us conceptualize the conditions under which international social movements emerge. While the Coxian notion of power highlights its ideological and material dimensions and incorporates both intended and unintended actions, it reduces power relations to the realm of production relations, neglects the discursive nature of power and privileges class at the expense of other forms such as gender or race.[1] In turn, while Laclau and Mouffe's conception of power brings to light the discursive, contingent nature of power and allows us to explore its diverse points of origin, it obscures the difference between the material and nonmaterial dimensions of power, on the one hand, and its ideational and discursive logics on the other. The question then is whether we need to choose between these two insightful yet seemingly incommensurable perspectives or if there is some way that we can reframe our questions and insights about power relations that allows us to sidestep this impasse?

A view from the Women's Reproductive Rights Movement

One way of tracing relations of power is in the light of the practices of resistance that it generates. Describing this line of inquiry, Foucault states that it 'consists of taking the forms of resistance against different forms of power as a starting point. ... it consists of using this resistance as a chemical catalyst so as to bring to light power, locate their position, find out their point of application and the methods used' (Foucault 1994: 329). This encourages us to do empirical research into practices of resistance and to map the imprint of power from its point of impact on the bodies, lives and actions of those who seek to resist them. It also requires us to take social movements seriously as producers of knowledge and the self-understandings of activists as one valuable source for theory building. Here, then, I offer an empirical mapping of a particular configuration of global governance from the point of view of one social movement that is seeking to resist it. More specifically, drawing on primary and secondary material including the self-understandings and analyses of women's reproductive rights activists, I foreground the specific *form* of power relation being resisted, that is, gender; identify the various *modalities* of power that sustain it and; locate the social *sites* or spheres in which this relation of power is collectively reproduced. This reading will then enable me to assess and intervene in the debate between Cox on the one hand, and Laclau and Mouffe on the other as outlined above.

The women's reproductive rights movement is part of a broader international women's health movement that emerged in the mid-1970s. As it embraces a complex array of local, national and global actors, I will focus here on one of its largest and most proactive members, that is, the Women's Global Network for Reproductive Rights (WGNRR) established in 1984 in Amsterdam.

The main structure of the WGNRR is a network of diverse, autonomous groups and individuals in every continent who are linked together by a shared concern for women's reproductive rights and health. Currently the WGNRR has about 1730 members in 157 countries working in a variety of capacities, some in feminist and women's organizations, others in medical organizations and still others in documentation centers or trade unions (WGNRR website). What holds these diverse 'members' together is their shared belief that any struggle for women's reproductive rights is both a political struggle – rather than a technical or management issue – and a feminist struggle to the extent that it recognizes *gender* as a particular form of power relation that implicates '*social structures* and practices of subordination that characterize relations between men and women in most societies' (Petchesky 2003: 11). Given the insistence of many feminists and women activists that current forms of global governance must be understood in terms of gendered social structures, I have chosen to deploy Cox's three historical structures as a starting point to explore the production and maintenance of global gender relations.

A. 'Modes of social relations of production': structural adjustment policies and women's material well-being

The debt crisis that began in the late 1970s and that continued during the 1980s prompted the World Bank and the IMF to 'save' both the flagging economies of the Third World and the bank accounts of creditor nations by imposing structural adjustment policies (SAPs). These policies have had varying effects depending on where and how they were implemented. Nevertheless, both critical economists and women's reproductive rights activists see their impact on the lives of Third World peoples, especially women, as generally negative (Gordon 1999: 31–4; *WGNRR Call for Action* 2004: 7–13; Nair *et al.* 2004b: 13). A recent comparative study, for example, suggests that SAPs have had a highly detrimental impact on women's reproductive health in Southern countries limiting the services available and the number and quality of physicians (Petchesky and Judd 1998).

In addition to the decrease in social services, SAPs have also required reductions in the subsidies of basic foodstuffs making products such as bread, rice, milk and fuel more expensive and difficult to obtain for the very poor. Given that it is often the women in the families who eat last and the least, this has meant an increase in the malnutrition of women. A third problem with SAPs is that they do not address the question of income distribution which is seen as a national domestic issue. But, as Hartmann and others have argued, it is precisely the unequal distribution of resources in the Third World that is one of the root causes of both overpopulation and underdevelopment (Hartmann 1995: 6). Bandarage, for example, argues that voluntary family planning has worked only in those countries where economic security, including access to material resources as well as health and education, has been improved for the general population and in particular women. She argues that it is exploitation and poverty that make many children a rational choice for most families in the South (Bandarage 1999: 28).

Alongside global economic policies implemented by international organizations, international commercial interests also have an impact on women's health and lives. For example, pharmaceutical companies play an important part in the promulgation of population control programs that seek to reduce women's fertility and create potentially profitable markets for these companies eager to test and sell their newly developed contraceptive technologies. For example, until recently trials of quinacrine, a contraceptive vaccine with harmful side effects, were taking place in the Philippines, Vietnam, Ecuador, Bangladesh and India. The women being tested were invariably poor and from minority communities (Hartmann 1999). In this way, gender overlaps with class and racial oppression.

In sum, members of WGNRR are seeking to resist what they see as forms of gender and racial oppression. To this end, they have identified the coercive force of the state and the financial might of corporations as one key modality of power that must be challenged. Recognizing that the 'material power' of the state is only part of the story, women activists have also sought to highlight the ways in which population policies are legitimized by a Malthusian ideology and sustained by specific discursive strategies embodied in family planning programs. Overturning gender relations therefore requires that these modalities of power are also resisted.

B. Forms of state: controlling the private sphere and the implementation of 'family planning' programs

By the 1970s 'over-population' became seen as a serious threat to world prosperity and as one of the root causes of underdevelopment in the South. Thus, along with SAPs, the South was also forced to swallow a variety of top-down, donor-imposed models of 'family planning' programs that were implemented with the primary goal of bringing down the population level in Third World countries and in fact today most countries have population policies of some kind. It is the argument of women's reproductive rights activists that these population control policies are not only an assault on women's health and bodily integrity but are also racist and sexist (Nair *et al.* 2004b: 22–5). Indeed, they go on to argue that they reproduce a population discourse that objectifies human beings and disempowers women physically, emotionally and psychologically (Keysers 1994a, 1994b, 1996; Hartmann 1995; Petchesky 2003; Lohmann 2003; WGNRR 2003a).

In a number of Asian countries, for instance, including Indonesia, Bangladesh and India, mass sterilization camps were created in the 1970s where both men and women were forced to undergo sterilizations or, in the case of women, the implantation of contraceptive devices. Coerced sterilization has also been practiced in Latin America. In Peru, for example, it occurred as late as 1996 when poor, rural indigenous women were forcibly sterilized in unsanitary conditions resulting in the deaths of three of them (Petchesky 2003: 207). If physical coercion is not permitted, then incentives and disincentives are often used to ensure that either long term acting contraceptives or sterilization are adopted. One example of this kind of incentive scheme is the dual track family plan implemented in Singapore in 1983 where uneducated women were penalized for having more than two children, while educated Chinese women were given incentives to have more children including priority access to the best schools and greater tax relief. It was only after the emergence of a popular protest that this policy was eventually dismantled (Hartmann 1995: 7). In addition to forced sterilization policies and racist incentive schemes, women have also suffered the consequences of strict anti-abortion laws. In Nigeria a staggering 20,000 women die every year from poorly performed illegal abortions. Not surprisingly, it is the poor, illiterate women who bear the brunt of maternal mortality risk (Osakue and Martin-Hilber 1998: 185).

Justifying this gendered and racist violence, according to women's reproductive rights activists, are spurious beliefs about the causes of population growth. In terms of this ideology, women's reproductive rights activists reject the idea that economic prosperity and the environment have been jeopardized by the sheer number of people on the planet. Indeed, they argue that environmental and population problems are symptomatic of an inhumane, unsustainable development model that ravages our natural resources and leads to high fertility rates among the impoverished. More specifically, they claim that the major causes of global environmental degradation have to do with economic systems that exploit nature, war and arms production that ruin the natural environment, disproportionate consumption patterns of the affluent, the displacement of small farmers by agribusiness, rapid urbanization and finally new technologies which rather than restore the environment are designed to exploit it (Keysers 1994a, 1994b; Hayes 1994).

Moreover, reproductive rights activists argue that the neo-Malthusian perspective underlying population policies incorrectly and unfairly focuses the blame for overpopulation on poor women from Third World countries. The tacit assumption seems to be that poor people are unable to control their sexual urges and breed irresponsibly without thinking about the social implications of their actions. This vision of Third World men and women indulging their sexual urges without consideration for the well-being of their families or communities has led many feminists to see the ideology behind these population policies as racist, sexist and imperialist and, therefore, as a key site of struggle. As Nair *et al.* state in a recent WGNRR Newsletter,

> The challenge today is not just to make demands for reproductive rights and social justice outside of a population framework, but also to challenge the very *thinking* that underpins many health, welfare, employment, immigration and education policies, to name a few (Nair *et al.* 2004a: 8).

In addition to opposing the ideology underlying the population paradigm, reproductive rights activists have also sought to expose the dehumanizing effects of the population *discourse*. The term 'population' itself is problematic as it originally was used to quantify insect life and when used to refer to people has the effect of objectifying them. Thus, the image conjured up by threats of a 'population explosion' is that of ants or rabbits multiplying uncontrollably as they yield to their 'natural' instincts to procreate. As Keysers states,

> Where 'population' is declared a development problem and the reduction of population growth through mass fertility control is coined a development strategy, people, that is men and women who relate sexually and get children, tend to disappear behind abstract statistical units (Keysers 1994b: 293).

The population control discourse also revolves around the concepts of 'reproduction' and 'fertility control' which not only renders procreation a process that can be bureaucratically and technically managed, but also separates discussions about fertility from those about women's autonomy and sexuality. By playing down the private, sexual dimensions of reproductive behavior, it becomes much easier and more acceptable to talk about 'controlling,' 'managing' or 'planning' a woman's fertility. Despite the fact that the question of sexuality is not explicitly addressed in population discourse, there are clearly two different conceptions of sexuality operating within it: male sexuality is associated with virility, lust and pleasure, while female sexuality is seen as expressing itself through procreation (Keysers 1994b: 295). In both cases, however, sexuality is conceived of as an instinctual urge rooted in our biology.

But as feminists remind us, a woman's fertility and reproductive capacity is intimately tied to her sexuality which, in turn, is socially and culturally mediated. In many societies, for example, young girls are groomed to be 'good' wives and mothers which requires them to be sexually subservient to their husbands and to bear many children, preferably boys. In this context, a woman's sexuality is completely subsumed to the requirements of her social role which is determined by the cultural beliefs and social practices of her husband and community. In this way, the intimacies of family life represent a crucial site of power relations through which societal norms, economic imperatives and particular conceptions of male and female sexuality are expressed.

In sum, women's reproductive rights activists seek to highlight how population policies target both the family and women's bodies transforming them into sites of power. Furthermore, they demonstrate how population policies are sustained through ideological elaboration and discursive practices which desexualize and even dehumanize human beings. Understanding that population policies reflect the beliefs, discourses and interests of a transnational configuration of social actors, they have launched an international movement which seeks to resist what they call the 'population establishment' and to bring their case to the global arena, particularly the UN.

C. World order and the discursive battle for reproductive rights

The neo-Malthusian population paradigm and, its attendant discourse, has become increasingly the subject of contestation and discursive struggle within the context of the UN over the past 30 years. One of the most important battlefronts was the International Conference on Population and Development held in Cairo in 1994 which, at the time, was hailed as a victory for women's rights and as representing a 'paradigm shift' on gender issues. Narrow family planning methods oriented to demographic targets were subjected to strong criticism and, at the discursive level, 'gender equity,' 'reproductive rights' and 'women's empowerment' became part of the lexicon of the Cairo Program of Action (POA). Indeed, DAWN goes as far as to say that the Cairo POA heralded a 'semantic revolution' in which 'family planning programs' everywhere were renamed 'reproductive health programs' in an effort to signify a move towards a more integrated, holistic approach to reproductive health (DAWN 1999).

Ten years on, however, the limitations of the Cairo POA have become glaringly evident. Apart from denying women's right to abortion, it said nothing about the social and economic inequalities that define the lives of women in the North and the South. Moreover, it refused to question the ability of neoliberal, market-oriented programs to secure the enabling conditions necessary for women to realize their reproductive rights. Finally, it did little to reallocate resources away from traditional family planning services (contraceptives and sterilization) to other vital services including gynecological health, prevention and treatment of AIDS and sexual health and education. Despite its progressive rhetoric and some important advances for women's rights, therefore, the Cairo POA (and the Cairo + 5 POA) remains fundamentally wedded to a neo-Malthusian subtext that has not been effectively challenged (Nair *et al.* 2004a: 5). In other words, rearticulating women's rights is not enough; an ideological struggle must also take place.

Another potential danger of focusing exclusively on the discursive battlefront is that of cooptation. As Yuval-Davis and Petchesky point out, the Vatican, fundamentalist groups, both Islamic and Christian, population agencies and the US government have all begun to adopt the language of women's rights (Yuval-Davis 1995: 7; Petchesky 2003: 40; WGRNN 2003b). So while the Vatican projects itself as pro-women to the extent that it is for 'mothers' and for 'parental rights,' Islamic states justify their opposition to abortion and sexual rights in the name of 'women's dignity' and 'women's right to keep their moral and cultural values' (Yuval-Davis 1995: 7). Population agencies have joined the bandwagon by insisting on 'women's right to control their own bodies,' meaning their right to use contraception.[2] As Yuval-Davis suggests, 'women's empowerment' is now on virtually everyone's lips (Yuval-Davis 1995: 7). In this shifting discursive field, women activists have been struggling to reappropriate, repoliticize and redefine these terms. Thus, while acknowledging the moral and the legal salience of embedding a reproductive rights discourse in UN texts, women activists are cognizant of the fact that resisting solely on the discursive front leaves both the dominant ideology and prevailing material inequalities safely intact (but see Amoore and Larner chapters for an alternative view).

Rethinking power through the politics of resistance

So how does exploring power relations from the point of view of women's reproductive rights activists help us assess and intervene in the critical theory-poststructuralist debate that we began with? Turning to the geography of power, feminists and women activists direct us to the realm of reproduction and the family as a crucial site of power relations. Moreover, they complicate the 'production' vs. 'discursive' debate by asking us to pay attention to the way gender relations are reproduced and sustained at the local and global level by overlapping, mutually reinforcing economic, political and cultural practices. To this extent, poststructuralist claims that power has no sovereign center and that it traverses all social relations resonate with those of feminists.

Moving on to the *form* that power relations take, feminists and women activists have clearly told us that gender must be understood as *sui generis* and that it is not reducible to class. Indeed, if we listen to them, the challenge becomes one of recognizing and mapping *diverse, multiple* forms of power relations and exploring why some congeal in particular historical circumstances and how they intersect. In this context, *pace* Laclau and Mouffe, gender cannot be seen as just one 'nodal point' among many which can be unknotted through contingent discursive practices. Rather it has to be understood in terms of an historically embedded relation of oppression that is pervasive in scope and intertwined with other power relations. From this point of view then, while Cox's notion of 'historical structures' provides a useful heuristic framework to begin one's analysis, Laclau and Mouffe's insistence on the plurality of power relations is well-founded.

Finally, the analyses of women's reproductive rights activists suggest that we need to think in more concrete terms about the specific operations of power. As we have seen, while Gramscians make a distinction between material and ideological modalities of power, and then go on to privilege the former, poststructuralists like Laclau and Mouffe deny any distinction. The problem, according to some, however, is that this conflation leads to the undertheorization of the materiality of power (Laffey 2000). For others, like myself, it is that they assume that the material and ideological manifestations of power operate according to the same logic and have the same effects. We are thus left to choose between the very problematic material/ideological dichotomy or the highly overburdened notion of 'discursive relations' (see de Goede 2003: 95).

In my view, feminists and women activists offer us an alternative route by guiding us to three *modalities* of power (the material, ideological and discursive), each having its own logic and each generating its own form of resistance. Material power refers to those practices and capacities that explicitly and materially constrain or enable our bodies and behavior. The expression of this modality of power is often, but not always, coercive in nature and is exercised in a range of contexts, that is, statist (for example, police, army), legislative (for example, national or international law), economic (for example, capital) or family (for example, wife battery). Discursive power includes not only the language that we use to speak and write about particular subjects, but also the cultural metaphors, stereotypes and representations that sustain our commonsense understanding about the world. Lastly, ideological power refers to the ideas, beliefs and normative values that we hold which can, and often does, exceed the language and metaphors that we deploy. Instead, these ideas form part of our background knowledge about what we take to be true and false, right and wrong and, despite not always being readily accessible to our conscious mind, they can be powerful to the extent that they provide the motivations for some of our actions.

Although interconnected and often mutually reinforcing, material, discursive and ideological power each have their own logic that must be understood if they are to be effectively challenged. While the logic of material power is to physically constrain or enable individual or collective action, the dominant logic of discursive power is that of representation. Discursive power is thus harder to pin down as it is produced in a seemingly less tangible form and permeates all aspects of social life. The underlying logic of ideological power is one of legitimization or moral condemnation. It is the least visible modality of power and perhaps most the intractable. Analytically separating these modalities of power, prompts us to explore both the politics of representation (a key poststructuralist concern) and the politics of redistribution (a key Marxist concern). It also reminds us that the constitution of our subjectivity cannot be reduced to our class positions or to a logic of identity differentiation and that our moral sense of the present and our utopian visions of the future must be part of the story.

The challenge facing any researcher interested in analytically mapping these sites, forms and modalities of power, however, is to avoid falling into the trap of assigning primacy *a priori* to any one of them. Any effort to conceptualize power relations requires us to engage in substantive empirical research and intersectional analysis in order to determine the specific interplay of gender, class and race in a particular historical moment. Furthermore, this structural analysis must be complemented by an effort to pay attention to *contingent* factors – whether that be the inauguration of a new US President, the development of a new contraceptive technology or the eruption of a new disease such as AIDS – that shape the power relations that social movements are seeking to respond to.

One broad line of inquiry following from this mandate is the need to do much more research into the 'politics of resistance.' How do these movements define and make sense of 'power' and 'oppression?' Do so-called 'progressive' social movements differ in their answers to these questions than so-called 'regressive ones?' And why and how, in each case, do power relations get transformed into relations of oppression? The first place to look for answers to these questions is the self-understandings and practices of those men and women who are actually engaged in resisting relations of oppression. From this vantage point we will be able to see more clearly the strengths and limits of our abstract debates over, say, the relative importance of material vs. discursive modalities of power or over the causal weight of economic vs. socio-cultural forces in shaping power relations. From here we can get a glimpse of what relations of oppression look like and a sense of how they are experienced by particular constituencies of people. Finally, it is from here we can begin to speculate about why we resist oppression when we do and, thereby, begin the real process of theorizing power.

Notes

1 Despite holding onto a class-based analysis which foregrounds 'skilled workers,' 'supporting workers' and those excluded from production, Cox does acknowledge that old production-related categories of class need to be rethought in the light of the fragmentation of both the proletariat and the bourgeoisie (Cox 1999: 118).

2 For an exploration of the tensions between feminist discourses and those of population agencies see Smyth 1998.

References

Bandarage, A. (1999) 'Population and Development: Towards a Social Justice Agenda,' in Silliman, J. and King, Y. (eds) *Dangerous Intersections: Feminist Perspectives on Population, Environment and Development.* Cambridge, MA: South End Press.

Cox, R. (1976) 'On Thinking about Future World Order,' *World Politics*, 28 (2).

Cox, R. (1987) *Production, Power and World Order: Social Forces in the Making of World Order.* New York: Columbia University Press.

Cox, R. (1999) 'Civil Society at the Turn of the Millennium: Prospects for an Alternative World Order,' *Review of International Studies* 25 (1): 3–28.

DAWN Platform for Cairo + 5 (1999) 'Implementing ICPD: Moving Forward in the Eye of the Storm,' January 1999.

de Goede, M. (2003) 'Beyond Economism in International Political Economy,' *Review of International Studies* 29 (1): 79–97.

Foucault, M. (1994) 'The Subject of Power,' in Faubion, J. D. (ed.) *Michel Foucault: Power.* New York: The New Press.

Gordon, J. (1999) 'The Intersection of Race, Class and Gender and the Biases of Economic Structural Adjustment Programmes,' *WGNRR Newsletter* 68/69: 31–4.

Hartmann, B. (1995) *Reproductive Rights and Wrongs The Global Politics of Population Control.* Boston: South End Press.

Hartmann, B. (1999) 'Women's Health Advocates Win a Victory Against Quinacrine Sterilization in Znet,' http://www.zmag.org/sustainers/content/1999-12/02hartmann.htm

Hayes, P. (1994) 'Taking Population out of the Equation,' *Political Environments,* a Publication of the Committee on Women, Population and the Environment, Amherst, USA: CWPE.

Keysers, L. (1994a) 'Women and Population Questions: From Rio to Cairo and Beyond,' *Vena Journal* 5 (2): 43–52.

Keysers, L. (1994b) 'Empowerment of Women: Constructing Global Humane Society,' Proceedings of the 1994 Tokyo Symposium on Women, unpublished paper, December 1994, 289–307.

Keysers, L. (1996) 'Is Gendering Population and Development Negotiations a Paradigm Shift? Alternative Body Building Exercises for Women's Reproductive Health and Rights,' unpublished paper presented at Lund Conference, Sweden, 14–6 June.

Laclau, E. and Mouffe, C. (1985) *Hegemony and Socialist Strategy: Towards a Radical Democratic Politics*. London: Verso.

Laffey, M. (2000) 'Locating Identity: Performativity, Foreign Policy and State Action,' *Review of International Studies* 26 (3): 429–44.

Lohmann, L. (2003) 'Re-Imagining the Population Debate,' *WGNRR Newsletter 80*: 9–12.

Nair, S., Sexton, S. and Kirbat, P. (2004a) 'A Decade After Cairo: Women's Health in a Free Market Economy,' *WGNRR Newsletter 81*: 5–8. (abridged version)

Nair, S., Sexton, S. and Kirbat, P. (2004b) 'A Decade After Cairo: Women's Health in a Free Market Economy,' WGNRR/Corner House Project Briefing Document pp. 1–36.

Osakue, G. and Martin-Hilber, A. (1998) 'Women's Sexuality and Fertility in Nigeria,' in Petchesky, R. and Judd, K. (eds) *Negotiating Reproductive Rights: Women's Perspectives Across Countries and Cultures*. London: Zed Books.

Petchesky, R. (2003) *Global Prescriptions: Gendering Health and Human Rights*. London: Zed Books.

Petchesky, R. and Judd, K. (1998) (eds) *Negotiating Reproductive Rights: Women's Perspectives Across Countries and Cultures*. London: Zed Books.

Smyth, I. (1998) 'Gender Analysis of Family Planning: Beyond the "Feminist vs. Population Control" Debate,' in Jackson, C. and Pearson, R. (eds) *Feminist Visions of Development: Gender Analysis and Policy*. London: Routledge.

WGNRR website at http://www.wgnrr.org/frameset.htm.

WGNRR Newsletter 78 (2003a) 'Vatican Says Word "Gender" is Anti-Church Code,' p. 42.

WGNRR Newsletter 80 (2003b) 'Women Population Control, Public Health and Globalisation,' pp. 7–9.

WGNRR Call for Action (2004) see website.

Yuval-Davis, N. (1995) 'From Cairo to Beijing: Feminists and Transversal Politics,' *WGNRR Newsletter 50*: 7–9.

13

'There is No Great Refusal': The Ambivalent Politics of Resistance[1]

Louise Amoore

> Let's face it. We're undone by each other. And if we are not, we're missing something.
>
> Judith Butler, *Precarious Life* (2004)

The streets around here are usually empty at weekends, but up ahead, a big crowd is making its way east towards Gower Street, and in the road itself, are the same nose-to-tail coaches he saw on the news. The passengers are pressed against the glass, longing to be out there with the rest. They've hung their banners from the windows, along with football scarves and the names of towns from the heart of England... From the impatient pavement crowds, some dry runs with the noisemakers – a trombone, a squeeze-ball car horn, a lambeg drum. There are practice chants which at first he can't make out. Tumty tumty tum. Don't attack Iraq. Placards not yet on duty are held at a slope, at rakish angles over shoulders. Not in My Name goes past a dozen times. Its cloying self-regard suggests a bright new world of protest, with the fussy consumers of shampoos and soft drinks demanding to feel good, or nice... On Warren Street he turns right. Now his view is east towards the Tottenham Court Road. Here's an even bigger crowd, swelled by hundreds disgorging from the tube station. Backlit by the low sun, silhouetted figures break away and merge into a darker mass... Despite his scepticism, Perowne in white-soled trainers, gripping his racket tighter, feels the seduction and excitement peculiar to such events; a crowd possessing the streets, tens of thousands of strangers converging with asingle purpose

> conveying an intimation of revolutionary joy... The sandwich bars along the street are closed up for the weekend. Coming towards Perowne, his back to the crowds, is a pink-faced man of about his own age, in a baseball cap and yellow Day-Glo jacket, with a handcart, sweeping the gutter for the council. He seems oddly intent to do a good job... What could be more futile than this underpaid urban scale housework when behind him, at the far end of the street, cartons and paper cups are spreading thickly under the feet of demonstrators gathered outside McDonald's on the corner... As the two men pass, their eyes meet briefly, neutrally. For a vertiginous moment Henry feels himself bound to the other man, as though on a seesaw with him, pinned to an axis that could tip them into each other's life.
>
> Ian McEwan, *Saturday* (2005)

Henry Perowne, Ian McEwan's protagonist in *Saturday*, drives to his weekly squash game through city streets filling with anti-war protesters. His feelings are starkly ambivalent. He registers antagonism – the map of London streets he traverses every day is reconfigured by the protests – he will be late for his game. He is indignant at the carnivalesque bright new world of protest that he sees subsuming the passions of sport, music (which he reads as incomprehensible rhythms and beats), and 'feel good' partying into the occupation of urban centers. He would like to be sure, in clear and unambiguous terms, what it is the protestors are 'against.' Yet, he simultaneously, if fleetingly, appreciates the aesthetic and emotional qualities of the event – the swarming crowd silhouetted against watery winter sun, the seduction and excitement of the crowd, the potential for a glimpse of revolutionary joy, however feigned. The protest has entered his field of vision not so much by its message or purpose, as by its interruption of his quotidian routine and its assault on his senses. In Perowne's encounter with the street cleaner we see the residue of his ambivalence, as the secure separateness of his everyday world, the practices of the protesters, and the lives of the workers at the borders and margins of the global economy, is momentarily shaken. As the man sweeps from the gutter the debris dropped by the apparent representatives of a concerned global civil society, Perowne sees the fragility of the axis that divides their lives, and that might otherwise 'tip them into each other's life,' render them undone.

Introduction: looking for the great refusal

The question of what it is that we 'refuse' when we say we resist is a central problematic of our times. The pervasive message that the events of 9/11 changed the nature of politics and our world forever; the projects of the war on terror that tell us that the civilized and globalized world must be secured against the uncivilized and fundamentalized world – these powerful discourses have been stitched together in such a way that elements of both the Right and the Left seek a great refusal. The temptation is to call for a clear and unambiguous declaration of the world we are against and the world we seek to secure. For the liberal state, this has led to a representational alliance between the categories of 'protestor,' 'illegal immigrant,' or indeed any 'deviant,' and the category of 'terrorist.' Among the manifestations of this is, for example, the news media's proclamation, in the aftermath of 9/11, that the 'anti-globalization movement is dead' (*Financial Times* 10 October 2001; *The Nation* 22 October 2001) amid an atmosphere, particularly in the US, where those who sought to be critical were branded 'excuseniks' or 'refuseniks' (*New York Times* cited in Butler 2004: xiii). At the same time, another form of resistance – a refusal to allow the destruction of American values – was celebrated: 'we were told to shop. Shop to show we are patriotic Americans. Shop to show our resilience over death and destruction' (Willis 2003: 122). The discursive alliance between the 'open,' 'liberal,' and 'progressive' processes of globalization, and the war on terror necessary to secure this world from the 'closed' and 'dangerous' global networks, was forged in the immediate weeks following 9/11. Anti-terror laws, together with policing and surveillance technologies developed under the auspices of the war on terror, are being deployed also to govern the limits of protest and public assembly.

In the face of such an effort, by the decentred liberal state, to define the nature and limits of possible resistance in terms of a 'permanent state of exception' where all critique or resistance may constitute suspicious behaviour (Van Munster 2004: 142), what is left for the Left? For a significant group of critical voices, as I have argued elsewhere, the response has been to seek to settle the terms of their own great refusal, to define more clearly and unambiguously the purpose and target of their political action (Amoore and Langley 2004; cf. Gill 2003; Mittelman 2000). The prevailing response appears as a desire to keep open the possibilities for alternative political visions by identifying and securing a common foe. Perhaps most clearly captured in the emblematic slogans of 'one no, many yeses' (Kingsnorth 2004), or the World Social Forum's 'another world is possible,' the simultaneous openness/closure is seen also in Naomi Klein's writings, where 'movements are indeed battling the same forces' (2002: 4). A sense of unity within a diverse movement is conjured through the securing of a single refusal – an identifiable enemy situated variously in global capitalism, neoliberalism, 'the west' and so on – to which multiple voices declare a clear and collective 'no.' Confronted with 'September 11 muffling the protests for a while,' some critical commentators have sought renewal in 'getting serious' and 'moving on from the playing of games and the staging of parties' (Monbiot 2003). This demand for a serious refusal also frames, for some of the Marxist Left, the view that surely it is time for postmodern and poststructural thinkers to 'get real,' to accept the bare materiality at the centre of serious political life, and to assign discourse its proper place in the realm that is 'ideal,' or 'merely cultural' (cf. Maiguashca this volume).[2]

In seeking to prise open a future for the global justice movement within the state of exception, commentators such as Klein and Monbiot establish a rationality for their refusal, a clearly bounded and unambiguously collective 'no.' In so doing, they articulate a desire for a settled world of for/against that replays the 'with us or with them' that is the discursive mainstay of their identified foes. 'A conventional pluralist,' William Connolly reminds us, 'celebrates diversity within settled contexts of conflict and collective action' (1995: xiii). Moreover, he argues, 'outside the warm and protected spaces of the normal individual and the territorial state, conventional pluralists project a lot of abnormality, anarchy, and cruelty in need of exclusion and regulation' (*ibid.*: xiv). Read in this way, the certainty and lack of contingency present in the claiming of an absolute 'no' will necessarily foreclose the possibility of multiple and contradictory 'yeses.' In order for the great refusal to be sustained, the boundaries of the possible futures are to be perennially regulated.

This chapter makes a number of interventions in what I observe to be a curious and politically problematic search for a great refusal. I work through some of the strands of poststructural and cultural theory that problematize our sense of what it is to resist within a global political context, in order to open up some of the possibilities of dissent that we may be less attuned to. In Michel Foucault's (1976: 96) famous formulation:

> Points of resistance are present everywhere in the power network. Hence there is no single locus of great Refusal, no soul of revolt,

> source of all rebellions, or pure law of the revolutionary. Instead there is a plurality of resistances, each of them a special case: resistances that are possible, necessary, improbable; others that are spontaneous, savage, solitary, concerted, rampant, or violent; still others that are quick to compromise, interested, or sacrificial... The points, knots, or focuses of resistance are spread over time and space at varying densities, at times mobilizing groups or individuals in a definitive way, inflaming certain points of the body, certain moments in life, certain types of behavior.

It is not the case, then, that there can be no resistance within Foucault's envisaged network of power relations (see for example, Davies this volume), but that there can be no categorical and unequivocal *Refusal*. Understood as both an instrument of power and a point of resistance or opposition, discourse 'transmits and produces power' while it also renders it fragile and 'makes it possible to thwart it' (1976: 101). Read in these terms, the search for a great refusal overlooks the very site where the fragility and vulnerability of power relations may lie – in the discursive articulation between power and knowledge (Keenan 1997: 153). To assert a great refusal implies a stepping outside of relations of power when, at least from Foucault's standpoint, this may be precisely the location of points of resistance. Yet, and particularly in Foucault's later writings, the possibility of a kind of refusal is not entirely ruled out. 'Maybe the target nowadays is not to discover what we are,' he writes, 'but to refuse what we are' (1983: 216). Understood in these terms, though we may not be able to think of refusing 'it' in a clear and unambiguous way (whether it is war, globalization, poverty...), we can think of refusing what it makes of us. Our double standpoint within the exercise of power and the instances of resistance implies that we may be both vehicles of discourse and the means by which that discourse is undermined (see also the introduction to this volume).

As a discussion conceived as an intervention in contemporary debates on the possibilities of a politics of resistance, this chapter cannot claim to fully flesh out, or indeed resolve, the many emerging dilemmas. Nonetheless, it can begin to work through some of the alternatives to the politics of a single locus of great refusal. First, I explore the problematic assumptions of agents as sources of *either* power *or* resistance. This has led, I argue, to a tendency to deny, or to seek to resolve, the contradictory subject positions that might otherwise become points of politicization. It is precisely the ambivalence of subject positions, I argue, that contains the potential for a recognition of the intimate connections between 'our' world and 'theirs.' Second, in response to the prevailing desire to settle and secure the identities of the powerful/powerless or the perpetrator/resistor, I suggest that it is, in fact, the insecure and incomplete nature of identity that contains the potential interstitial spaces for dissent. Contrary to the drive to identify and delineate the political interests of the 'migrant,' or 'women,' or 'workers,' for example, I argue that these identities can never be singularly located and realized. Drawing on examples of the struggles to identity and to disidentify the 'migrant' at the US-Mexico border, I argue that the state, the social movements and the migrants occupy ambiguous positions, and that this ambiguity has promise from the point of view of a politics of dissent. Finally, I argue that where we are tempted to look for an openly declared refusal, we should consider that the most marginalized and displaced peoples of the world have the most to risk in making such declarations. Moreover, the insistence on a great refusal consigns the prosaic and everyday struggles and contests, the carnivalesque or simply coping strategies, the world of art and the aesthetic, to a realm that is seen as subordinate to the 'real' world of the global political economy. Following Homi Bhabha, Stuart Hall and others, art and literature are capable of making extraordinary intrinsically ordinary experiences. I will argue that it is often the least obtrusive moments of dissent, hidden away in the seams of the global political economy (at the borders and boundaries), that most effectively disrupt our sense of normalization, our almost tacit sense of what has a place and what is 'out of place' in the normal run of our daily lives – in the commute, the journey, the border crossing, the financial transaction.

Power, resistance, ambivalence

Understanding the contemporary politics of resistance tends to be framed by the idea that agents stand 'counter to' relations of power. In the neo-Gramscian tradition, for example, the potential for 'counter hegemony' is located within a civil society sphere understood to be a form of collective agency. Similarly, the Polanyian notion of a 'counter movement' has been deployed to suggest a necessary uprising against the neoliberal self-regulating market. As I have argued elsewhere, these traditions significantly and problematically underplay the ambiguities and contradictions of subject positions within the interplay of power and resistance (Amoore and Langley 2004; Amoore 2005). Put starkly, how do we understand the Amnesty International Visa card holder who stands opposed to the human rights abuses that characterize much of contemporary world politics, but whose debt is bundled up and sold on in the global financial markets? Or, Ian McEwan's protagonist Henry Perowne, who observes the congruence of 'fussy consumers' with protesters who decry the injustices of the global economy? The tendency to oppose power/resistance leads to a drive to seek to resolve or overcome such contradictions, resulting in a concealment of the difficulties at the heart of political life. Moreover, it actively obscures the extent to which we (as 'resistors,' 'protesters,' 'consumers,' 'workers,' or 'citizens') are implicated in the everyday practices of governing the global political economy, and in the life experiences of those who suffer most in that governing.

Writing this chapter in spring 2005, in the months preceding July's G8 summit to be held in Gleneagles, Scotland, I find myself surrounded by the political difficulties of the relationship between power and resistance. The Make Poverty History (MPH) campaign, allied, at least for the moment, with the celebrity-studded Live 8 concerts, plan a series of protests and festivals to coincide with the G8 summit. Consider an example of the acutely ambivalent politics that is being played out. In 2004 the MPH campaign drew on a practice instituted by Lance Armstrong's 'Live Strong' campaign: the selling of wristbands that clearly communicate allegiance to a cause. An unambiguous enough statement, one might think, of what is being resisted and what is proposed as the alternative future. Soon enough, though, the ambivalent double binds of the wearing of the band begin to emerge. The internet auction site eBay began to sell on 'rare' and 'collectable' charity wristbands, and the high profile wearing of the wristbands by fashion-conscious celebrities has seen them directly implicated in the very circuits of global capital and multinational power they seek to oppose. Jonathan Glennie, of Christian Aid, part of the MPH coalition, identified the dilemma in 'wanting everyone to be wearing a white band' but 'not just for the sentiment or the fashion statement' (*The Guardian* 31 May 2005).

If media commentators and MPH activists registered surprise that their symbol was so readily incorporated into the mainstream multinational making of style commodities, they were appalled by what was to follow. It was revealed that the wristbands were being produced in sweatshop conditions in China, where wages fell below 16p per hour and new workers faced a form of bonded labor (*The Scotsman* 30 May 2005). Similar contradictions emerged when tickets for the Live 8 concerts, allocated for a nominal sum by text messaging, emerged on the eBay website, where bids exceeded hundreds of pounds. Though the campaign was content to use multinational information communication technologies to distribute the tickets and publicize their campaign, Sir Bob Geldof called for internet Hacktivists to 'bring down the eBay site' on the grounds that they made 'filthy money on the back of the poorest people on the planet' (BBC News 15 June 2005).

Of course, these tales reveal the extent of the prevailing assumption that the exercise of power in the global economy can be clearly distinguished from the 'counter exercise' of resistance. The MPH wristband was used to convey a fictional 'unity' – both of those on whose behalf the campaign speaks, and of the movement itself – that could not be sustained. It never existed in a sphere that was unambiguously identifiable as 'resistance,' for it could never be abstracted from the relations of power that gave rise to it. Indeed, I would reinterpret the shock and surprise that greeted the news that the wristbands were bound up with the marketized relations of power in the global fashion economy and the everyday lives of workers so often invisible in the offshore export processing zones. We should not be shocked and surprised – these are the difficulties and dilemmas we encounter in our everyday entanglements with the global political economy. It is perhaps within these difficulties that we find the possibilities of politicization, where in their negation (such as in the attempt to reposition the MPH wristband within ethical production practices) we find a curious denial of the political. As Thomas Keenan argues in a discussion of the dilemmas of political action, 'it is political because it is impossible. If negotiation were merely possible, politics would be unnecessary. But there are double binds, every day, which is why politics is difficult' (1997: 171).

Rather than a politics of 'speaking on behalf of,' which as I have argued, aims to resolve the difficulties and dilemmas of everyday political life, perhaps there is potential for a politics of ambivalence that acknowledges the ambiguity of how we speak and for whom we speak. Our sense of agency as a secure and identifiable source of power, as Judith Butler suggests, 'shores up the first person point of view,' mitigating against alternative accounts that might 'decenter the narrative "I" within the international political domain' (Butler 2004: 7). So, how might the acknowledgment of ambivalence contribute to a questioning of the solid 'I speak' within international politics? Foucault's proposition that that the subject is 'either divided inside himself or divided from others *via* dividing practices that objectivise him' has been taken up to explore the contemporary governing of the subject (Foucault 1983: 208; cf. Rose 1999; Larner and Walters 2004; Larner this volume). Meanwhile, postcolonial reflections on the subject positions that are produced by dividing practices, locate 'antagonistic and ambivalent moments' that make it possible to 'disrupt authority' (Bhabha 1994a: 88). Similarly, Butler's concept of resignification acknowledges that, in the act of resisting, agency is perennially caught in an ambivalent bind, within which the speaker revitalizes hegemonic discourse at the same time as 'talking back' to 'perform a reversal of effects' (1997: 14).

Consider, by way of example, Max Stafford-Clark's staging of Robin Soans' play, *Talking to Terrorists*. We might interpret this play to be motivated by a desire to capture the ambivalence at the heart of the discourse of the war on terror. The dividing practices that oppose citizen/terrorist, homeland/strangeland, civil/uncivil and so on, are articulated through a discourse that says we can unambiguously distinguish 'us' from 'them.' Soans' script, derived from dialogue with resistance fighters (from the PKK to Al Aqsa and the IRA), peace activists and politicians, conveys the sense that 'the difference between terrorists and the rest of us is not that great' (Soans, cited in *The Guardian* 20 April 2005). Told through interwoven oral testimonies, the play juxtaposes, for example, witness accounts of British government-backed torture in Iraq, with the experiences of a 13-year-old Ugandan child soldier who has supervised torture. The play powerfully reflects on the coexistence of relations of power and resistance, unsettling our sense of 'us' and 'them,' and suggesting that the agency of the protagonists and victims is not so clearly identifiable. As in Niza Young's use of Bhabha's concept of ambivalence to explore the hatred experienced by Jews and Palestinians, *Talking to Terrorists* acknowledges the 'split recognition of similarity and difference' that works as 'a point of identity for both sides of the relation' (2002: 74). Both the colonizer and the colonized, Young argues, perceive the ambivalent coexistence of similarity and difference from their specific and situated locations in discourse and culture. Soans' play, in its presentation of the domestic household, urban, national and global contexts of terror, effectively disrupts the settled categories of 'same' and 'different' which we can see deployed by the contemporary war on terror. We are, even if only momentarily, exposed to our culpability in, and vulnerability to, the experiences of others, and confronted with the many 'ways in which our lives are profoundly implicated in the lives of others' (Butler 2004: 7).

Identity, difference, dissent

Many of the dilemmas that arise in the debates about global civil society and resistance movements are centered on the question of identity. It is conventionally understood that an effective politics of resistance must be somehow rooted in a form of shared identity – whether this be derived from class, gender, race, ethnicity, or from some shared basis for action, such as the environment, peace or development (Walker 1994). What is often denied, though, is that the process of defining an identity is itself subject to ongoing contestation and struggle. 'New social movements often rely upon identity claims,' write Butler, Laclau and Žižek, 'but "identity" itself is never fully constituted; identification is not reducible to identity' (2000: 17). Rather than a sense of a complete and secured identity that can be used to anchor the source and strategy of resistance, then, the ongoing processes of identification are themselves representative of the essence of political struggle.

Within cultural studies, where the question of identity has long been the focus of critical inquiry, the problematic is clearly stated: 'in common sense language, identification is constructed on the back of a recognition of some common origin or shared characteristics with another person or group, or with an ideal, and with the natural closure of solidarity and allegiance established on this foundation' (Hall 1996: 4). The assumed naturalness of identity presupposes that the lines that bind and divide social solidarities are themselves naturally emerging. In contrast to this understanding, as Stuart Hall has it, 'identification is a construction, a process never completed – always "in process"' (1996: 2). Rather than producing sameness and difference as natural categories that bind agents together, identification operates *through* difference, through the practices of differentiating. Identification can thus be understood as part of the discursive work of dividing practices, as the 'binding and marking of symbolic boundaries, the production of "frontier effects"' (Hall 1996: 3). Contrary to the hope that locating an identity for resistance politics will help to build some form of inclusive progressive politics, identification requires always its constitutive outside, its 'other' that, by the marking out of difference, secures its position.

The ever present gap between identity and identification, or what is unrealizable in the discursive making of the subject, has been a central preoccupation of social and cultural thought (cf. Laclau and Mouffe 1985; Butler 1997). Despite radical differences of approach, there is some sense of valuing the 'gap' politically as a potential space for contestation and dissent. Since the identity of the subject can never be entirely secured, the practices that rely upon the calling into being of specific subjectivities can never consider their work complete. Thus, for Homi Bhabha, what is 'politically crucial' is the necessity of thinking beyond 'initial categories and initiatory subjects and focusing on those *interstitial* movements or processes that are produced in the articulation of difference' (1994b: 269). For Bhabha, the interstices that emerge at the frontiers or borderlands of our contemporary world have particular significance – the negotiations and struggles of workers, migrants and minority populations 'against the authorities' that would seek to identify them in particular ways (270). As the migrant and refugee become the 'unhomely inhabitants of the contemporary world,' writes Bhabha, 'how do we rethink collective, communal concepts like homeland, the people, cultural exile, national cultures, interpretive communities?' (271). Identifications of 'homeland' and the threat of the 'unhomely' abound in the discursive practices of contemporary world politics. It is to one site of the contests and negotiations surrounding the identification of homeland, migrant and citizen that I now turn by way of exploring these ideas: the securing of the US-Mexico border.

Nicholas de Genova has described the border, and specifically the US-Mexico border, as the 'exemplary theatre for staging the spectacle of the illegal alien' (2002: 436). If we are to take seriously the negativity within all identity claims, this theatre is a site that must continuously stage and restage the show of the illegal alien, and which can never fully realize an end point to identification. There can be little doubt that international borders are increasingly being used to stage other spectacles that seek to fully 'identify' – the terrorist, the 'bogus asylum seeker' or 'health care tourist,' and so on. The question here, though, is how to keep open the possibility of the staging of other shows that actively underscore 'disidentification' from regulatory norms (Butler 1993: 4).

In May 2005 the US saw two political issues of particular significance for the identificatory practices of migrants and citizens. The first was legislation giving the Director of Homeland Security the right to override human rights and environmental laws in order to build a triple-security fenced zone between San Diego and Tijuana. Among many other measures, the REAL ID Act authorizes the Secretary of Homeland Security 'to waive all laws as necessary to ensure expeditious construction of the San Diego border fence.' The second was the proliferation of vigilante anti-immigration forces at the Arizona section of the US-Mexico border. The

Minuteman project calls for volunteers to 'assist the government in their monumental task of turning back the tidal wave of people entering our country illegally' (www.MinutemanHQ.com). Hundreds of armed and uniformed volunteers, equipped with shortwave radio, night sights and light aircraft, now patrol a 23-mile stretch of the border. They draw their identity, not only from their namesakes the minutemen of the war of independence, but also from the imagery of frontierland cowboys: 'it's a dangerous place down there. It's the wild west reincarnated' (cited in *The Guardian* 2 April 2005). The vigilante border guards, supported and encouraged by the council representing official border patrols, play the courageous and brave cowboy citizens to the cowardly coyotes or 'Indians' of the Latino migrants.

From the Mexican government we find, in part, a similar identification of the border struggles with the historical characteristics of the Wild West. In January 2005, Mexico's foreign ministry published *The Guide for the Mexican Migrant,* distributing the border crossing advice free in the popular cowboy comic book *El Libro Vaquero*. Mimicking the cartoon-style drawings of brave heros in the comic, the guide ostensibly offers practical advice on how to cross the border safely and how to live unobtrusively in the US once 'you have made the difficult decision to seek new work opportunities outside your country' (Secretaria de Relaciones Exteriores 2005: 3). The migrant is disassociated from the homeland security discourse of wily, cowardly or cheating behavior, and identified instead with bravery and responsibility (for income for the family, for the nation of Mexico, and so on). The illustrations depict men and women in their physical prime crossing the frontier and evading the authorities. In one frame, for example, a group of migrants are running from a border patrol vehicle, alongside the text 'do not resist arrest.'

Not only does the guide illustrate the identification gap experienced by migrants crossing the border, but it also reveals the displacement of risks that takes place with increased fortification and private policing of the border. On desert crossings, for example, it offers advice on how to avoid dehydration and to follow power lines or train tracks when lost. On 'using the services of a coyote' to cross the border, it warns of the 'deaths of hundreds of people,' illustrating with immigrants climbing into the back of a tractor-trailer (19 migrants died in Texas in May 2003 after being sealed inside a tractor-trailer). In this way, what appears as a pragmatic guide to survival strategies segues into the simultaneous identification of brave 'frontier masculinities' more commonly associated with international financiers or IT entrepreneurs

(Hooper 2001: 160), and the exposure of the acute risks borne by border crossers. The *Guide* can be read as a momentary glimpse of the other possible identities of the migrant subject, beyond the discourses of various threats to security.

Culture, translation, transcendence

In his seminal discussion of the transformation of the idea of culture from the eighteenth and nineteenth centuries, Raymond Williams notes that 'where *culture* meant a state or habit of the mind, or the body of intellectual and moral activities, it means now, also, a whole way of life' (1961: 18). Taking my cue from Williams' sense of culture as comprising both the body of the arts and our everyday apprehension of meaning and understanding, I want to ask here whether the cultural sphere can shed different light on the contemporary politics of resistance.

Everywhere, or so it seems, we are faced with rationalities that seek to 'secure,' to insulate our lives from vulnerability and uncertainty. Such is the message pervading the discourses of vigilance in the war on terror, as in the advertising for armoured sports utility vehicles, and in the calculative rationality of global financial markets (de Goede 2005). So long as we deploy the correct practices of management, accounting, audit and personal security and insurance, we are told, we can render the future less contingent and more knowable and certain. Indeed, the connectivity of a shrunken globe that is peddled by the management consultants as much as by the politicians at the World Economic Forum, functions precisely by seeking to insulate one set of circuits (capital, business, leisure, tourism...), from the effects of others (global terrorism, illegal migration, trafficking...). The question, then, is how this fiction of invulnerability can be challenged. As Butler notes, 'to foreclose vulnerability, to banish it' is to withdraw 'one of the most important resources from which we must take our bearings and find our way' (2004: 30). Butler offers the experiences of grief, passion, and extreme emotions of many kinds, as a potential basis for a community held together by mutual complicity in, and vulnerability to, loss. Butler writes with much in common with other commentators who suggested that out of the trauma of 9/11 there was an unfulfilled opportunity to reflect on the proximity of 'our' practices in relation to 'theirs' (Sassen 2002; Beeson 2003), and to recognize in others 'the distilled version of our own essence' (Žižek 2003: 133).

I want to suggest here that the arts offer another means to transcend our apparently secure state of existence (as, for example, commuter, internet surfer, gallery visitor), to be, as Butler puts it 'outside of oneself' (2004: 24), and momentarily connected to the layers of subordinate everyday lives that make our lives possible. So, just how can the cosmopolitan city-dweller artist convey or connect to the experiences of the Latina immigrant living without papers in Los Angeles, or the migrant domestic worker cleaning the London hotel room? Is the idea that the arts offer a means of politicization not neglecting the inequalities of power between artists and marginalized groups? (cf. Young 1990). For Bhabha the question of culture makes the place of desire, pleasure and the affective body 'critical to our understanding of the ambivalent mechanisms of social authority' (1994b: 271). Art and literature are capable of making extraordinary intrinsically mundane and ordinary experiences, translating, if only for an instant, the everyday experiences of ourselves and others. Moreover, cultures, in the broadest sense of ways of life, and in the narrow sense of artistic practice, have political potential because they challenge our sense of occupying an insulated and immune individuality. They may temporarily call into question the site of individual identities that neoliberal modes of government take as their very life source, creating a 'temporary autonomous zone' in which a specific or limited refusal can take place (Bey 1991; Balliger 1995).

An example can be explored here, in the shape of the experience of a daily commute on the London Underground, a space variously constructed as commercial (advertising space, arteries of the city/global economy) and secured (*via* new surveillance technologies). When artistic and creative practices enter this space though, the sense of everyday normality and the 'usual run of things' is disrupted. A recent exhibition at the Crafts Council Gallery in London, for example, exhibited the work of *Cast Off*, a group of artists whose medium is wool and technique is knitting. The work seeks to juxtapose the homely safety and security of knitting with the violence and insecurities of the global political economy. 'Once a devalued craft,' states the exhibition catalogue alongside images of their knitted hand grenades and balaclavas, 'knitting is now taking on capitalism, consumerism and war' (*The Guardian* 31 January 2005). The artists engage in their group knitting in public spaces where, they note 'it is odd that you are allowed to read a book on the tube, but knitting is abnormal.' Their work illustrates the many ways in which our prosaic daily practices become part of what is represented as normal or suspicious social behavior. Of course, public spaces are increasingly subject to the discourse of vigilance that says we should be on the alert for suspicious behavior and identify potential threats. *Cast Off* shed satirical and humorous light on these practices, photographing knitted balaclavas and weaponry against a backdrop of New York streets. Ejected from the Savoy Hotel for knitting in the lobby, the artists staged a 'knit in' on London's Circle line, encountering variously, surprise, laughter and discomfort from their fellow passengers.

The Underground, it seems, has become a metaphor for the arteries and circuits that connect our daily practices to the organs of the global city and, thus, is a site where the commute to work or the tourist's journey confronts the world of artistic representation. Choreographer Mark Baldwin's new work for the Rambert Dance Company, *Constant Speed,* made its surprise premiere on London's Jubilee line. Commissioned to mark Einstein's century, the work sought to 'disrupt the external perception of space and time' with movement that suggests 'different rates for different observers' (Rambert Dance Company 2005: 7). Performed on the escalators and train carriages of the London Underground by dancers in white boiler-suits, *Constant Speed* interrupted the daily life of the commuter and the tourist, evoking a sense that scientific laws and practices 'reach far into our daily lives' (Rambert Dance Company 2005: 11). Commuters between Canary Wharf's business district and Waterloo's Eurostar terminal 'sensed that this was not going to be a conventional ride' (*The Guardian* 18 January 2005). It is precisely the disruption of the conventional ride seen in the work of *Cast Off* and *Rambert* that embodies the potential for a disruptive politics – an unsettling of the apparent ubiquity of our part in the making, and the governing, of the global political economy. In her study of the politics of 'making strange' the accepted and almost unnoticed rationalities of the global financial markets, Marieke de Goede explores the performance art of British artists *foreign investment.* In common with *Cast Off* and *Rambert, foreign investment* involves the passer-by in an encounter with the unexpected, in a disruption of their daily routines. 'The performances of *foreign investment,*' writes de Goede, run 'a kind of interference... like sending another wavelength into a certain jargon' (2005: 384). Though these kinds of practices 'may not form a consistent counter-hegemonic programme,' de Goede concludes, 'they do transform people's experiences' (390). Read alongside Butler's insight that to be transformed 'out of oneself' has the potential to break down our sense of being insulated from the workings of world politics, artistic practices contribute by intervening in and transforming our experience of taken-for-granted public spaces.

Art, comedy and laughter, as many writers have suggested, may confront us with the conditions and contingency of our place in this world and make it possible to see the world anew (Odysseos 2001). An encounter with an alternative experience of the commute, the hotel lobby or multiple privileged spaces of the global political economy changes our future perceptions of those spaces. As in the opening passage of this chapter, Henry Perowne's usually ordinary and uneventful journey from his West London home to the sports club is transformed by his encounter with the city streets as changed by the anti-war protests. It is not so much the slogans, banners and chants of the protesters that invoke this transformation (indeed these strike him as faintly ridiculous), but the disruption to the access to which he has become accustomed within the global city, and the aesthetic qualities of the day itself. His residual feelings of discomfort and vulnerability are expressed in a fleeting feeling that his life may be less secure and more vulnerable than he had recognized. Though, as Butler reflects, 'one may want to, or manage to for a while,' one cannot help but be 'undone in the face of the other, by the touch, by the scent, by the feel, by the prospect of the touch, by the memory of the feel' (2004: 24). The aesthetic realm, then, though not unproblematically or naturally politicizing, has a capacity to call us into question, to challenge our sense of invulnerability to the problems of the world, and to make us feel a certain discomfort.

Concluding reflections

In the opening citation of this chapter, Butler suggests that it is in our encounters with one another that we are rendered undone, that the threads of our everyday lives can begin to unravel. Ian McEwan's protagonist experiences just such a momentary tear in the apparently safely woven fabric of his everyday journey, the city streets of London so often traversed briefly appear to him anew. 'For a vertiginous moment,' Henry feels bound to another man, 'as though on a seesaw with him, pinned to an axis that could tip them into each other's life.' I have suggested that it is this moment of vulnerability and contingency, sought by artistic practices that intervene in everyday contexts, that conveys a sense that the apparent materiality of our lives may be less certain and secure. So many aspects of the contemporary global political economy appear to us as an immutable and material architecture – the commute on the underground arteries of the global city, the operations of the global financial markets, the presence and policing of the international border – that we become somewhat anaesthetized to what they make of us, and to how this could be otherwise.

To ignore the insights poststructuralism brings to a politics of resistance is to risk a particular concealment of the multiple points and knots of dissent that are possible. As the editor argues in her introduction, there is a perception that claiming multiple and contested identities is part of a kind of thinking that is dangerous to the project of critical thinking. For some, poststructural thought is dangerous because it underplays the materiality of the fabric of the global economy, whether this is capital or the relations of production, or surplus value, or whatever. And so a great refusal is sought because this makes it possible to envisage a clear and absolute cut through the fabric of neoliberal global capitalism. We are left with the somewhat frustrating impression that we must make a choice, between discourse and materiality, between the ideal and the real, between class protest and cultural practice, between refusal and complicity. But what does such a choice imply for those who share a sense that, in a world dominated by the demand that we choose between 'us' and 'them,' there remains something politically important at stake? As Butler (2004: 48) has put the question:

> We could disagree on the status and character of modernity and yet find ourselves joined in asserting and defending the rights of indigenous women to health care, reproductive technology, decent wages, physical protection, cultural rights, freedom of assembly. If you saw me on such a protest line, would you wonder how a postmodernist was able to muster the necessary 'agency' to get there today? I doubt it. You would assume that I had walked or taken the subway.

And so, in the hope of a future for scholarship that is driven by a desire to politicize that which is so often presented as a technical choice, we should refuse the choice between a critical thinking driven by political activism/class struggle and one concerned with identity/ambivalence, and recognize what this is: a false choice that does more to govern and contain dissent than to make it possible.

Notes

1 In the preparation of this chapter I wish to acknowledge the support and encouragement of the editor, Marieke de Goede, who has generously allowed me to pursue avenues of thought that took me to dance and knitting. For comments on drafts thanks to the editor and to Paul Langley. I must also thank here the students on my masters course, *Politics of Global Change*, who

sent me almost daily updates on what became for us the saga of the multiple binds of the MPHwristband.

2 For critical debate on the question of dissent in poststructuralist thought, and particularly in the work of Michel Foucault, see Campbell (1998) and Keenan (1997).

References

Amoore, L. (ed.) (2005) *The Global Resistance Reader*. London: Routledge.

Amoore, L. and Langley, P. (2004) 'Ambiguities of Global Civil Society,' *Review of International Studies* 30 (1): 89–110.

Balliger, R. (1995) 'Sounds of Resistance,' in Sakolsky, R. and Ho, F. W.-H. (eds) *Sounding Off: Music as Subversion/Resistance/Revolution*. New York: Autonomedia.

BBC News (2005) 'eBay prevents Live 8 ticket sales,' transcript of television news, 15 June, available at www.news.bbc.co.uk/1/hi/entertainment/music/4090774.stm.

Beeson, A. (2003) 'On the Home Front,' in Leone, R. and Anrig, G. (eds) *The War on Our Freedoms: Civil Liberties in an Age of Terrorism*. New York: Public Affairs.

Bey, H. (1991) *TAZ: The Temporary Autonomous Zone, Ontological Anarchy, Poetic Terrorism*. Brooklyn: Autonomedia.

Bhabha, H. (1994a) *The Location of Culture*. London: Routledge.

Bhabha, H. (1994b) 'Frontlines/Borderposts,' in Bammer, A. (ed.) *Displacements: Cultural Identities in Question*. Indianapolis: Indiana University Press.

Butler, J. (1993) *Bodies that Matter: On the Discursive Limits of Sex*. New York: Routledge.

Butler, J. (1997) *Excitable Speech: A Politics of the Performative*. New York: Routledge.

Butler, J. (2004) *Precarious Life: The Powers of Mourning and Violence*. London: Verso.

Butler, J., Laclau, E. and Žižek, S. (2000) *Contingency, Hegemony, Universality: Contemporary Dialogues on the Left*. London: Verso.

Campbell, D. (1998) 'Why Fight: Humanitarianism, Principles, and Post-structuralism,' *Millennium: Journal of International Studies* 27 (3): 497–521.

Connolly, W. (1995) *The Ethos of Pluralization*. Minneapolis: University of Minnesota Press.

de Genova, N. P. (2002) 'Migrant Illegality and Deportability in Everyday Life,' *Annual Review of Anthropology* 31: 419–47.

de Goede, M. (2005) 'Carnival of Money: Politics of Dissent in an Era of Globalizing Finance,' in Amoore, L. (ed.) *The Global Resistance Reader*. London: Routledge.

Financial Times (2001) 'Clamour Against Capitalism Stilled,' 10 October.

Foucault, M. (1976) *The Will to Knowledge: The History of Sexuality Volume 1*. London: Penguin.

Foucault, M. (1983) 'Afterword: The Subject and Power,' in Dreyfus, H. L. and Rabinow, P. (eds) *Michel Foucault: Beyond Structuralism and Hermeneutics*. Chicago: University of Chicago Press.

Gill, S. (2003) *Power and Resistance in the New World Order*. Basingstoke: Macmillan.

Hall, S. (1996) 'Introduction: Who Needs Identity?' in Hall, S. (ed.) *Questions of Cultural Identity*. London: Sage.

Hooper, C. (2001) *Manly States: Masculinities, International Relations, and Gender Politics*. New York: Columbia University Press.

Keenan, T. (1997) *Fables of Responsibility: Aberrations and Predicaments in Ethics and Politics*. Stanford: Stanford University Press.

Kingsnorth, P. (2004) *One No, Many Yeses: A Journey to the Heart of the Global Resistance Movement*. New York: Free Press.

Klein, N. (2002) 'Farewell to the End of History: Organization and Vision in Anti-Corporate Movements,' *Socialist Register*, pp. 1–13.

Laclau, E. and Mouffe, C. (1985) *Hegemony and Socialist Strategy: Towards a Radical Democratic Politics*. London: Verso.

Larner, W. and Walters, W. (2004) 'Introduction: Global Governmentality: Governing International Spaces,' in Larner, W. and Walters, W. (eds) *Global Governmentality: Governing International Spaces*. London: Routledge.

McEwan, I. (2005) *Saturday*. London: Jonathan Cape

Mittelman, J. (2000) *The Globalization Syndrome: Transformation and Resistance*. Princeton: Princeton University Press.

Monbiot, G. (2003) 'Stronger than Ever,' *The Guardian*, 28 January.

Odysseos, L. (2001) 'Laughing Matters: Peace, Democracy and the Challenge of the Comic Narrative,' *Millennium: Journal of International Studies* 30 (3): 709–32.

Rambert Dance Company (2005) *Constant Speed: Physics in Motion*, London: Institute of Physics/Rambert Dance Company.

Rose, N. (1999) *Governing the Soul: Shaping of the Private Self*. London: Free Association Books.

Sassen, S. (2002) 'Governance Hotspots: Challenges we must confront in the Post-September 11 World,' in Booth, K. and Dunne, T. (eds) *Worlds in Collision: Terror and the Future of Global Order*. Basingstoke: Palgrave.

Secretaria de Relaciones Exteriores (2005) *Guia del Migrante Mexicano*, available at www.sre.gob.mx/tramites/consulares/guiamigrante/default.htm

Soans, R. (2004) *Talking to Terrorists*. London/Royal Court: Out of Joint.

The Guardian (2005) 'Rambert Dancers Take to the Tube,' 18 January.

The Guardian (2005) 'Political Protest Turns to the Radical Art of Knitting,' 31 January.

The Guardian (2005) 'US Vigilantes Begin Border Stake-out,' 2 April.

The Guardian (2005) 'It could be you,' 20 April.

The Guardian (2005) 'Wrist watch,' 31 May.

The Nation (2001) 'Signs of the Times,' 22 October.

The Scotsman (2005) 'Anti-poverty Wristbands Produced in Sweatshops,' 30 May.

Van Munster, R. (2004) 'The War on Terrorism: When the Exception Becomes the Rule,' *International Journal for the Semiotics of Law* 17: 141–53.

Walker, R. B. J (1994) 'Social Movements/World Politics,' *Millennium: Journal of International Studies*, 23 (3): 669–700.

Williams, R. (1961) *The Long Revolution*. London/New York: Columbia University Press.

Willis, S. (2003) 'Old Glory,' in Hauerwas, S. and Lentricchia, F. (eds) *Dissent from the Homeland: Essays After September 11*. Durham and London: Duke University Press.

Young, N. (2002) 'Hatred as Ambivalence,' *Theory, Culture and Society* 19 (3): 71–88.

Young, R. (1990) *White Mythologies: Writing History and the West*. London: Routledge.
Žižek, S. (2003) 'Welcome to the Desert of the Real!' in Hauerwas, S. and Lentricchia, F. (eds) *Dissent from the Homeland: Essays After September 11*. Durham and London: Duke University Press.

Index